NEVER
DAUNTED

ALSO BY RANDALL TOBIAS

Put the Moose on the Table: Lessons in Leadership from a CEO's Journey through Business and Life
with Todd Tobias

NEVER DAUNTED

A Life and Legacy of Embracing Change

RANDALL L. TOBIAS

INDIANA UNIVERSITY PRESS

This book is a publication of

Indiana University Press
Herman B Wells Library
1320 East 10th Street
Bloomington, Indiana 47405 USA

in cooperation with

Randall L. Tobias Center for Leadership Excellence
801 West Michigan Street
Indianapolis, Indiana 46202-5151 USA

iupress.org

© 2025 by Randall L. Tobias

All rights reserved
No part of this book may be reproduced or utilized in any form or by any means, electronic or mechanical, including photocopying and recording, or by any information storage and retrieval system, without permission in writing from the publisher.

For customers in the European Union with safety or GPSR concerns, please contact Mare Nostrum Group B.V., Mauritskade 21D, 1091 GC Amsterdam, The Netherlands. Email: gpsr@mare-nostrum.co.uk

First printing 2025

Cataloging information is available from the Library of Congress

ISBN 978-0-253-07497-3 (paperback)

To my grandchildren—and theirs.

CONTENTS

Foreword **ix**

Chapter One   From Plow-Hand to Banker   *1*

Chapter Two   A Remington Childhood   *7*

Chapter Three   Work to Do, Lessons to Learn   *15*

Chapter Four   School Days   *23*

Chapter Five   From a Small Town to a Big School   *31*

Chapter Six   My First Summer in the "Real World"   *39*

Chapter Seven   Active Duty   *47*

Chapter Eight   A New Wife and a New Life   *57*

Chapter Nine   My First Lap on the Fast Track   *65*

Chapter Ten   A Mysterious Medical Crisis   *71*

Chapter Eleven   Life in Indianapolis   *77*

Chapter Twelve   Getting Out of My Comfort Zone   *83*

Chapter Thirteen   A Whole New Ballgame in Illinois   *91*

Chapter Fourteen   Earning a Spot in the AT&T Boardroom   *99*

Chapter Fifteen   A World Turned Upside Down   *115*

Chapter Sixteen   Out of the Blue   *137*

Chapter Seventeen   A Fast Start   *151*

Chapter Eighteen   Tragedy Strikes   *169*

Chapter Nineteen   Pain, Joy, and New Beginnings   *181*

Chapter Twenty   Moving On   *191*

Chapter Twenty-One   Keeping Busy   *205*

Chapter Twenty-Two   Collaborating with Todd on a Magazine and a Moose   *221*

CONTENTS

Chapter Twenty-Three	The Challenge of a Lifetime	*229*
Chapter Twenty-Four	The Long, Vexing Road to Senate Confirmation	*241*
Chapter Twenty-Five	A New Agency with a New Strategy	*253*
Chapter Twenty-Six	Getting (Almost) Everyone on the Same Page	*265*
Chapter Twenty-Seven	Seeing AIDS Up Close	*277*
Chapter Twenty-Eight	Navigating Washington and Tackling an Even Bigger Job	*289*
Chapter Twenty-Nine	Public Service and Philanthropic Causes	*317*
Chapter Thirty	Another Terrible Loss	*329*
Chapter Thirty-One	Meant to Be	*335*
Chapter Thirty-Two	Full Circle	*359*
Acknowledgments		*377*
Index		*385*
About the Painting		*414*
About the Author		*417*

FOREWORD

Over the generations the Tobiases have been farmers, bankers, teachers, military officers, lawyers, magazine publishers, business executives, and more. As the world changed, we changed with it.

The Tobias family's American story begins in Scott County, along the banks of the Muscatatuck River, a 40-mile waterway in south-central Indiana. But our known roots stretch all the way back to Wales, to Carmarthenshire County, near the banks of the River Tywi.

We know that on November 2, 1736, Catherine Richard and Thomas Tobias (my fifth great-grandparents) were married in St. David's Church in Abergwili, Carmarthenshire, Wales, where both are now buried. In 1743, Catherine and Thomas had a son they named David. In about 1780, David Tobias (my fourth great-grandfather) and his wife, Elizabeth Jones Tobias, while residing in Llanfihangel Aberbythych, Carmarthenshire, had a son named Tobias Tobias (my third great-grandfather). On February 24, 1780, Tobias was baptized in St. Michael's Church in Llanfihangel Aberbythych. We have not located a marriage record for Tobias

FOREWORD

Tobias and Margaret William, but on June 22, 1816, they had a son named David T. Tobias, my second great-grandfather. David T. was baptized in St. Tybie's Church in Llandybie, Carmarthenshire, on June 30, 1816. We don't know what happened to Margaret beyond that event, but sometime around 1820, Tobias Tobias, along with his eight-year-old son from an earlier marriage, John, and four-year-old David T., departed Wales for the United States, where they took up residence in Scott County, Indiana.

Records indicate Tobias Tobias, who had been a carpenter in Wales, was initially a farm laborer. On August 1, 1833, he was granted ownership of forty acres of land by the United States government. While we'll never know for certain, achieving land ownership may well have been among the primary reasons for his decision to leave Wales, where all land was owned by the aristocracy and there was no prospect of him ever owning some of his own. It was there in southern Indiana, in 1849, that David T. Tobias established a business enterprise that served as a community landmark for decades, and which still looms large in our family's history.

In 1849, two years after his marriage to Maryland native Ann Mayfield, he and a Baltimore doctor named Isaac Mayfield, Ann's brother, decided to acquire land next to the Muscatatuck River and build a water-powered mill.

The project was something of a community effort. In the spring of 1849, residents of Scott, Jennings, Jefferson, and Jackson counties banded together to help construct a two-story frame building with an attached water wheel to both saw lumber and grind grain. Built from timbers hewn at a nearby farm, the mill was sited on the river's south bank. Under my great-great-grandfather's supervision, the work was finished by Christmas of that year.

The mill quickly became both a commercial and social hub. In those days, farmers who wanted trees cut into lumber or their wheat or corn ground into flour or meal had to visit the nearest mill, where water wheel-powered saw blades and grinding stones did the work. My great-great-grandfather's mill (like many at the time) took one-eighth of each grinding as payment. Since the farmers who brought in the grain sometimes needed to wait for some time to have it processed, the mill became an informal meeting place where locals relaxed and discussed the issues of the day.

Some probably also fished near the mill's stone dam. Built to create a dependable reserve for the water wheel, it formed a large millpond that became a prime site for swimming and fishing in summer and skating and ice cutting in winter. With water powering the saw, the mill could cut between 1,200 and 1,500 board feet of lumber per day.

My family's relationship with that building spanned generations. David Tobias trained his son, Theopolis, to operate it, and he in turn taught his own son, Harry, to do the same. But new technology —in the form of steam engines—changed the game. It was much more cost-effective to take steam-powered machinery directly to the fields to grind the grain than it was to haul the grain to the river-powered mill. As a result, the mill became obsolete.

At the dawn of the 20th century, the mill closed its doors. In 1906 high winds toppled the main building.

In the summer of 1949, on the 100th anniversary of its construction, Roy Tobias, great-grandson of David T. Tobias, attended a centennial celebration in honor of both the mill and the nearby one-room Alpha community school and visited the mill site with his wife, Fern, and his seven-year-old son—me. As I recall, there wasn't much to see. Today there's even less—just some stonework from the ruins of both the old stone dam and the mill foundation, as well as an abandoned iron bridge over the

Muscatatuck, known as the Tobias Bridge. These are the only signs that it was ever there.

Yet in a very real sense, that old mill lives on. It comes to life in the stories passed from generation to generation by our family. That simple structure, where a Welsh immigrant first found his footing in a new land, still has lessons to teach—most importantly, lessons about resilience in the face of inevitable change. We started out in this country as laborers and then sought further opportunities as millers. But the end of that business wasn't the end of our family. Over the generations we've also been farmers, bankers, teachers, military officers, lawyers, magazine publishers, business executives, and more. As the world changed, we changed with it.

The mill's influence on our family—and our perseverance after its demise—is a tale worth sharing with future generations of Tobiases. And it's not the only one. That's why I wrote this book. I wanted to set down our story so far and commit to print my personal recollections of times past, the challenges and triumphs of my own life, and the lessons that can be drawn from them.

In these pages, I will share my own story, from my childhood in the small Indiana town of Remington to my days as vice-chairman of AT&T and then chairman and CEO of Eli Lilly and Company, to my service as a U.S. ambassador and the first head of PEPFAR (the U.S. AIDS program), the first Director of U.S. Foreign Assistance and, concurrently, the Administrator of the U.S. Agency for International Development (USAID), and more. But I'll also recall those who came before me—my parents and grandparents—and the examples they set that helped shape my attitudes and character.

Of necessity, this work includes some strong parallels with an earlier book, *Put the Moose on the Table: Lessons in Leadership from a CEO's Journey Through Business and Life*. It was written by my son Todd and me in 2003, a few years after I retired from Lilly. I'm quite proud of it, not least because I got to spend hours collaborating with Todd, a talented writer. It was an incredible way for a father and son to further bond.

That effort was primarily a summation of my observations about the lessons I'd learned during my life and business career to that point. Some important, illustrative personal anecdotes from my own life and those of my ancestors were included, but it wasn't a true memoir. And of course, the story stops at roughly the turn of the 21st century, nearly a quarter century before the conclusion of this book.

This work pays much more attention to the Tobiases' personal—and sometimes very personal—history. These family matters may be of little interest to most of the general public, but that's not who this volume is primarily for. This one is first and foremost for my family.

I hope that you, whether you're one of my grandchildren, or perhaps one of their grandchildren, will find the tales of those who came before you both interesting and instructive. Because, while businesses crumble and people pass away, the lessons and examples they leave behind live forever. All you have to do is heed them.

NEVER
DAUNTED

FROM PLOW-HAND TO BANKER

Chapter One

Money was tight during the 1930s, but my parents persevered.

My father, Roy Tobias, graduated from college on a full-ride scholarship in an era when simply finishing high school was cause for celebration. Yet he started first grade one year later than the other kids at his small rural school. It wasn't for academic reasons, however. It was because, at six, his parents didn't think he was old enough to take care of a horse!

He was born in 1906 near our family mill, which had just closed after nearly six decades of operation. Shortly thereafter, the Tobias family moved to northwestern Indiana, in Pine Township, Benton County, near my hometown of Remington, where my grandfather, Harry Tobias, worked some rented farmland. Though Harry farmed his entire life, to the best of my knowledge, he never owned his own property.

His wife, my grandmother on my father's side, was named Leva Sparks Tobias. She was a remarkable woman—self-educated and very curious and energetic. She taught school for a while in southern Indiana before the move north. One of her earliest students was a young girl named Hanna Milhous, later to be Richard Nixon's mother.

Harry and Leva had four children: my father first, his brother, Clifford, and his two sisters, Hazel and Helen. When it was time for my six-year-old father to start school, it was simply too far for him to walk. He'd need to ride a horse. However, my grandparents didn't think he was old enough to provide the proper food, water, and care for the animal, which would stay with the horses of the other students in the school's barn. So, they held him out of school until he was seven and better able to shoulder the responsibility.

For years thereafter he dutifully saddled up his horse and rode to Gilboa Township's schoolhouse, which he would attend all the way through high school. He worked hard and graduated in 1925 as part of a class of 10 students. And there his education might have ended, as it did for most families without the means to pay for college even if they had the inclination.

But one of my father's high school teachers noticed his abilities, took an interest in him, and helped him take the next step. My father won a highly prized Rector Scholarship to DePauw University, a very fine liberal arts college in Greencastle, Indiana. Back in those days, as still today, the scholarship covered room and board as well as tuition. It paid for pretty much every expense, which was the only way he could afford a college education.

My father liked to read and study, and he worked hard at DePauw. He used to tell me that he worried constantly, knowing that if his grade point average fell, he would lose his scholarship. But he made sure that didn't happen because he knew a college diploma could change the trajectory of his entire life.

And so it did. Though he first faced some very hard knocks.

He graduated in the spring of 1929 with a degree in economics, joining the work world just a few months before the stock market crashed and the Great Depression began. He was hired as an accountant with an electric utility, the Northern Indiana Public Service Company, but as the economy worsened, the company started laying off staff. Dad had to take a demotion, from office worker to lineman, with the understanding that he could move back up the ranks when things improved.

But things didn't improve. At least, not for a long time. Eventually, even his lineman job went away. He returned to Remington and worked for one of his uncles as a farm laborer.

It was a huge step down for a recently minted college graduate. But one day in 1931 his luck turned. Two members of the board of directors of the State Bank of Remington visited him while he was plowing a field behind four horses and asked if he might be interested in a job at the bank. Not surprisingly, he said yes. As he often said in the years following, it sure seemed a lot more promising than continuing to look at the rear ends of those horses!

It was the start of a 44-year career in small-town banking. But it was by no means a ticket to quick riches. The bank wasn't a huge operation, with fewer than a dozen employees at any given time. So, there were many years of careful family budgeting to come. During the Depression, my father picked up an understandable lifelong aversion to financial risk and a strong tendency toward frugality. For instance, he and my mother told me that after they were married, they would buy just one stick of butter at a time. They didn't have a refrigerator, and the only way to keep it cool was to put it on a shelf in the basement of the house they rented.

The two met in high school. My mother, Fern Beatrice Harwood, was born in 1904 in Kansas. However, she spent most of her childhood in and around Gilman, a small town in northeastern Illinois. In

1922 she moved with her family to Gilboa Township, near Remington. As a high school junior, she found herself in the same school as my father, who was two years younger. They hit it off immediately, but it's my impression they didn't become romantically involved until much later.

My mother was an amazing person. When she graduated from high school, she took an exam that earned her a teaching license. She used it to teach back in Gilman, Illinois, about 45 miles from Remington. She taught in the winter and then used the money she earned to attend summer school. After several summers of this, she went back to school full-time for a year and finished earning a college degree from Illinois State Normal University, now Illinois State University. It was a herculean effort and something not many women accomplished in those days.

My parents began seeing each other seriously in the early 1930s and were married in 1934. The ceremony was low-key, and for a while they kept the happy news mostly to themselves. It's hard to believe now, but back in those days, a female school teacher was expected to be single. And with jobs so scarce during the Depression, two-income families were frowned on.

My mother kept teaching throughout much of her adult life, though she took a break while my brother and I were very young. But I never felt that she taught because we needed the money. I think it was more about personal fulfillment. Not that the second paycheck wasn't helpful. Indeed, it was probably more helpful than I realized at the time. It allowed my parents to do things for our family they otherwise couldn't have done.

Money was tight during the 1930s, but my parents persevered. The State Bank of Remington survived the Depression, as did the town's other bank. These days it seems remarkable that such a small community, which in 1930 had only 879 residents plus those living on surrounding farms, could support two financial institutions.

My father developed an extremely long-term investment strategy. Every time someone who owned stock in his bank died, he would scrape together all the extra money he could get his hands on and buy perhaps one of those shares. By the time he retired at the age of 70 as the longtime president, he owned a significant part of the bank. But he was in good health and spirits for a long time afterward. He would sometimes say that he knew he did the right thing by retiring because he knew his predecessor stayed too long and he didn't want that to happen to him. However, he certainly missed everything associated with going to the bank every day.

During his final year on the job, he didn't see a bright future for independent small-town banks, so he orchestrated a merger of his and two other small banks. The institution they put together operated for about two years and then was acquired by Bank One, a multi-state Midwest institution. So it all had a very happy ending in that regard. In the later years of his life, all of those quarters and dollars he put together amounted to roughly $1.25 million in Bank One stock at the time of his death. This was a large amount of money, but a particularly large sum when you consider how it all came about.

My father never regretted those years in the early 1930s when he worked on a farm. Far from it. Those trials, he believed, helped him build character and develop good work habits.

When I was growing up, he was offered a job at a significantly larger bank in Crawfordsville. I remember that it sounded kind of exciting to me, and I think my mother agreed. But Dad saw an opportunity ahead to become the president of the State Bank of Remington and run his own show. He knew that's what he wanted, and he was willing to take the risk and stay put. I'm happy he made that choice. If he hadn't, I'd have missed out on all the fun I had and the lessons I learned by growing up in Remington. And he might never have become a bank president.

A REMINGTON CHILDHOOD

Chapter Two

It's a miracle no one was hurt by my grandmother's stove lighting technique.

Like most little kids, I thought my parents' house was huge. Though of course it wasn't. Honestly, nothing in Remington was all that big.

The place where I grew up was a square, brick, two-story home with a front porch overlooking Brown Street. It didn't have a house number, or an actual street sign for that matter, because in a town that small it just wasn't necessary.

Nevertheless, my years in "the brick house on the hill," as our family called it, hugely impacted my worldview.

We moved there in the summer of 1945, when I was three years old. It was my home until I graduated from high school in 1960.

On its first floor were the living room, kitchen, and a separate dining room. I remember how much my mother loved that dining room. The kitchen, when I think about it now, seems small. But it didn't at the time. There was a very simple counter with a vinyl top and three stools on one side and one on the other. My father sat on one end, I sat in the middle, and my brother at the other end. My mother sat on the other side. We had a lot of meals at that counter.

The second floor contained my brother's bedroom, my bedroom, my parents' bedroom, a guest room, and the only full bathroom in the entire house.

There was also a basement with a large, semi-finished room that was big enough for a ping-pong table that my father constructed from a large sheet of plywood and painted green with regulation white lines. An unfinished area housed the washing machine and the furnace. I remember in the early days we had a coal furnace equipped with a stoker—a big container that automatically fed coal chunks into the fire. In winter I'd watch my dad shovel in coal to keep it full. There was also a coal storage bin adjacent to the furnace. Periodically, the local coal supplier would back his truck up to the basement window that opened to that area and fill the bin with new coal.

In the basement, there was also a space we called the fruit room. The walls were covered with shelves. In late summer my mother would put up in glass Ball jars tomatoes, green beans, and other vegetables; grape jelly from our grape vines; and other things from our garden, and store them there.

During summer there was certainly plenty of produce. The house sat on roughly six acres of property. I was never sure quite how much land we had. We always raised a lot of vegetables in our large garden. My mother and father both gardened, but my father especially enjoyed it and continued doing it until shortly before his death. We had everything—lettuce, radishes, potatoes, corn, tomatoes, and more. You name it, and it was probably out there.

Next to the garden lay a fenced pasture where we kept a half dozen sheep. Their principal function was to "mow" the pasture grass. The sheep also produced wool, and someone came once a year to shear them. One of my earliest responsibilities was to fill a bucket with water from a hand pump in the yard and empty it into a trough in the pasture so the sheep could drink. I gave them water every day, winter and summer. For a while, we also kept several rabbits in a cage, and it was also my job to feed them.

Our actual lawn, however, was cared for by a man named Dutch Atkinson, who was sort of a local hermit. He never bathed, always smoked a pipe, and wore the same dirty bib overalls every day. My brother and I took over his lawn-mowing duties when we got older.

The remaining several acres of our land were rented out to a farmer down the road, Wilson Bellows, the father of my lifelong friend Janet Bellows Biddle, the wife of Bill Biddle. Their house was at the end of our street, just within the town boundaries, and backed up to their farm, which was officially outside Remington. Wilson alternately planted our small field with corn and soybeans. When he was working there, he would sometimes ask me to fill his thermos with fresh water. Once, when I filled it from the garden hose rather than from the kitchen sink as instructed, he tasted it, detected the rubber-like flavor imparted by the hose, and sent me back to do as I had been instructed. I've always remembered that.

It was a great place for a boy to grow up. There were a couple of sheds on the property: one was used to store hay and another in the pasture to feed and shelter the sheep. We kids used the hay bales to build forts and other things. This was only a few years following the end of World War II, and I remember one year we played army all summer. I have wonderful memories of digging a fox-hole in the ground and constructing a sod-covered top with a trap door. You could go inside and then cover it up so no one could see it. That took us all summer to build.

We also played lots of sports. We had an area in the backyard with a tree-mounted basketball goal and backboard, and we played there so much that the ground became as hard as a wooden gym floor.

For a couple of years, we also had a neighborhood football team called the Southside Bulldogs. I don't remember who we played, maybe just each other, but I recall spending as much time on the accouterments as we did on actual games. We got lime from the local feed store to make lines for the football field. Before games, we used a record player to play the national anthem.

We even had our own makeshift uniforms. We sent away for some felt bulldog heads we found in a mail-order catalog, and our mothers sewed them onto our jerseys.

This was truly a kids' paradise. There was even a creek that ran through the edge of our property. I remember having lots of good times in that. One of my friends had an old aluminum canoe, and we paddled it up and down the stream.

Naturally, after a day of running around, my brother and I worked up big appetites. I must say that my mother was not, nor did she ever claim to be, anything approaching a gourmet cook. We were always well-fed, but cooking just wasn't one of her favorite things. Her meals were enjoyable, but often rather plain. One of her specialties was a truly great meatloaf. In the summer we often had sweet corn and tomatoes from the garden, along with things like fried chicken, or ham slices.

Mom also baked cherry and blueberry pies. My father liked the blueberry ones in particular. It was easy to get the fruit because people sold truckloads of blueberries and strawberries on the roadside when they were in season.

My mother always kept a coffee can on the back of her stove, into which she'd pour bacon grease. As with most country cooks in those days, grease was essentially her all-purpose cooking oil. We even popped popcorn in bacon grease! If this sounds a bit gross to you, all I can say is, don't knock it until you try it.

Every school morning my brother and I would race down the stairs to the kitchen counter, where we'd find a small glass of orange juice waiting for each of us. My mother served it in little jelly jars with designs painted on them. It was pretty common back then for preserves to come in glass containers that could be repurposed as drinking glasses.

For breakfast, my brother Roger would always eat a bowl of Cheerios and I always had a bowl of Wheaties. We couldn't go out the door until we polished that off.

Actually, there was one other morning ritual to attend to before we grabbed our books and left. We always had a bottle of Multicebrin vitamins, manufactured by Eli Lilly and Company. Our family doctor, Dr. Richard Schantz, was a strong proponent of anything Lilly made, so each of us took one of these vitamins every morning. Dad would take the cap off the bottle, put four pills in the cap, and set them on the counter. My father took one, then my mom, and then my brother and I. It was my first introduction to the company.

When my grandfather and grandmother (on my dad's side) retired, they moved into town in Remington. My grandmother was an excellent cook and loved to prepare huge meals. While she still lived in the country, she did it all on a wood-burning stove. I remember watching her get things started by first placing wood in the stove's firebox. Then she removed one of the burner covers and inserted a handful of kerosene-soaked corn cobs. She kept a large stock of those on hand. She tossed a lit kitchen match into the open stovetop, and it would light with a loud "whoosh." It's a miracle no one was seriously injured by her lighting technique.

After she and my grandfather retired, my brother and I became intimately familiar with her culinary skills thanks to numerous visits to her house for lunch. During the years when my mother taught school, she of course didn't have time to fix lunch for us. My brother and I weren't particularly impressed by the options available in the school lunchroom, so at lunchtime, we became regular guests at my grandmother's. My father paid her and encouraged us to eat there, I now suspect, because it was a way to give her money that he knew she needed but didn't want to admit to needing.

The food she made for us was wonderful. There were fairly standard dishes like meatloaf and fried chicken, plus garden vegetables, as well as hominy and okra, and also fried mush—a cornmeal batter that's fried in a skillet like pancakes and served with butter and syrup. I still think about that mush with great affection.

Fortunately for us kids, nearly everything in the way of entertainment in Remington was either free or pretty cheap. A ticket at the town's movie theater cost 14 cents and a bag of popcorn a dime. So a quarter got you a movie and popcorn, plus a penny candy.

My chief childhood hobby was design and construction. It seemed like I was always building something. I used any spare cash I had to buy lumber, bolts, and nails from the hardware store. I built a lot of things out of scraps I scrounged, but occasionally I had to spend money on specialty parts.

The most complicated thing I ever built as a kid was a gasoline-powered car that, in simple terms, was similar in size to what we think of today as a go-kart. I bought four wheels at the hardware store that were meant, I think, for a wheelbarrow. Then I designed a steering mechanism using a steering wheel I scrounged from the automotive junkyard. It was attached to a steel rod that went down at an angle. I put two pulleys on that rod, with a clothesline strung to a mechanism I mounted on the front wheels. When you turned the wheel, it tightened the clothesline on one side and loosened it on the other, pointing the wheels left or right.

I mounted an old lawnmower engine on the back, attached a pulley to the inside of one of the back wheels, and linked the pulley on the engine's drive shaft to the wheel pulley using a slightly loose automobile fan belt. There was a little device I created out of a piece of pipe and yet another small pulley. The bottom end of the pipe was attached to the lower side of the car's frame, and the top half was covered with a grip from a bicycle handlebar. When you pushed the pipe forward, it tightened the belt against the pulley on the pipe, which in turn tightened the belt against the pulley on the gasoline engine and the pulley inside of the wheel, causing the car to go forward. I'm not sure where I got the idea, but I think mostly I just made it up through trial and error.

I never had a lot of chores, other than giving water to the sheep and mowing grass, because I was so busy with school activities. In the fall, because our town was too small to support a football team, I played softball. Of course, basketball practice started in October and continued every weeknight until March. This was, after all, the height of our state's enthusiasm for high school hoops. In towns like Remington, Friday night games were the only show in town.

Besides my sheep and rabbit duties, I was also in charge of picking up sticks in the yard and leaf raking in autumn. We raked them into piles at the edge of the street or on bare ground and burned them. To this day, I still remember it as the smell of autumn.

One thing I don't remember is ever having a key to our house. But this wasn't a problem because I never came home to a locked door. That's just the way it was. There were never any strangers in town, and we knew everybody. And I don't recall crime of any kind.

Growing up in that house, at that time, was an incredible experience. It seemed like a live version of old TV shows like

Ozzie and Harriet and *Father Knows Best*. It was a terrific place. It allowed me to have the sort of innocent, unspoiled childhood that, in retrospect, seems almost magical. And it taught me life lessons that no amount of money can buy.

WORK TO DO, LESSONS TO LEARN

Chapter Three

---

*What you say doesn't matter
nearly as much as what you do.*

In retrospect, I understand that during my childhood my family's finances were often much tighter than I realized. But it's a testament both to my parents and to the world in which they lived that I never felt the least bit disadvantaged. Quite the opposite, in fact. To the degree I even thought about it, I assumed we had plenty.

There was never anything that I wanted to do that I couldn't do or anything I needed that I couldn't get. But I didn't really want things that were particularly expensive. My desires were fairly modest and perfectly in scale with everyone else in the rural corner of the world where I grew up. Everybody worked hard and pulled their weight, but nobody could by any stretch of the imagination be called wealthy. We were mostly all in the same economic boat.

This made it very easy to be happy with what we had.

Or even delighted, as was the case for me on Christmas Day, 1944, one of my earliest memories. I got an old-school, all-metal, pedal-powered fire truck. I was so excited that I drove it in circles from room to room. But I learned years later that in 1944 you simply couldn't get something like that. It was the height of World War II, and metal stocks were used for bullets and tanks, not toys. My father purchased it secondhand from a friend whose own son had outgrown it years earlier. Dad painted it up like new, and I, at the age of two and a half, was none the wiser.

During my youth in Remington, I got many such object lessons about the importance of frugality, hard work, and dependability—both from personal experience and from watching my parents' conduct.

One of the most influential lessons was watching how my dad treated his banking customers. In those days, the State Bank of Remington kept what were known as banker's hours. It opened at 9 a.m. and closed at 3 p.m. on Monday, Tuesday, Wednesday, Friday, and Saturday. It was closed in the afternoon on Thursdays. But my father never kept banker's hours. Far from it. He was at his desk at 7:30 a.m. every morning, and in the afternoon he wouldn't leave until after 5 p.m., once the books had been balanced for the day. Keep in mind that this was accomplished not with computers, but with bound ledgers, paper transactions, and pen and pencil entries.

And his day didn't stop then. Even after all these years, I can still see my dad sitting on the back steps of our house with his knees bent up, smoking a cigarette with a farmer who'd stopped by the house after hours, knocked on the back door, and asked to talk about a crop loan. "This man can't come to the bank during banking hours because he's out in the field," my dad told me. "Of course, he's got to come and see me here."

He held these back-step, after-hours meetings all his adult life, and I never thought it unusual. In my mind, it was just how you treated people. It was one of my first lessons in proper customer service.

My dad understood that when it comes to integrity, what you say doesn't matter nearly as much as what you do. For instance, he took great pains to uphold the image of the bank in the community. My father would occasionally, though not with any great regularity, sip a Canadian bourbon before dinner. But he never bought it in Remington because he didn't want to create a negative impression and be seen going into or coming out of a liquor store. That would have been unthinkable to him because he was a banker. He had an image to uphold, and reputation was important to my parents. He took it very seriously because the image of the bank was just as much at stake as his own.

While my parents were my strongest role models when it came to learning about work, they weren't the only ones. Some things I learned from others, or from firsthand experience.

I started my first "job" while still in grade school. I received an allowance for mowing the lawn and then started mowing a handful of other yards around town. I would push my lawnmower to my various clients. If they were far away, my father, who came home for lunch most days, would put the lawnmower in the trunk of his car and drop me wherever I needed to go. Then, I'd either push it home or he'd pick me up later.

I typically got around $2 per yard, but I'd get $4 for a particularly large one. At my father's insistence, I kept a passbook savings account at the bank, and I was always encouraged to save at least some of my earnings—as I recall, maybe half. The rest was spending money.

During the winters of my high school years, I worked at Peck's, the local grocery store. I went in at 8 a.m. on Saturday and stayed until 9 p.m. I made five dollars a day, under the supervision of a wonderful man known as "Doc" Milner. I have no recollection of his actual first name. For a very long time, he ran the grocery store for the Pecks, who also owned an adjacent dry goods store.

On Saturdays, farm families came into town to do their shopping, and whoever was available would help them. You'd literally go around the store with them while they picked out things they wanted and carry their items back to the counter.

When we weren't helping customers, there were always other things to do. You stocked shelves with cans and boxes. The truck from the grocery wholesaler would come to the back door, and you unloaded the boxes and put them in the storeroom. I also learned, among a great many other things, how to cut pork chops from a pork loin and slice cheeses and luncheon meats with an electric slicer.

When it was time for a customer to check out, we totted everything up on an adding machine with a paper tape. There was also a huge old cash register. We each had an assigned key that we pushed to indicate whose transaction it was, and there was a crank on the side that you wound to open the drawer. Customers paid by cash and check. Doc Milner knew whose checks he shouldn't take and taught me how to handle such situations quietly and gracefully.

A few years after I stopped working there, Doc Milner died. He was found by an employee early one morning, collapsed in one of the aisles with his white butcher's apron on and the little device that stamped the prices on the tops of cans still in his hand. It was probably the way he would have wanted to go. I learned a lot of things from him, about life and running a business.

That grocery store was my first experience dealing with money and people and with the art of keeping six different balls in the air at the same time. I enjoyed it immensely. I also enjoyed the people who worked there and made many friends. One was Alice Dalton, a pretty young woman who was seven years older than me and a full-time store employee. Her boyfriend and soon-to-be-husband,

Bill Medley, would pick her up after work every Saturday night, and I would cash his paycheck for him.

She was a mentor of sorts for me. I sang at their wedding when she and Bill were married, and their first child was named Randy Lee. Sadly, he died in an automobile accident along with both of his grandparents when he was a young boy. I was able to stay in touch with both Alice and Bill over the years. Alice passed away in 2022 at age 87, after 67 years of marriage to Bill.

During my high school years, I landed a summer job that taxed my organizational abilities to their limit, not to mention my sheer capacity for hard work. My brother started working at a summer camp in the Tippecanoe River State Park near Winamac, Indiana. When I turned 15 or so, I signed on too, laboring there for many summers.

The camp, which sat on the banks of the Tippecanoe River, was built during the Great Depression by the Works Projects Administration and named Camp Potawatomi. It was full of rustic log buildings, and quite nice. Initially, I mostly did odd jobs, like helping around the kitchen and supervising campers assigned to assist with meals. The kids were Brownie Scouts and Girl Scouts, so they were maybe seven or eight, and no older than 12.

I worked at Camp Potawatomi every summer from age 15 until part of my junior year of college, spending 10 or 11 weeks away from Remington, which was about 50 miles from the camp. The experience profoundly impacted my life. The man who ran the place, Channing Vosloh, was a very successful, well-known Southern Indiana basketball coach. He and his wife, Rowena, were my surrogate parents during the summer, and their values were very consistent with what I grew up with. Over the years, the Voslohs and my parents became good friends and continued to socialize long after I grew up. I'm still in touch with their daughter, Channa Beth.

My parents would visit me every Sunday while I was away. My mother, bless her heart, would pick up my dirty laundry, wash it, and bring it back the following Sunday. I learned a lot of important lessons there: about working hard, but not working all the time; about honesty; and about getting along with people. This last bit of knowledge was vital in a place where you lived with the folks you worked with.

It also taught me not to be too rigid (or too proud) to tackle whatever jobs needed to be done. Even though you might be, say, a swimming instructor, if there was a toilet that needed unclogging, that was your job too.

For instance, prior to my last several years at the camp, I had become a certified Red Cross Water Safety Instructor, meaning I could test, certify, and license Red Cross Lifeguards, a requirement for anyone seeking such a summer job. It was kind of a big deal. One of my biggest tasks was helping to oversee the camp's swimming pool. But I didn't spend my days sitting regally in a lifeguard chair. Overseeing the pool meant keeping it in good condition, which meant changing the chlorine tank, cleaning filters, and washing the pool itself. And when there was a lot of canoeing on the river, I helped with that. I also had major responsibilities in the dining room, supervising the kids who helped with place settings and cleanup. To this day, when I set a table, I still hear my instructions to those campers in my mind, "forks on the left, spoons on the right, knives inside the spoons, blades to the left!"

In that mess hall's kitchen, I learned the beginnings of almost everything I know about cooking. The camp was managed by a staff that remained in place all summer while the campers and their counselors came and went. The food was prepared by two or three elderly ladies (or so they seemed to me, a teenager) who worked in winter as school cooks. Part of my role was to help them as needed, and I learned to make everything from pancakes to mashed potatoes to fried chicken—for 150 people. When you cook in those quantities, you really learn to do it without fear. For instance, if you put too much milk in the mashed potatoes, you fix it by adding another few pounds of potatoes. Simple!

For several summers I also had the privilege of working with one of my best high school friends, Mike Merkel. He also played the cornet and sat next to me in the high school band, actually just ahead of me because he played it very well! We spent several summers together at camp, sleeping on metal-frame, military cots in a room we shared. When he graduated from high school, he went to Purdue University, got a degree in engineering, and went to work for Western Electric in Indianapolis, which at the time was the manufacturing arm of AT&T.

But he was also an ROTC graduate and was commissioned as a second lieutenant. He was called to active duty in Vietnam, where tragically he was killed by a Viet Cong attack on a remote communications site he commanded. He was my closest friend to die during the war. He's buried in the Remington Cemetery, not 30 feet from my parents.

Obviously, I got a lot more from the various jobs I held in my youth than mere money. As for my parents, of all the intangibles they passed along to me, I think the most important work-related wisdom was a sense of value—a belief that it didn't much matter what you did in life as long as you kept your commitments and did the very best you could.

If you had an assignment in school, that was a commitment. If you promised to be someplace at 8 a.m., you showed up on time.

And in sports, if the coach told you to do something a certain way, you didn't complain or second-guess. You just did it.

At about the same time, I got another notion in my head that also came straight from my parents—most strongly from my mother. I believed that if I worked hard and learned to think beyond the moment, there were all kinds of things I could do with my life. I hope this idea didn't give me an inflated ego. Just what I would call a reasonable level of self-confidence. It served me well during my high school academic career and my college days.

SCHOOL DAYS

Chapter Four

I loved words and writing, and that's stayed with me all my life.

The Remington Public Schools, where I studied from the first grade through the 12th, consisted of two side-by-side buildings: one for the first six grades and the other for grades seven through twelve. The elementary school building had stood for years and years, and like many such places, it had a distinctive smell. It came from the cleaning products they used. Even today, if I catch a whiff of that odor, it takes me right back to my time as a young student.

Of course, I recall a lot more about my academic career in Remington than just the smell of the building. It was a wonderful experience. There was plenty of hard work, but I felt that I learned a lot and that I was doing it at an institution that my town took very seriously.

The teachers and students were in many ways one big family—or at least one family. I'm guessing the entire high school student body was about 150, and all twelve grades totaled about 400 to 450 students.

Different grades were of course taught in different rooms, but in such a small facility there were lots of overlaps.
Elementary classes usually stayed in the same room all day, but starting in the seventh grade, students went from class to class. And from seventh grade on, different grades shared the same teachers.

Though the school was small, there were still a respectable number of academic options. If you didn't plan on going to college or planned to go directly to work on the family farm after graduation, there were practical courses such as farm shop, which was like an old-time shop class, but with an emphasis on servicing agricultural equipment. You probably also joined the Future Farmers of America.

If you wanted to go to college, which was the path I chose, the curriculum included a foreign language option—either Latin or Spanish. I chose Latin, along with things like chemistry, physics, and math. I was okay with physics and chemistry but wasn't really passionate about them. I worked hard at both, however, because during high school I entertained the idea of becoming a doctor. In retrospect, this was probably not because I had a deep love of the field, but because it seemed like a good career choice.

The subject I really enjoyed was English. I loved words and writing, and that's stayed with me all my life. I pay a lot of attention to words and to the importance of accurate communication. I think I owe this trait to both of my parents, who cared very much about reading and literature. In his eighties, my father would still recite a number of poems he'd memorized as a boy. For as long as I can remember, I've always read lots of books.

I also had a wonderful English teacher named Mary May. She and her husband Bill were great friends with my parents. She was an amazing lady who died several years ago at the age of 101. I saw her at an event in Remington when she was in her mid-90s and asked if she was still driving. She said, "Oh my, yes. There are several older ladies here in Remington who rely on me for transportation!"

She was just one of a long list of excellent teachers from whom I had the privilege of learning. I have to say that during my Remington schooling, I don't recall having any weak ones. They were all very capable, dedicated, and hardworking. Watching how they conducted themselves was perhaps just as instructive as the academic knowledge they shared.

Our school principal, Donald Utter, made a huge impression on me. He came to Remington after serving in World War II, working first as the high school basketball coach and math teacher and then later as the principal. During my senior year, I enjoyed the distinction of being selected by him to work in the school's office, answering the phone from 11 a.m. to noon when his secretary was at lunch.

Though it was never described in such terms, I realize now that being allowed to cover for his secretary was quite an honor. It meant he thought you were dependable. I certainly thought the same of him. I remember being impressed by his organizational skills. He had big calendars on the wall that mapped out everything going on throughout the life of the school, and he kept it all running like a finely tuned machine. He was a man who was admired and respected, and I certainly felt that way about him.

We also had a wonderful music program for a school our size, and it was all thanks to its long-serving director, Robert B. Shearer. He taught me how to play the cornet. But he also taught me deeper lessons about succession planning and how to organize, energize, and constantly refresh a large, ongoing enterprise.

Mr. Shearer grew up in Remington and graduated from DePauw University just a few years after my father. The town and the school's music program were his life. Parents and kids just sort of accepted the fact that everyone was going to take part in it. He started me on the cornet in the second grade, which wasn't at all unusual. At some point, he would approach pretty much every child of that age and tell them what instrument they were going to learn.

By starting us so young, by carefully selecting our instruments, and then by providing high-quality lessons and high expectations, he knew he would always have a steady supply of well-trained recruits for the high school concert band. We didn't have enough bodies to field a conventional marching band, and since we also didn't have a football team, there weren't any halftime shows where it could regularly perform. One of the few times we actually marched was during Remington's Memorial Day parade.

You'd think this would have put us at a distinct disadvantage in music competitions, but it didn't. Indeed, this was where Mr. Shearer's succession planning and high standards really bore fruit. Every year we competed with much larger schools and bands in the statewide concert band competition, and every year we won first place. This was all thanks to the expectations of excellence that began when he started our early musical training, with an eye toward filling slots in the high school concert band that wouldn't need filling for a decade.

But Mr. Shearer's methods taught me a lot more than just proper succession planning. He also taught me to aim high—that if you worked hard, there was no limit to what you could accomplish.

Almost all of my teachers were also pillars of the community—leaders in local organizations and active in their churches. I've thought about that so much in recent years because I think the way teachers are perceived, supported, and admired these days is too often quite different—and not for the better.

My teachers were mostly women. They lived in a time when education was one of the very few professions open to them. This limited their career aspirations, but it helped me and my classmates greatly. We had the benefit of sitting in the presence of some very high-quality individuals who in today's world might well have careers in other fields.

In my case, that list of teachers never included my mother. After my brother and I got older, she taught sixth grade at Remington for a number of years—that is, until I finished fifth grade and was ready to move up. She didn't want to teach her own son, which she feared might look unseemly. So she swapped grades with the fifth-grade teacher, Mr. Casey, and our class was taught by him two years in a row.

During the school year, my social calendar was just as packed as my academic roster. I participated in anything and everything, from the town's big Halloween celebration to dozens of extracurricular activities, including school dances, plays, and of course sports.

This could have led to some interesting scheduling problems. For instance, I was on both the high school basketball team and Mr. Shearer's concert band. As a freshman, when I played in the preliminary game on the "B" team, as soon as the game was over (and while I was still in my uniform), I grabbed my cornet and performed with the spirit band before the varsity game.

Our basketball team played in the state tournament every year, back when there was just one class for all of Indiana's 700 or so high school teams. We never went very far because we were so small, but our games were the focus of Remington's winter social life.

In addition to playing basketball, I also ran track, which was my best high school sport. I set some school records in both junior and senior high that stood for a long time. They were in the broad jump (now called the long jump) and the 100-yard dash.

There were plenty of other activities besides athletics. We staged junior and senior class plays, and I was in both of those. I don't remember the name of either production, but I do recall that I had to kiss a girl in one of them. What an embarrassing experience—so embarrassing at the time that I remember it to this day.

Because Remington was such a stable town, the cast of characters from my school years, be it teachers or students, didn't change all that much. The kids in my first-grade class were by and large the same ones with whom I graduated from high school.

Besides Mike Merkel, one of my best school friends was Bill Biddle, the son of Chester Biddle and his wife Edith, who were also very good friends of my parents. The Biddles owned a farm that had been in their family for several generations. Bill and I, and our families, did a lot of things together when we were growing up, including a couple of summer vacation fishing trips. Along with his wife Janet, we have remained good friends over the years. Bill and his son Bryce now operate the 320-acre farm that I own near Remington, where they also run a very large farming operation of several thousand acres and produce hybrid seed. Having that farm, which I purchased in 1998, helps me stay connected to the Remington community.

Another boyhood friend was Jeff May, who lived down the street. We used to get up very early and run for about four miles together before school to condition ourselves for basketball. This was long before people commonly went out jogging so we got a lot of strange looks and offers of a ride. He was quite a comedian and a very talented musician. Living next to Jeff on our street was another friend named Roy Hansell. His father was the local pharmacist. It was Roy who had the old canoe we used to take out on the creek.

Around the corner, within a block and a half of where I grew up, was a girl in my class named Carol Schantz. Her father was Remington's doctor, and she was a very talented pianist. She got a degree in music from Southern Methodist University and has been involved with music all of her life.

I was also very good friends with Ronnie Q. Gillam, the son of the town's lawyer. We went to college together and became fraternity brothers. Having Ronnie Q. around when I got to IU was a great comfort. We're still very connected and try to see each other once a year back in Remington.

When I first arrived at college, I felt more than a little intimidated. I graduated from Remington High School in 1960 with a class of just 42, and now I found myself at a university with around 15,000 students.

But I soon realized I had an education that, though perhaps it lacked some of the options available at larger schools, nevertheless prepared me as well as most. In some ways, it was probably better because I got so much personal attention. There were of course some areas where I hadn't enjoyed the same breadth of curriculum as others, but I suspect the teachers I had were as dedicated and hardworking as one would find in most places. Honestly, on balance, I couldn't have asked for more.

FROM A SMALL TOWN TO A BIG SCHOOL

Chapter Five

It would have taken a quarter of Remington to fill some of my big IU lectures.

I wasn't sure about my career path when I graduated from high school, but I was sure about which college I wanted: Indiana University.

There was never any thought of going out of state, so that meant attending one of Indiana's two big state schools, IU or Purdue University, both of which seemed incredibly glamorous to me—like moving up from a small town to the big leagues.

Then as now, the universities drew from different academic pools. Purdue attracted mostly people who wanted to work in engineering, agriculture, and certain scientific fields. But if you wanted to be a doctor, pursue a business degree, or get a classic liberal arts education, you leaned toward IU.

I knew that a career in engineering or agriculture wasn't for me. Plus, my brother went to IU, which I know had some influence. While my father would have loved it had I chosen DePauw and applied for a scholarship there, I didn't want to go to a small school, so I don't think I ever seriously considered anyplace other than IU, nor did I apply anywhere else. IU just seemed like the logical spot for me. Little did I realize, when I reported to campus in the fall of 1960, that my college experience would take place at a peculiar cusp in American history, as an era of relative calm (and social conformity) gave way to years of turmoil and change.

My parents weren't concerned about the fact that I hadn't yet chosen a major. They said I shouldn't try to make up my mind until I saw all the things that might be available—things that hadn't even occurred to me in Remington.

It was sound advice. I remember thinking about my father, who had been very happy, as far as I know, essentially sitting at the same desk in the bank, doing generally the same thing for 45 years. I knew that I didn't want any part of that. The opportunity to face new challenges and do new things appealed to me. Even if, for the moment, I wasn't sure what those new challenges and new things might be.

I saw myself, almost by default, as premed. At least that's what I wrote on my entrance forms. Truth be told, I also entertained thoughts about becoming a broadcast journalist. It wasn't until my sophomore year that I found my calling in business.

My first task as a freshman was simply to get my footing. I grew up in a town with fewer than a thousand people. It would have taken a quarter of Remington to fill some of my big IU lectures I attended. It was rather daunting until I got to know other students personally and learned that they were just as apprehensive as I was. So I rapidly overcame any fears that being from a small school meant I was not "good enough."

Not that there weren't still difficulties. My first semester was a real struggle. For one thing, I took on too much coursework. School had always been easy for me, so I assumed college would be more of the same. I found out just how wrong I was in French class. The language wasn't even offered at Remington, but now I found myself in a room with students who had taken years of it in high school. I felt fortunate to escape with a "C." Those early struggles put me on notice that the game had changed.

One of the things that helped me deal with both the academic load and the culture shock of attending such a large school was my involvement in extracurricular activities. I've often said that in many ways, they were my true major and the real source of my career. I saw going to class as a necessary evil and wasn't all that focused on it. I just didn't yet understand that taking a particular literature or economics class would give me knowledge of great importance. Later, of course, I understood that formal learning was far from pointless. There are concepts I learned in IU classrooms that I've remembered and used all my life. But the overall college experience was my true learning environment. In essence, I learned how to learn. It was wonderful, and it shaped who I am today.

I was caught up in volunteer work almost from day one, when I joined the organizing committee for Fall Carnival, one of the major annual campus events. I was surrounded by talented people with the creativity and willingness to think outside the box and to do things in ways that energized me. I was fascinated and stimulated by this, and I worked hard to make sure my part of the event went well. After that, I worked my way up the volunteer structure until, by my junior year, I served as the event's general chairman.

A love of politics also drew me into student government. I served in some appointed positions and then was elected to the student senate. Eventually, I was elected president of my senior class. Though honestly, there wasn't much for the president to do once elected.

During my senior year, I also had my own Sunday evening radio show, which I enjoyed very much. It was part of a slate of programs put together by the Student Union, including someone who did sports and another who was the main disc jockey, playing popular music on the studio's turntables. I did interviews as well as an hour of classical music. I didn't know much about classical music, so I just read the liner notes from the album jackets over the air. That seemed to convince the audience I knew what I was doing.

I also joined the Greek fraternity system—specifically the Theta Chis. My brother had been a Theta Chi and had very good friends there, so when I got on campus, I moved directly into the house as a pledge. My friend from Remington, Ronnie Q. Gillam, moved in after the first semester. Our house was located at pretty much the center of the campus. A year or two after I graduated, it was purchased by the university, torn down, and replaced with the magnificent IU Musical Arts Center. But some of the original trees and a parking lot from when I was a student are still there, so whenever I visit the campus, I can still visualize where I lived.

IU's football stadium (Memorial Stadium) was brand-new when I was a freshman. I attended the very first game ever played there in the fall of 1960—while serving as a sideline dog walker! Our fraternity's big English bulldog named OX would frequently escape and liked to wander around campus. He started showing up at football practices. Pretty soon the cheerleaders adopted him as the team's unofficial mascot. So, on game day, I, as a Theta Chi pledge, was given the task of parading our bulldog back and forth behind the home team's bench.

I was never interested in becoming an officer of the fraternity or really got much involved. I made several lifelong friends there (Fred Buckingham, Dr. Tom Hayhurst, and my roommate, Larry Contos, for example) and was active socially, but I typically focused on things that were happening in the broader campus community. That's where I made the most lasting friendships, including Jim Morris and his wife Jackie Harrell Morris, Jim Kittle, Dave Frick, Jay B. Hunt, Curt Simic, Terry Clapacs, Rich Woosnam, Dave Gibson and his wife Ginny Shaw Gibson, and Bill Hunt to name a few.

In spite of my earlier reference to academic work as a "necessary evil," I do recall several classes that I liked very much. For instance, Business Law, taught by Dr. Charles M. Hewett. This was my first experience with the law and my first with studying, analyzing, and presenting cases. I found it fascinating, and it caused me to eventually apply to law school after getting my undergraduate degree. Honestly, it's an unfulfilled aspiration that I still harbor.

There were a few women in my business classes, but the vast majority were men. I remember that one of my female classmates was admitted to law school, which seemed very unique at that time. In the early 1960s, women just didn't do that. Now, they often make up the majority of law school students.

I also recall that female undergrads were required to be locked in their dormitories or sororities at 11 p.m. on Sundays and weeknights and at 1 a.m. on Fridays and Saturdays. But men weren't. Hard to believe today. The powers that be asserted that if they locked up the women, the men would stay out of trouble.

It really was a different world back then—especially when it came to campus social life. Each year in early December, there was a dance sponsored by the Student Union called the Opening of Formal. The fraternities and sororities weren't supposed to host their own black-tie events before this dance, which served as the gala opening for the campuses' formal dance season. Needless to say, it's been a few years since anyone had to bother with prohibiting college students from dressing up for black tie events.

The tradition of holding formal dances didn't last much longer. In fact, at about the time I graduated and in the following years, many such traditions started to go away. Students were for the most part still focused on getting a degree, getting a job, getting married, and having fun, but we also started to see the very first peace marches and "ban the bomb" rallies. The campus was no longer an oasis of tranquility, isolated from the "real world."

This brings me to perhaps the most memorable lecture I ever attended—or didn't. It was a finance class that took place on November 22, 1963. The fact that it's burned into my mind has nothing to do with the subject matter.

The class was large and met twice a week rather than five times. It was so long that there was a short coffee break in the middle. On this particular occasion, I left the business building during the break and walked to the Student Union with a group of other students. It was a beautiful fall day of my senior year. I can still picture it. But when we got inside the union, everyone was just standing around in the lobby. No one moved, and the only sound came from the speakers of the building's music system. Only no music was playing. Instead, a voice on the radio told us that President Kennedy had been shot.

The turmoil of the 1960s had begun. And it was about to intrude on my own life in an even more personal way.

We still had the military draft back then, and the war in Vietnam was about to ramp up. If you were over 18 and out of school, it was very likely you were going to be called up. So, based on the experiences of a number of people—including my brother, who had been in the Reserve Officers' Training Corps (ROTC) and then on active duty—I decided that if I was going to go, I'd rather go as an officer. So I joined the ROTC.

Actually, "joined" is probably the wrong word because, at the time, two years of ROTC were mandatory for boys who went to state schools. However, I stayed enrolled for the program's full four years, at the end of which I was commissioned into the army as a second lieutenant. It turned out to be a very good decision for reasons I didn't fully grasp at the time. My stint in the military gave me leadership training and a host of experiences that served me well for the rest of my life.

MY FIRST SUMMER IN THE "REAL WORLD"

Chapter Six

If we don't have it and we can't get it for you, you're better off without it.

So I graduated from Indiana University in June of 1964 with a degree in business, an ROTC commission, and orders to start a two-year tour of duty in the army come October. My parents of course attended the graduation ceremony which, as president of the senior class, I actually played a small part in. I gave a short speech and participated in the induction of the entire class into the alumni association.

And then I joined the "real" world.

My ROTC commissioning ceremony was held that same weekend. We were all dressed in our uniforms and had our gold second lieutenant's bars pinned on us. Mine were pinned on by a girl I dated during my junior and senior years. We'd grown up together in Remington and been good friends, but then we began seeing each other fairly seriously at IU. More about her later.

I started interviewing for jobs well before graduation, and the times created what was very much a seller's market for graduating seniors with business degrees. In my case, anyone who hired me would have to do so with the understanding that, come October, I was going away for two years. And yet, I still was invited to have a large number of interviews and received several offers. Of course, I focused on companies that would commit to taking me back after my military service. Some would, and some wouldn't.

I also applied and was admitted to the Indiana University School of Law. I then wrote a letter to its dean, explaining that I couldn't enroll in the fall class and asking for a two-year delay, which was granted. In later years I liked to tell the attorneys I worked with about this reserved spot. I never got around to going to law school, but I like to think there's still a place waiting for me if I change my mind!

At the time, my interest in the legal profession was far less whimsical. I wanted to go to law school because at some point I thought I might eventually pursue a career in politics and public service. An IU law degree would have provided some extremely useful statewide networking contacts.

In addition to a large number of corporate interviews, including with Procter & Gamble, Pepsi, Cummins, and a Wisconsin-based paper company, I was also approached by the college recruiter for AT&T, Jesse Overman, who worked for the company's wholly owned local subsidiary, Indiana Bell. He called on behalf of the Bell System recruiting team and said that he'd visited IU's placement office, looked through the files of graduating seniors, and wanted to talk to me in a couple of weeks when he planned to return to campus.

I was of course very flattered that, at a time when some students were working valiantly to obtain interviews with companies, I was actually approached by one. I agreed to a meeting even though I knew almost nothing about their business and had no preexisting interest in working for the phone company.

I'd acquired a certain attitude about telephone companies during my youth in Remington. Our town's phone company was a small, independent outfit with two operators and one installation-and-repair employee. He wasn't exactly the most admired person in town. But he was the face of the only telephone organization I'd known, and I didn't see myself becoming associated with something like that.

Nevertheless, I took the interview. It was part of a relatively new AT&T initiative called the Initial Management Development Program (IMDP).

What the AT&T human resources people had discovered was that if you took a group of academic standouts from any college class and then looked at their performance and career progression 10 or 25 years later, you'd see that high grades weren't, by themselves, a good predictor of what they went on to accomplish. Rather, college graduates who successfully carried an academic load, but also demonstrated strong and significant leadership skills in campus activities and organizations, most often rose to the top of the company's leadership ranks. AT&T recruiters were particularly interested in students identified and selected as leaders by their own peers.

I was of course president of the senior class, had my own radio program, and even ran a small company that I called Tobias Enterprises. I'd had some great business cards printed that included the slogan, *"If we don't have it and we can't get it for you, you're better off without it."* I thought it was very descriptive!

Actually, it was quite a lucrative little enterprise. I took orders on behalf of several suppliers of custom novelty goods from social chairpersons of sororities, fraternities, and other organizations who needed bling for various events such as beer mugs with people's names on them, personalized sweatshirts, or whatever. I would buy things for a dollar and sell them for two. It was pure profit. One year, with a friend and partner named Bill Godfrey, we were even awarded a contract to supply Christmas trees to campus dormitories. I got into all of this because a company that sold those kinds of products contacted me. They liked to approach student leaders because they figured they had the best campus contacts and could serve as a ready-made distribution system. Perhaps this business experience, which I of course listed on my resume, was also one of the things that attracted AT&T, but it was mostly because I was president of my class.

The job interview itself was pretty typical for the time. I put on my suit and tie and went to the School of Business Placement Office for a sit-down. I was to have read AT&T's annual report and prepared some questions about the company. They, in turn, asked some fairly standard questions about my background and career aspirations, and then asked me to talk about life experiences where I felt good and experiences where I felt disappointed about what I'd done. I also took some kind of personality test.

As a follow-up to that initial screening and get-acquainted interview, I had lunch with a man who, interestingly, worked for me later in my career. At the time, he was responsible for all of the telephone service in the southern half of Indiana, and his office was in Bloomington. I ultimately was invited to Indianapolis to meet some more senior people.

After all that, I was offered a job. I would go to work a week or so after I graduated in June of 1964 and stay until a week or so before I went on active duty in October. When I came back two years later, assuming it all went well and that I wanted to return to the company, I would have two years and four months of seniority, which would be considered when deciding what assignment and compensation I would then be given. So I would have options. I could return to AT&T or go to law school as originally planned.

This sounded like an excellent arrangement, and of course it was. However, I was in no sense a "made man." The philosophy of AT&T's IMDP program was basically "up or out." Participants were expected to meet a certain number of performance and evaluation benchmarks. If, at the end of your first year, a decision hadn't been made that you were a likely candidate to be promoted to the district manager level in the first five years, then you were probably going to be counseled out of the business. Your boss was always a high-potential person, and part of his evaluation was how well he developed you.

My very first boss, when I started out at AT&T's Evansville office, was just such a young, very high-potential manager. I was 22 at the time, and he was 29. His name was Bob Allen. To say that things worked out for him, and for me, would be an understatement. Less than 25 years later, I became the vice-chairman at AT&T, and Bob was the chairman and CEO, the two most senior people in the company. Following our days together in Evansville, we remained in touch and friends throughout our careers. But perhaps surprisingly, even though we worked in close proximity on several assignments, I did not work directly for Bob again until he became AT&T's CEO. It was pure coincidence and quite amazing that both of us, after starting out together in Evansville, ended up at the top of the company. But that's a story for a later chapter.

An important part of the IMDP program was that you were given immediate responsibility. In my very first position, two weeks after graduating from IU, I had eight people reporting to me, some of whom had worked for the company for 10 or 15 years. It was a test to see how quickly I could learn one particularly important lesson: that whether you're a low-level manager or the CEO, you'll never get anything done all by yourself. Leadership is about getting the people in the organization to want to do the job—for themselves, for the company, and perhaps to some degree, for you. Some people understand this instinctively, and some don't.

It was a great experience, and I had wonderful people working for me. They just couldn't have been more helpful. I also assisted with a big technological advancement that took place in the small town of Boonville, 20 miles east of Evansville on the Ohio River. Boonville was the last Indiana town still using "manual telephone service." This meant that when you picked up a phone, an operator answered and said, "Number please." You then gave the operator the number you wanted and they connected you.

Even in 1964, this system was very antiquated. But instead of upgrading the town to rotary dial phones (another now-vanished technology in which one dialed using a circular, rotary ring with a finger hole for each number), we skipped straight to the then-new Touch-Tone system, which basically computerized local calls through an electronic switching system, eliminating the need for an operator. Touch-tone phones used transistors to generate tones to operate the switching equipment when you pushed numbered buttons on the phone, whereas rotary dial phones used mechanically generated pulses. Boonville became the first Indiana Bell-served community to receive this upgrade.

So I spent the summer of 1964 working for AT&T in Evansville, for $6,500 per year. This was so much money for a brand-new college graduate that I couldn't spend it all. I rented an apartment that was carved out of an old house on the banks of the Ohio River. The owner had just recently divided it into four or five rental units. The floor plan was a little "off." For instance, there was no room in my kitchen for the refrigerator, so it sat in the dining room. But compared to my college living arrangements, it was a palace. And it was mine. I thought it was quite grand.

This was the first time I had my own place and my own money. I was so excited and interested in my new job that I neglected another huge project that was supposed to be under development at the time—my impending marriage.

Remember the girl I mentioned earlier, who pinned on my second lieutenant's bars at my ROTC commissioning ceremony? In the latter stages of my senior year, we became engaged and planned to marry at the end of 1964, just before I went into the military. It is certainly not as usual today, but in the 1960s it was often the norm to develop a relationship in college and get married shortly after graduation. She graduated when I did, and that summer she found a job in Indianapolis while I worked in Evansville. During the very early part of the summer, we would visit each other on weekends when we could.

But very soon, it became apparent that this plan was an ill-conceived mistake. I focused more and more on my work and had less and less interest in finding time to spend with her, or to spend thinking about a wedding. I soon began to question whether we were on the right path. I'm sure she must have too. By early July we both began to understand we were headed for a train wreck. I don't recall exactly who said what to whom, but at the end of a conversation held shortly after she arrived in Evansville on a Friday evening, we ended it all peacefully, and she got in her car and drove away. That was the last time either of us saw each other until our 50th high school reunion.

It wasn't at all a bitter breakup. We just realized we were about to make an enormous mistake. Our relationship could have formed the basis for a good, lifelong friendship, but it shouldn't have gone as far as it did. I'm incredibly grateful we called a halt when we did, and I assume she is too.

Shortly thereafter, I went on active duty. So I was essentially gone from Indiana for two years. By the time I got back, she was married to someone else and so was I.

As for AT&T, I apparently performed up to or beyond expectations during my initial summer IMDP assignment because after my military service I would return and spend decades with the company. That first summer was a life-altering experience and one that can be chalked up almost entirely to serendipity because, if they hadn't called me, I certainly would never have called them.

ACTIVE DUTY

Chapter Seven

Block House Signal Mountain, known to artillerymen the world over.

The summer I spent with AT&T (of which Indiana Bell was a wholly owned subsidiary) was a momentous time not just for me but for the country as well.

Two months after I started my first "real" job in June of 1964, the U.S. Senate passed the Gulf of Tonkin Resolution. It was in response to an August incident in which a small United States Navy vessel named the *Turner Joy* was allegedly attacked while cruising the Gulf of Tonkin off the coast of Vietnam. North Vietnamese gunboats were reported in the ship's area by radar operators, and at some point, during a significant thunderstorm, a lookout thought the *Turner Joy* had been fired on by the North Vietnamese. However, there were no hits, and no gunboats were actually seen.

News of the encounter, which historians refer to as the Gulf of Tonkin Incident, quickly made its way to the Pentagon and the White House. At the time, there was already controversy about whether the U.S. should withdraw its military advisors from South Vietnam. President Lyndon Johnson, who wanted not only to keep them but to increase their numbers so they could better defend themselves, seized on the incident as justification for a larger deployment. In the passion of the moment, the U.S. Congress gave the President the authority he sought by passing the so-called Gulf of Tonkin Resolution by a vote of 414 to 0 in the House of Representatives and 88 to 2 in the Senate.

In later years, political leaders advocating for the escalation of our involvement would point to the Gulf of Tonkin Resolution as all the authorization required for further expansions of America's presence in Southeast Asia.

Interestingly, the lookout who reported the incoming rounds was later quizzed closely about the encounter by military investigators and admitted to some uncertainty. Many historians later concluded that what he thought was gunfire was more likely thunder and lightning. By that point, however, it was not an assessment anyone in Washington wanted to hear.

I reported for active duty in October of 1964, a few months after these events, and at the very beginning of the national buildup for war. I went to Fort Sill, Oklahoma, where only a few officers were wearing the shoulder patch of the Army's Military Assistance Command Vietnam or MACV, indicating they'd already been to Vietnam. The patch was still a fairly rare sight. Before long, the absence of a MACV patch on an officer's uniform meant it was highly likely he would soon be headed to Vietnam. The presence of the patch meant it was likely he would be going back.

I drove to Fort Sill in a beige-colored, four-door, hand-me-down Ford sedan that was given to me by my father—definitely not the sort of vehicle a young man would have chosen for himself. I packed it with all my worldly possessions for the two-day drive from Remington to Oklahoma. I reported for active duty with some apprehension. As a second lieutenant, I was officially an officer and a gentleman, fully trained on the basic responsibilities of a junior officer. But I still wasn't trained on the additional complexities required of a newly minted artillery officer. But at least I had company. I reported along with about a hundred other brand-new second lieutenants to become the members of the next Field Artillery Officers Basic Class (FAOBC) at the artillery school, to undergo 13 weeks of artillery officer initial training.

At that moment, I had other problems besides not knowing anything about artillery. For instance, I had no place to live. In those days, because of capacity issues at Fort Sill, junior officers received a monthly housing allowance of $110.20 and found their own accommodations instead of living in the bachelor officer quarters. So I pooled my resources with three other lieutenants toward a three-month lease on an apartment in a very nice complex with a swimming pool. I mean, it was luxurious. The four of us stayed there together throughout the 13-week program.

I had no idea where I was going after my training, which was to wrap up in late January. None of us had orders for our next assignments, which meant I was going to be there during Christmas, with neither the time nor the money to get home.

As it turned out, I did have the opportunity to spend the Christmas break with my good friend and fraternity brother Fred Buckingham and his wife, Diane. I had been the best man at their wedding just a few months earlier. Fred was a graduate of the IU Air Force ROTC program and was undergoing pilot training at Vance Air Force Base in Enid, Oklahoma, not far from Fort Sill. For Fred, it was the beginning of a long and distinguished military career. He ultimately retired as a Brigadier General—at the time, the first IU Air Force ROTC graduate to reach flag rank.

For all three of us, it was the first Christmas of our lives away from Indiana. And to add to my own melancholy, I fully expected to be sent to Vietnam.

But that's not what happened. My orders were to stay at Fort Sill and become a member of the artillery school faculty. My mother was always convinced this had everything to do with my demonstrated leadership as an artillery officer. I could never convince her, and eventually stopped trying, that it just as likely had more to do with chance. In the military, sometimes it's a bad thing when your number comes up, but sometimes it's not.

So I spent the balance of my two-year assignment teaching at Fort Sill's artillery school. Oddly, I taught courses that had to do with communications. And this, once again, was pure chance—not because someone found out about my AT&T job and thought it would be a good fit. That, as anyone familiar with the sometimes arbitrary nature of the army's personnel assignment decisions (at least in those days) understands, just isn't how it works. I've always suspected that if they had known I was on a leave of absence from AT&T, they would have put me in the gunnery department!

Yet, my two years of service turned out to be fortuitous, both in the kind of work I did and the people with whom I did it. Both impacted the rest of my life. For instance, I found myself teaching classes to officers who in almost all cases outranked me. And during my last months of service, I gave briefings and training to colonels and generals who were on their way to Vietnam from duty assignments elsewhere. They were passing through Fort Sill to get up to speed on new equipment with which they weren't familiar.

This was extremely helpful to me because during my business career I learned that the ability to teach, motivate, communicate, and be able to defend every word to your superiors are arguably some of the most important attributes of a leader. In the army, I got two years to practice these skills. Looking back, it was a terrific experience. I didn't always see it that way at the time, but I later realized that I liked the military discipline, order, and traditions. To this day, I'm a proud member of the United States Field Artillery Association, the Association of the United States Army, and the American Legion Post 280 in Remington.

Firing artillery is a unique experience. We would do our target shooting against junked cars painted in bright colors that you could just barely see with binoculars out on the Signal Mountain firing range, a place, as the saying goes, that is a landmark "known to artillerymen the world over!" Your task as a student forward observer was to learn both the technique and terminology for radioing your assessment of the precise location of the target back to the fire direction center or FDC, which in turn calculated the settings for the guns needed to put the shells on the target and transmitted those instructions to the gun crews. Today this would be accomplished using GPS coordinates and computers. In those days it involved a lot of manual assessment and calculations.

This was just as complicated and demanding as it sounds. The method was to drop a shell from a single gun somewhere just past the target by 100 to 200 meters. Then, by spotting where it landed and referencing that spot on a map, you calculated how far you needed to fire a round to drop the shell exactly the same distance *just short of* the target. A perfect demonstration of your ability would be to put the first round 100 meters beyond the target, drop the second round 100 meters short of the target, and then split the difference on the third round, exactly on the target. This is called "bracketing."

On the range, we would first bracket and then, if the gunnery instructor confirmed you were actually precisely on the target, as a reward for your performance, you were permitted to give the command to have all six guns in our training battery "fire for effect." If you'd bracketed properly, the car you shot at would explode into a million pieces. Controlling those guns and seeing what they could do was a very intimidating experience. I've never done anything like that since. It's why the artillery branch proudly refers to itself as "The King of Battle."

When I wasn't on the artillery range, I was doing my best to live my life. Lawton, Oklahoma, neighboring Fort Sill, was in some ways a fairly typical town, except for the fact that its main industry was the military. There was a lot of vice and not much culture. The Vietnam buildup meant that business was booming—especially for bar owners, with a whole string located just off-post. It was kind of a gritty place.

My apartment stint with my three bunkmates didn't last. After basic officer training, the other three were transferred overseas. So I struck up a friendship with two other artillery school instructors, and the three of us joined two others who were already renting a rundown house in a not-very-nice part of town. The landlady had no idea who was living there at any given time. She'd rented the place out years earlier to several young officers like us, but the lineup of tenants changed one at a time as they transferred. The first she heard of it was when a tenant told her, "Lieutenant so-and-so left, so I'm now going to be paying the bills."

The landlady never complained. She had a good thing going because she never had to look for tenants. The place just sort of rented itself.

The house even had its own eclectic, crowdsourced furnishings. People left things behind when they moved on, so we probably had enough mismatched cooking utensils and silverware for fifty people. And there was a three-legged sofa that was propped up at the missing leg with a (disarmed) mortar shell laid on its side that was just the right size. Every once in a while, the couch would get moved, and the legless corner would fall off the shell. You'd have to pick it up and scoot it back under there.

We split a total rent of about $100 per month three ways on this place, so with our housing allowance of $110.20 we were doing pretty well. We made more money on housing than we spent. But it definitely wasn't the Ritz. In fact, I'm sure that if we'd been put in base housing that looked like this place, we'd have been incensed.

I remember going to Dallas on weekends with some of my friends while I was at Fort Sill. In fact, I was in Dallas, in Dealey Plaza, on November 22, 1964, a Sunday off and the first anniversary of President Kennedy's assassination. It was a strange feeling to stand right there in the street exactly one year later. There weren't yet any permanent monuments—just flowers and other mementos that people had left.

The social life of Fort Sill officers could be quite interesting. You had access to the officers' club, which was the first experience I had with something like a country club. The food was good and relatively inexpensive, and it was a great place to take a date, if you could find one.

During my base time, I also pursued something one doesn't often associate with army duty—a pilot's license. I've always been interested in flying, and I got my chance to join a flying club that was part of the base infrastructure. The club owned a half dozen single-engine prop planes, and the fuel was cheap, so I signed up for lessons. I completed enough hours of instruction to get a private license, but my tour of duty ended before I could take my final FAA check ride. I enjoyed being in a plane all by myself, flying over Oklahoma's wide-open spaces.

I remember the very first time I soloed. That's always a very big deal because you never feel like you're ready. I probably had eight to ten hours of experience at that point. I was practicing landings and takeoffs on a bumpy, sod-covered strip in the middle of Fort Sill with my instructor. At one point, when we landed, he said, "I'm going to get out."

He explained that he wanted me to take off, fly around the pattern, touch down, and then take off and do it again a total of three times. That procedure is called doing "touch-and-gos." Three times in succession was the requirement for soloing. After you accomplished that, you were licensed to fly by yourself but with no passengers.

My plane was a yellow Piper Cub. It had a metal frame that was covered with lightweight metal. The plane was very narrow, with a single seat in front and another behind it. The side doors split into two parts, with one going up and the other down. When the doors were open, it was like the entire side of the plane disappeared. This is important because when the instructor got out so I could fly solo, he didn't properly latch the doors.

I realized this as I bumped down the grass strip on my first takeoff. Just as my wheels left the ground, the top part of the door flipped up and the bottom part flipped down. So there I sat, my first time alone in a plane, with half the cockpit basically wide open. I remember thinking there were only two ways I was going to get back to the ground, and one of them was not acceptable!

Instead, I decided to just ignore the door and focus on flying. I wheeled around the strip and came in for a landing, as agreed. But instead of doing a "touch-and-go" and then immediately lifting off again, I landed, took the Cub to the very end of the runway, stopped, and closed the door.

After that, I took off and landed two more times, taxied over to my instructor, and parked. He congratulated me but immediately wanted to know why I'd stopped after the first landing. So I told him about the open door, and I think he was pretty embarrassed. I had a few interesting experiences during my days as a student pilot, but that was certainly the most memorable.

A NEW WIFE AND A NEW LIFE

Chapter Eight

Given our financial situation, the beginning of our marriage was hardly glamorous.

My years in the army changed my life in more ways than one. During my service at Fort Sill, I also met my first wife, Marilyn.

She was completing graduate school and teaching at a public school for students who were children of military personnel, which was located on the fort's grounds. I think our initial attraction was pretty straightforward. In that rough-and-ready setting, finding an intelligent, attractive woman with a master's degree was like finding a needle in a haystack—or a diamond in a coal mine.

We struck up our first conversation at a cocktail party at a mutual friend's house.

Her maiden name was Marilyn Salyer. She'd grown up in Lawton, Oklahoma. Her father, Erwin "Blue" Salyer, had recently died in a pedestrian automobile accident, and she'd left her teaching job in

South Carolina to come home to live with her mother, Ruth, for a year and help her cope with all the changes in her life.

We met sometime in 1965, and I got out of the army in October of 1966, almost exactly two years after I went in. We were married in September, just before I was discharged.

She came from a family that, for reasons I'll explore later, I never learned a lot about. Oddly, I didn't fully understand how unusual this was, or the impact it had on my life, until after we'd been married for 28 years. Marilyn was always fairly closed off about a lot of things having to do with her childhood and family, and over the decades the subject just never came up much. Her mother would visit us from time to time and stay a couple of weeks, but there was nothing unusual in that. I liked her mother a lot and was very much in contact with her until her death some years ago.

Marilyn also had an older brother, Jerry, with whom I became very close. At the time of our marriage, he was a lawyer and later became a judge in Oklahoma City. He too passed away several years ago. I'm still in touch with Jerry's three adult children, Cindy, Derek, and Michelle, and am very proud of their significant successes in life. But other than those relationships, I didn't have much contact with Marilyn's extended family or understand much of its history.

Thinking back on it, I may have accepted this somewhat unusual state of affairs because I was raised in roughly similar circumstances.

I loved and deeply respected my mother and consider her one of the fairest, most level-headed people I've ever known. But she also had family stories she kept close to her heart—stories I wouldn't learn about for years.

What I knew, as a child, was that her mother's name was Grace Harwood, she had three brothers, and she grew up in Illinois, where her father farmed. During my youth, members of my father's family, who all lived in Remington, were always around, but not my mother's brothers—two of whom lived near Detroit and one in Illinois. They visited occasionally, but they and their families weren't intimate acquaintances.

As for my mother's father, he not only never visited, he was never mentioned. It wasn't just that he never came up in conversation. It was because we must have known, from a very young age, not to ask. Over the years, after doing extensive family genealogical research and thinking carefully about all of this, I think I've connected the dots and figured out much of what happened.

My mother's mother (my grandmother), died long before I was born, and fairly young—at the age of 49. I remember my mother once saying, when I asked, that she died of a broken heart. It just never seemed appropriate to ask any questions after that.

While I was in high school, I was surprised to learn that my grandfather, Mark Harwood, was alive and living in a town about 20 miles from Remington. I don't recall how I discovered this, given it was something we never talked about.

But that wasn't the end of the revelations. Many decades later I discovered that my mother had much younger twin sisters, who I later learned were both still living. Two years after my mother died and a few days before my father died, when he was in and out of consciousness, he casually mentioned the twins to my brother and me as if we knew all about it. I remember looking at Roger and asking, "Who is he talking about?"

I didn't know she had sisters, and I at first incorrectly suspected they were half-sisters—maybe the product of a second marriage by her father. However, my mother must have been so upset about whatever happened that, as far as she was concerned, this was no longer a part of her life.

It was so uncharacteristic of her. My mother was very upbeat and wasn't ever bitter about anything. Something must have hurt her very, very deeply to make her react in such an extreme way. But it would be decades until I got even the merest inkling of what it might possibly have been.

Around the year 2020, while I worked on tracing my family's genealogy, I discovered an unknown first cousin of mine named Jeannine Syrstad Klingbeil, who was the child of Lois Nadine Harwood, one of my mother's mysterious younger twin sisters (the other was named Betty Jean Harwood). Jeannine knew as little about my side of the family as I did about hers but was eager to begin a helpful correspondence with me.

Her help cast at least a bit of light on a family mystery that I've tried and so far failed to unravel. It's a tangled narrative that's full of gaps, but I'll try to relate it as simply as possible.

My mother's mother, Grace, died on August 12, 1932, at the age of 49, from (at least as indicated on her death certificate) gallbladder surgery complications. When this happened, my mother's father (my maternal grandfather), Mark Harwood, with four grown children (my mother among them), was left with the twins, who were 6 at the time. Shortly thereafter he hired a local woman named Nora Weir to help care for them. She'd divorced her husband in October of 1932, two months after my grandmother's death.

"Our father, who was farming, hired Nora Weir, a close family friend, to get his twins ready for school each morning and fix lunch, etc.," Lois wrote in a family memoir she prepared for her grandchildren, and which Jeannine was kind enough to share with me.

Their relationship must have deepened quickly because, on December 2, 1933, Nora and my grandfather got married. The nuptials were a surprise to the twins, according to Lois's memoir. One day, she reports, she and her sister got in the family car with the housekeeper and their father, who told them, "Today, you're going to have a new mother."

Could this have been the incident that angered my mother? It seems unlikely because her father remarrying almost one and a half years after her mother's death wouldn't have seemed unusual at the time—or today, for that matter. But though I hesitate to speak ill of people who have been gone for decades, and I've uncovered no hard evidence to support such a supposition, it might be within the realm of possibility that Nora and my grandfather's relationship predated my grandmother's passing. It would certainly explain my mother's claim that she "died of a broken heart."

It might also explain why, when the twins were seven, my mother and her three brothers brought a suit against their father, trying to get his parental rights revoked. Though my evidence is only circumstantial, it's possible that my mother, who was in her early 20s at the time, wanted to become their legal guardian. But, of course, none of that happened. The court decided for my mother's father, and he and his second wife raised the twins, according to the twins themselves, without incident.

Again, from Lois's memoir, "When we were seven, our older brothers and sister had a custody trial and tried to take Betty and me away from our Daddy! One day Aunt Betty, Aunt Ethel, and Uncle George Fleming came to be with us when the case went to court. With our clothes laundered and ironed and laying in a big oval basket, we realized we didn't know who we would be going home with. Our youngest brother, Ray, told us later that he was only 18 and just went along with what our older siblings wanted to do. Praise the Lord, the judge threw the case out of court and we got to go home with our Daddy!"

This is pretty much all I know—and all I will ever know—about the affair. I've been unable to locate any records of a court proceeding, and everyone who could tell the full story is gone, leaving only questions behind.

Anyway, perhaps given that my mother never spoke of her family, Marilyn's reticence about hers didn't seem that strange to me. Based on what I now know, her ancestors on both sides, going back a couple of generations, were laborers and farmers in Oklahoma. Her late father had been an electrician and was traveling on a job constructing high-voltage power lines at the time he died in the accident.

I also now know there was a history of clinical depression in her family, and based on what I later learned from Jerry about his own speculation, I think it's not beyond the realm of possibility that her father may have committed suicide by walking in front of an automobile. However, no one will ever know. I don't believe Marilyn's mother ever worked outside the home before her husband's death. But after his passing, she had to find a job to support herself. So she went to work as a nurse's aide in a nursing home associated with a hospital in Lawton, Oklahoma. She stayed there a long time until, after retirement, she moved to Oklahoma City to be near Jerry. I know she had a lot of friends there, and that it was a reasonably comfortable experience for her. She lived a modest life but always seemed like a happy person.

Marilyn attended grade school and high school in Lawton but was born in Binger, Oklahoma, a town with a current population of 426. We visited there once while I was still in the army and I remember the short main street was unpaved. Her family moved to Lawton when she was quite young. Incidentally, Johnny Bench, the Hall of Fame Cincinnati Reds catcher, was also born in Binger. Once, at an AT&T Pro-Am golf tournament at Pebble Beach, Marilyn had the opportunity to meet him and compare their Binger memories. In high school, she was very active in a number of things, including debating. She won a contest that the local Democratic Party sponsored, the title of which was "Why I am a Democrat."

She got a trip to Washington, D.C., which included a visit with one of the United States senators from Oklahoma.

She attended Cameron College (now Cameron University) in Lawton for two years while living at home and then transferred to what was then the Oklahoma College for Women in Chickasha, about thirty miles away. It's now called the University of Science and Arts of Oklahoma. She earned an undergraduate degree in education and speech therapy and then got a series of jobs teaching school. At the time we met, she worked full-time. In addition, a couple of nights a week she drove 81 miles each way to the University of Oklahoma in Norman to earn her master's degree—all of which impressed me greatly.

We were married on September 2, 1966, by her brother's father-in-law, Dr. J. Clyde Wheeler, who was the minister of the Crown Heights Christian Church in Oklahoma City. We had very little money, so for our honeymoon, I took my handful of leave days and we drove from Oklahoma City to Dodge City, Kansas, and from Dodge City to Denver. Then we spent a day or two in the mountains around Denver, drove to Colorado Springs and spent a couple of days there, and then drove back to Lawton.

Given our financial situation, the beginning of our marriage was hardly glamorous. For the two weeks or so before I got out of the army, we lived with Marilyn's mother.

Honestly, I don't think either of us was ready for such a huge change. The timing wasn't opportune because I think we both probably would have preferred to wait another year or so to tie the knot. But we also thought that all these relatively minor hassles would work themselves out. After all, I was leaving the army and returning to my AT&T career, which meant I was done with Oklahoma, and people just didn't easily fly back and forth to keep relationships going as they do now. It seemed to us like it was then or never, and we didn't want it to be never, so we decided to get married.

After I left the army, we returned to Indiana, where AT&T had offered me a new position and a big raise. My AT&T salary went from the $6,500 a year, which I'd made in the summer of 1964, to $9,000 a year. I also got promoted to a much bigger job in Lebanon, Indiana, where I was to manage the local telephone company operations.

It was the true start of my business career—and a relationship with AT&T that would last nearly three decades.

MY FIRST LAP ON THE FAST TRACK

Chapter Nine

Within a few months, I'd gone from being a bachelor officer to a married civilian with a new life, a new job, and a new address.

For some reason, I've always coped well with change. It's an odd talent for me to possess, given that I lived in the same small town and the same house for most of my first 18 years. That was, in retrospect, by far the longest period of geographic stability in my life until post-retirement.

Though I've changed jobs and addresses many, many times since then, it never fazed me. It's a good thing because, after I left the army, I faced several years' worth of transformative events, including the birth of my two children, numerous new jobs, a family health crisis, and moves to Lebanon, Bloomington, Evansville, and Indianapolis.

The saga began about six months before my military discharge, when I was contacted by Bob Allen, the man who was my first boss at Indiana Bell before I went into the army. The company wanted me to return to the fold, with (as mentioned earlier) a big pay bump that far outstripped my government check. When I entered active duty, I got the base pay for a second lieutenant, which was $222.30 per month or $2,667 a year. I was able to manage with my $110.20 monthly housing allowance tacked on, plus the subsidized prices at the Post Exchange, the Commissary where we bought our groceries, and the Officers' Club, but going to $9,000 a year felt like winning the lottery.

This certainly helped clarify my civilian career path. Before then, I wasn't sure if I wanted to return to Indiana Bell or go to law school, my original plan. But Bob's offer settled the matter. I took a position overseeing telephone service in and around Lebanon, Indiana. My territory included the now-thriving communities of Carmel and Zionsville, both of which were not a great deal larger than Remington at that time.

Within a few months, I'd gone from being a bachelor officer to a married civilian with a new life, a new job, and a new address. And I loved it.

I didn't salute anyone anymore, no one saluted me, and I wore a suit instead of a uniform, but I don't recall having to make any great attitude adjustments to cope. The military was of course very regimented and hierarchical, and AT&T and the Bell System weren't that different. The company employed roughly one million people, and it was probably the closest thing there was in civilian life to the Department of Defense in terms of practices, procedures, rules, regimentation, and rank. I never thought about it at the time, but maybe that helped ease the transition from the military to the civilian world.

Though we didn't stay in Lebanon very long, that posting was still very eventful. I supervised a staff of five, handled customer service operations, collected revenue, oversaw the people who handled service requests, and generally served as Bell's face to the community.

That last task was quite important because of the company's unique nature. Indiana Bell was fully owned by AT&T, a regulated monopoly. The inter-state operations were overseen by the Federal Communications Commission (FCC), and state operations were regulated in Indiana by the Indiana Public Service Commission. Among other things, the commission approved the prices the company charged. Keeping things running smoothly in Indiana thus depended on the decisions made by those appointed officials and therefore, in the end, the political goodwill of the people of the state. You needed to keep the community as happy as possible with its service, and with the company in general.

That's why an important part of my role was to cultivate good relationships with community leaders, including members of the Indiana state legislature who lived in or near Lebanon. This is how AT&T handled this sort of thing. In Indiana, in addition to a centralized corporate headquarters lobbying effort, every manager in every city and town across the state was dispatched to talk to their local representatives. So it wasn't just the telephone company's headquarters in Indianapolis trying to get members of the state legislature to support something. It was the job of frontline managers, such as myself, who regularly attended high school basketball games, Rotary Club meetings, and church with these same people in places like Lebanon to help influence decisions.

However, I wouldn't want to imply that public affairs work was an overwhelming part of my job. The biggest portion was just what you'd expect—making sure that, when someone picked up a phone, they got a dial tone, and that customers' monthly bills were correct and got paid.

I wasn't, however, the person directly responsible for maintaining the equipment. That was handled by another supervisor named Milo Wert who was part of a different chain of command. He'd been around for probably 25 years and knew everything about the technical operations. All the technicians—the guys (and in Lebanon just one woman) who actually kept the system running—answered to him.

This posed a management challenge not unlike what I faced in the army, when I gave orders to men who'd served for decades, or when I instructed officers who outranked me. If somebody was screaming because phone service at their business had gone out for the third time in six months, I needed to move them to the front of the service line. But I couldn't just issue an order to get it fixed because that was Milo's responsibility. So I had to develop a strong working relationship with my partner to make sure crises were dealt with in a timely manner.

There was a lot to do at work, but it was definitely not the only thing on my plate. It's funny that in today's world people can be 30 years old before they think about getting married and starting a family. It wasn't that way for Marilyn and me. She was 27, I was 24, and we were already well behind our friends, many of whom were wed right after college and already had children.

We both very much looked forward to starting a family. Marilyn became pregnant with our daughter, Paige, while we were still in Lebanon. It was an unusual pregnancy because for the last three months or so she constantly salivated. Her doctor said it was a hormonal reaction to being pregnant, and though it wasn't typical, it wasn't unheard-of either. As a result, during those final months, if we went out for the evening, it was often to the drive-in movie. For obvious reasons, Marilyn felt more comfortable sitting in the car holding a towel to her mouth than she would have in public.

In July of 1967, I was promoted and transferred to Bloomington to head Indiana Bell operations there. Marilyn, who was due in December, started seeing a very well-known Bloomington obstetrician, which led, I've always suspected, to the very interesting timing of Paige's birth.

The doctor was a huge Indiana University football fan, and the 1967–68 season would see the team make it all the way to the Rose Bowl. There was no doubt in Marilyn's obstetrician's mind that he was going to Pasadena, California to watch the game in person. We always suspected he cooked up some reason to induce her labor early. Paige was born on December 14, even though her predicted due date was 10 days later.

We were convinced that he wanted to get all the pregnant mothers cleared off his schedule so he could go to the big game. Which, by the way, IU lost 14–3 to the University of Southern California. Over the years, I've become very good friends with Harry Gonso, the team's quarterback. We have a running joke that it was his success with the football team that determined Paige's birthday.

We were only in Bloomington for a little over a year before I was transferred to a similar but higher-level position in Evansville, which was a more challenging job. And then we moved to Indianapolis in late 1969, where I became a district manager, overseeing a significant part of the company's operations in Central Indiana. I supervised 100 or so service representatives and their supervisors and managers who, among a great many other things, arranged telephone installations and service calls, collected overdue bills, and made decisions about turning off people's phone service for nonpayment.

My son, Todd, was born in Indianapolis in 1970 at Methodist Hospital. Today a big deal is made about fathers being in the room and participating in some fashion in the birth of their children. But you didn't see much of that back in 1970—especially in my case.

Marilyn and I were together in the labor room, which was essentially a bed with curtains pulled around it to provide some privacy. Her doctor came by to do an examination and asked me to step out for a moment. I did so, thinking somebody would come and get me in maybe five minutes. I was out there for something like 20 or 25 minutes, still expecting someone to come and get me. I didn't know what was going on.

The next thing I knew, a nurse came out of the door holding Todd and told me it was okay to go back in. What a shock!

Unfortunately, visiting hospitals would soon become a regular part of my family's existence and turn our Indianapolis years into a rollercoaster of highs and lows. On the one hand, I saw the birth of my son and rose steadily through the ranks at Indiana Bell. But on the other hand, our family also faced a health crisis that proved as mysterious as it was dangerous.

A MYSTERIOUS MEDICAL CRISIS

Chapter Ten

Paige started having very severe asthma attacks—ones so dangerous that she was hospitalized more than 60 times.

The division of labor in our family fell along traditional 1960s lines. Marilyn's responsibility was to raise the kids and manage the home and mine was to get up and go to work and financially support the family. But I was definitely not an MIA dad. I changed plenty of diapers back in the days before disposables were invented. Paige's were made of cloth and secured with big, clunky diaper pins.

But this was no Ozzy and Harriet sitcom family. Far from it.

When Paige was about a year old, she started having very severe asthma attacks—ones so dangerous that she was hospitalized more than 60 times. We never discovered all of the things to which we thought she was allergic, but it was a long list and included pollen and mold.

To say that it disrupted our lives would be an understatement. What made it even more frightening was the fact that the science regarding allergies and pulmonary disease wasn't nearly as advanced as it is now. In fact, it's safe to say that none of the experts we consulted truly understood—or *could* have understood, given the level of the then-current science—exactly what caused her difficulties, let alone how to help.

Many of her hospitalizations and much of her early treatment took place at Methodist Hospital in Indianapolis, the same place where Todd was born. Her doctors tried all sorts of things, such as putting her in an oversized metal crib that was sealed in clear plastic and filled with a pumped-in medicated mist. She was only a year or two old, but she would sit for hours or days inside that plastic bubble, dripping wet from the humidity and crying her eyes out. It was pitiful and heart-wrenching to watch. And we saw quite a bit of it. One year she went into the hospital in late April and checked out in June. She missed the entire month of May.

Marilyn usually sat by our daughter's hospital bed from 8 a.m. to 8 or 9 p.m., coming home only to sleep. I would work and then go to the hospital. My parents, who still lived in Remington, were a huge help. If we had to rush Paige to the hospital, they would drive to Indianapolis, pick up Todd, and take him home with them. He spent lots of time in their company. Todd was happy in Remington—or as happy as he could be, given the circumstances.

It's hard to overstate how tough Paige's illness was, both for her and for the rest of us. On two occasions a doctor called us in the middle of the night to tell us we needed to get to the hospital right away.

"We don't want to overly frighten you, but this is serious enough that we're not absolutely convinced Paige is going to make it to morning," they would say.

Of course, her condition was never far from my mind. But I was helped somewhat by the fact that I had a job to do. Like it or not, every workday I had to focus not on my fear alone, but on Indiana

Bell business. But Marilyn had no such buffer and was utterly consumed with worry and care. Paige herself was of course sickly and miserable, and Todd was shuttled around on short notice from one house to another.

We tried every medical approach that showed the remotest promise, and even remedies that were far from scientific. Once, Marilyn read somewhere that Chihuahuas might help people get over asthma. She got it into her head that maybe this might be worthwhile, so we bought one and kept it for about six weeks. Obviously, it didn't work. I now think we were so desperate we got the facts confused. Chihuahuas didn't cure asthma, but it was thought they didn't trigger attacks in people who were already allergic to dog dander from other breeds.

For a very long time, nothing seemed to help.

During those dark days, I talked to the powers that be at AT&T about a job transfer from Indianapolis to Phoenix, on the theory that the dry climate was better for asthmatics. A potential transfer was arranged. It would have meant a demotion and a pay cut, and I don't know what it would have done to my career, but I didn't care. However, our asthma specialist advised against it. He said that so many people had moved to the Phoenix area and brought so many non-native plants with them that now the pollen situation was no better than anywhere else. Also, the area actually had two high-pollen growing seasons, whereas Indiana only had one.

Not that we didn't travel far and wide in search of help. We visited the Mayo Clinic and the University of Alabama in Birmingham Medical Center's renowned infectious disease program. When she was almost six years old, we placed Paige in the long-term pediatric inpatient treatment program at the National Jewish Hospital and Asthma Research Center in Denver, which remains to this day a worldwide leader in pulmonary research. Because the doctors wanted to determine if there was an emotional component to young patients' asthma attacks, they permitted only minimal contact between the family and the child. This meant that at age six we had to leave Paige in their care.

Even worse, we were only permitted to talk to her once a week, via telephone, for maybe five to ten minutes.

Dropping off Paige at the hospital was a traumatic time for Marilyn and me. We couldn't have direct contact with our daughter, but we didn't want to leave the Denver area until we had some sense of how things were going. So instead of moping around a hotel room, we drove up to Vail for a few days. And for the very first time, each of us took ski lessons. That was the beginning of a lifelong family commitment to the sport.

Paige stayed at the National Jewish Hospital for the entire first semester of her first-grade year, taking classes at a school inside the hospital. At the end of her first semester, she came home for the Christmas holidays, but only briefly, because they wanted her back. That was tough for all of us. But as I recall, once she returned to the hospital, she only stayed for perhaps a month before she came home again for good, both because she was getting better and because we'd had all we could handle emotionally. We never learned if her improvement was because the doctors finally found an appropriate combination of medications for her or she was just beginning to outgrow the worst of her asthma symptoms, the way many children do. Perhaps it was a mix of both.

Whatever the reason, by the middle of the 1970s, Paige's life-threatening episodes and long hospital stays were things of the past, though she still experienced periodic asthma attacks. She came back from Denver to our home in Carmel. She too became a skier, and as a young adult, she took up running because her principal pulmonary physician, who was also an asthmatic, believed in the benefits of heavy aerobic exercise. She has continued a significant exercise regimen all of her adult life, but nearly always with a rescue inhaler in her hand.

Though Paige has never completely outgrown her asthma, its symptoms have vastly diminished. She's enjoyed a normal life, complete with four children, which is something of a miracle in itself. Early in the crisis, the doctors told Marilyn that, because of all the steroids and other drugs Paige was given, as an adult she might not ever be able to get pregnant. If she didn't tell you she has asthma, you'd never know.

LIFE IN INDIANAPOLIS   *Chapter Eleven*

During my Indianapolis years, much of Indiana was still equipped with rotary phones.

While Marilyn and I struggled with Paige's medical issues, I also dealt with the challenges posed by my Indianapolis job, or rather my series of Indianapolis jobs. During the first half of the 1970s, I moved from position to position at Indiana Bell, tackling new and sometimes wildly unfamiliar responsibilities with each promotion.

It wasn't just that my duties changed. During this time, the telephone business underwent wave after wave of drastic, tech-driven developments that remade the industry for decades to come.

To give you an idea of how rapidly this happened, consider the phone system I grew up with back in Remington. My father's office phone number was 100, with no three-digit prefix or area code—just 100. Our home number was 179, and my grandmother's was 198. All the calls were routed by hand via a human operator sitting at a switchboard. This was the basic setup, though steadily refined, that served the nation from the beginning of the telephone industry to roughly the middle of the 20th century.

But then things started to change. And kept changing. During my adult life, we've moved from what was basically an electromechanical system relying on metal relays and the constant intervention of human operators to handheld, wireless phones that can call anywhere in the world. Now, we take for granted that one can take and display movies and photos, procure pretty much any product or service online, and pinpoint your location within inches, all from the phone in your pocket.

The first rumblings of this gathering technological storm could already be felt when I arrived in Indianapolis. I started out as one of three district commercial managers who reported to the Indianapolis division manager. I oversaw the massive call center where Indiana Bell assisted customers with everything from the installation and removal of lines to disputes about long-distance service charges. Back in those days, the individual long-distance charges used to be itemized on your monthly bill.

More about that in a moment.

Around 1971, I became a district accounting manager. It was a real switch for me, but ironically also a very good sign for my career. When you joined AT&T, you typically started out on a career track that mirrored your educational background. If I'd graduated from Purdue University with an engineering degree, I might have likely been assigned to the organization responsible for installing phones or operating and maintaining switching equipment.

The first sign that people in the upper echelons were watching your career was if you were moved to a different track outside your "comfort zone." It meant they wanted to give you a broader set of experiences and, of course, to see how you handled curveballs. This is how I found myself a district accounting manager, responsible, among other things, for the workers who prepared customer billing data for input into our computer system.

At that time, computers certainly existed, but they were far, far less capable and ubiquitous than they are now. These were the days when data processing systems consisted of numerous IBM mainframe machines built on raised and refrigerated office floors. These systems possessed less power than the chip inside your current phone, which meant paying your Bell bill "online" simply wasn't an option.

So every month, tens of thousands of our customers wrote out paper checks to Indiana Bell, sealed them in envelopes along with paper receipts, and then dispatched them to us via the U.S. Postal Service. As district accounting manager, I was ultimately responsible for getting all these analog documents ready for computer processing.

In retrospect, and certainly in light of how such things are handled today, this was an almost unimaginably complex, Rube Goldberg-ian process. As I mentioned earlier, it was the tail end of an era when calls were made with the assistance of a human operator. Local calls were mostly connected automatically, but long-distance connections could still be very "hands-on."

Vital information about every such call was manually recorded on its own punch card literally as it happened. First, the operator would record the originating number and the number being called and then timestamp the card. Then she (it was almost always a "she") watched a light that told her the call was taking place. When that light went out, she put a "stop time" on the card showing how long the conversation lasted and, thus, how much should be charged.

That card then wended its way to the accounting department, where it was run through a card reader. This process turned the information into computer data, which would then be applied to the bill of the person who made that particular call. That is why people regularly disputed individual long-distance charges. Given that the typical operator monitored maybe seven or eight such calls at any given time, human error was entirely possible.

Even at that time, we were acutely aware of how labor-intensive this was. We used to talk about the fact that if everything—local and long distance—still had to be done via manual switchboards, every female in the United States over the age of 18 would need to become a switchboard operator just to keep the system functioning.

Technological advances meant that such a situation never came to pass. For instance, manual long distance was rapidly being replaced by "direct distance dialing." Three-digit "area codes" were added to the usual seven-digit numbers, and dialing a "1" before the new, ten-digit sequence meant you were making a long-distance call. Thus, the human was taken out of the process, expediting both the connection and the collection of billing data.

During my very first summer with AT&T, I had of course helped oversee just such a sweeping technological upgrade in the town of Boonville, the last AT&T-served location in the state that used a manual operator to handle even local calls. That had been a huge leap for Boonville, and the rest of the state (and nation) would shortly follow in its footsteps. During my Indianapolis years, much of Indiana was still equipped with rotary phones. As I mentioned earlier, instead of simply typing out a phone number using buttons or a screen, one used a rotary dial with holes in it—one for each number between 0 and 9. Whenever you "dialed" a number, it would trigger physical, metal relays at the phone company switching center. Those centers sounded like a million typewriters, with thousands of relays constantly opening and closing.

The Touch-Tone system that replaced them was not just more efficient but also far less clunky. For the most part, it utilized new handsets like the Trimline phone, developed in 1966. It was basically a rudimentary computer, handling calls using transistors, not electromechanical relays. In most versions, the old-fashioned dial was replaced with buttons.

These advances meant AT&T would never again have to hypothetically contemplate dragooning half the nation's adult population just to keep the phones functioning. However, the efficiency of the new equipment, along with massive changes to how phone services were delivered, also meant that a portion of the people already working for us would soon be made redundant.

But at this point in my career, that reckoning was still (mostly) in the future.

GETTING OUT OF MY COMFORT ZONE

Chapter Twelve

I'd already developed the habit of willingly embracing change and challenge and taking on tasks I'd never done before.

In the previous chapter, I digressed somewhat to talk about the technological changes gripping the phone industry. Now I'd like to do so again—though more briefly—to provide an overview of AT&T's corporate hierarchy and my place therein.

The company's management was very well-organized and formal. A Level One job was typically a supervisor or a foreman who might oversee a group of home phone installers, or perhaps six or seven service representatives in a call center. A Level Two usually carried the title of manager and might run a call center with half a dozen supervisors reporting to him or her.

A Level Three was a district manager with several Level Twos under him. A Level Four was a division manager, and a Level Five was a general manager. Level Sixes were AT&T's assistant vice presidents and the subsidiary companies' vice presidents. Level Sevens were AT&T's vice presidents and subsidiary companies' presidents.

Obviously, the number of people occupying each succeeding level diminished almost exponentially. Level Eights were AT&T's executive vice presidents. Level Nine was the vice-chairman or president of AT&T. And out of roughly one million Bell System employees, the only person holding a Level Ten post was the chairman and CEO.

My first job with the company that was part of the IMDP initiative—the one that I held for a few months after I graduated from IU and before I reported for army service—was in a special category. My first post-military job, as manager of the Lebanon office, was Level One. My Bloomington and Evansville positions were both Level Two, with the Evansville job being a Two-A, one of the highest Level Twos in the state, giving me responsibility for everything phone-related along the Indiana side of the Ohio River in the southwestern part of the state.

My first Indianapolis job, which I started in 1969, was a Level Three position as a district manager, responsible for providing customer service in a significant part of central Indiana. During my years in the city, I also held a series of Level Three and then Level Four jobs in the commercial call centers and in accounting and advertising, before being promoted, at age 32, to a Level Five position as general commercial manager with responsibility for all customer service in Indiana, heading an organization of well over two thousand people. It was one of the twenty-three most senior positions in a twelve thousand-employee organization. I still have in my office a framed copy of the org chart from those days, with pictures of each of those twenty-three executives. Sadly, because of my young age relative to the others, I'm the only one still living.

After my time as a district accounting manager, which I described in the previous chapter, I was promoted to become Indiana Bell's general advertising manager. I worked in the company's public relations department and—as my title implied—handled all of the company's advertising as well as other public relations duties. For example, during that period, the company was constructing a new downtown office building at 220 North Meridian Street that was covered with black reflective glass. It looked like a giant cube and was quite a departure from the city's more traditional-looking business district limestone and brick structures.

In my new capacity, I was responsible for telling the public what was going on with this new edifice. So I came up with what I thought was a pretty cool slogan: "Reflecting a New Indianapolis." We had a billboard with those words put up on the corner of Meridian and New York streets, where the building was under construction.

That project also reflected the range of disparate responsibilities I'd been given. Often, I dealt with tasks I knew absolutely nothing about and had no training for—one of the biggest of which was handed to me by Indiana Bell president Jim Olson himself.

I was working in my office one day when Olson's secretary called and asked me to come to the president's office. So I went up to the hallowed halls of Indiana Bell building's top-floor executive suite, where the carpet was deep, the paneling walnut, and everything was as quiet as a library. I'm pretty sure it was my first time ever in the president's office. Olson told me he'd accepted a request to co-chair an event with J. Irwin Miller, longtime chairman and CEO of the Cummins Engine Co. in Columbus, Indiana, and a member of parent AT&T's board of directors. It was the annual national meeting of a group called the Business Committee for the Arts, which brought together heavyweights in the national arts scene and Fortune 500 CEOs from all over the country to discuss the importance of supporting arts and culture and why and how corporations should focus on those endeavors.

Bringing all these nationally known arts and business leaders to Indianapolis, energizing their interest, and keeping them fed and happy was a very, very big deal.

Jim Olson turned to me and said, "I want you to take care of this for me."

And so, along with someone from Cummins with a role similar to mine representing J. Irwin Miller, we were charged with organizing the Indianapolis edition of this significant national gathering. Needless to say, neither of us had any relevant experience in such matters. But of course, that was part of the reason I was chosen. It wasn't just that Olson needed someone to put the conference together. It was also part of the development and testing process in the Bell System—throwing managers on an upward career trajectory into unfamiliar situations and seeing how they performed.

I will admit that, when I was first told of this, I experienced a brief "deer in the headlights" moment. But it quickly passed, as it always seemed to when I was thrust into unfamiliar situations. During such moments, my first step was always to ask myself, "What do I need to know to get this done?" And that's exactly what my Cummins partner and I set about figuring out. We talked to people who'd previously staged the event and found out how they handled it. We inventoried what sorts of unique capabilities and attractions Central Indiana offered. And we brainstormed our own ideas.

It wasn't rocket science. However, I learned over the years that the ability to deal with such novel assignments isn't a particularly common trait.

Fortunately, I was already accustomed to operating outside my comfort zone. During my time at Indiana University, I'd already developed the habit of willingly embracing change and challenge and taking on tasks I'd never done before—everything from becoming a radio deejay to (later) learning to fly a plane. This event was just one more item on that list. And the conference turned out to be a phenomenal success. National leaders in business and the arts were involved in all this, and they said privately to Jim and J. Irwin Miller that this was one of the best gatherings they'd attended, and the most creative.

No one ever said so, but I'm confident my role in that project launched a series of decisions Jim Olson made over the years to advance my career. I think the overarching lesson of that encounter (one I've shared many times with people who ask me about the "secret" of success) is to get up every day and do the best you can at whatever you're asked to do because you never know which opportunity might change everything, and it may arrive when least expected. It could be the most important moment of your life, and you won't know until after the fact.

My out-of-the-box assignments didn't end there. Indiana Bell sponsored the television coverage of the Indiana High School Athletic Association's Boys Basketball State Tournament, which effectively made me, as the general advertising manager, the executive producer of the event's television coverage.

The tournament was no small affair. High school basketball was the state's primary form of sports entertainment, and each small town had its own high school team. For decades, the Final Four games were held at Butler University's Hinkle Fieldhouse, which was for a very long time Indianapolis's largest hoops venue. Getting a ticket was almost impossible for the average person. It was Indiana's version of the Super Bowl.

Movies such as the iconic *Hoosiers* have been made about this legendary tournament, and I was responsible not just for bringing it to the state's television screens but also for making sure fans knew Indiana Bell was the sponsor.

Covering the early rounds, when many dozens of games might be played on a given weekend, was a huge logistical challenge. Obviously, there were no computers to collate stats and crunch numbers. But we did have plenty of telephones and willing employee volunteers, and we used them to maximum effect. During our halftime broadcasts of the games, the camera would switch back to a sort of "tournament central" studio set, where Indiana Bell employees could be seen sitting at a large phone bank. This wasn't window dressing. They were actually talking to game venues around the state, where other Indiana Bell employees were feeding them scores and floor updates. That information was then written on cards and placed on a board that the TV camera would zero in on.

I also had a hand in producing Indiana Bell's commercials for the tournament. We used actual employees to introduce every telecast. I remember that for the final championship game, we used a cable repairman to introduce the telecast. He popped out of a manhole and said, "Hi, I'm so-and-so, I'm a cable repairman at Indiana Bell, and on behalf of the 12,000 Indiana Bell employees, welcome to the Indiana High School Basketball Tournament."

Of course, those telecasts earned the company goodwill by bringing the tournament to the state's TV viewers. But they also excited Indiana Bell's employees by getting them involved in what was, at the time, the state's hottest ticket.

Not too long after this, my time as a TV producer and advertising executive came to an end when I was promoted to become Indiana Bell's general commercial manager. All of my previous positions presented unique challenges, but this one was in a vastly different league. Up to this point, my supervisory roles kept me close to the rank and file who did the "boots on the ground" work—the employees who actually dealt with customers and operational issues. My situational awareness was excellent because I spoke daily with the people who got things done. Now, for the first time, I was more than one step removed from them. My chief interactions were with people at the district level or above, meaning that instead of talking mostly to the troops, I now more typically talked with their bosses and the other senior leaders of the company.

The issues I dealt with also changed. I focused more on strategic problems instead of tactical ones. For instance, getting Indiana's Public Service Commission to approve a request for a telephone rate increase.

This new job also put me within two levels of the president of Indiana Bell himself, who during part of the time I was in that role was a man named John "Jack" Arbuckle. Jack had himself been the general commercial manager at the time I'd been hired. I later learned that at some point, while in that role, Jack had asked to see the list of the ten people in the organization most likely to someday have his job, and my name was included. That, I'm certain, was an important career milestone for me. So that promotion was no small thing—and not a bad achievement for a guy who'd mustered out of the army only eight years earlier. It was an unusually rapid rise, and in the ensuing years, it would only accelerate.

I have to say that when I received these promotions, I was certainly surprised and grateful but typically not "floored" that I was selected. I had known since my first day at the company that if I kept proving my ability, my career would stay on a fast track. And that if I didn't, I'd be sent packing. I suppose my aspirations, after I'd been with the company for my first five years, could be summed up like this: "If I could someday become a vice president of Indiana Bell, that would be terrific. I could live in Indianapolis and be at the top of the company and do things for my family and in the community."

But that wasn't in the cards because that first Level Five position was also my last job at Indiana Bell. My next challenge would take me out of state to my final stop on the road to AT&T's corporate headquarters.

A WHOLE NEW BALLGAME IN ILLINOIS

Chapter Thirteen

It was important to always remember that achievement begins with opportunity and deserves humility.

E‌arlier I mentioned that I'd begun receiving job assignments designed to take me out of my managerial comfort zone. It was of course crucial that I performed as a leader among my peers in my regular, day-to-day assignments. But things like running a national gathering of arts experts and business leaders and overseeing the TV production of the Indiana High School Athletic Association's Boys Basketball State Tournament were key indicators of even greater potential. Each of these, had I failed, would have been sterling opportunities to fall on my face.

But, because I didn't, they became stepping stones to greater responsibility. Those experiences, I've since come to realize, made all the difference in my career.

I was astute enough to realize that it was about more than just my own abilities. It was also about developmental opportunities. Whenever I took a new position, I could usually look to my left and right and find people with skill sets and experience levels very similar to mine. But once I got promoted and they didn't, I would gain new skills that they lacked because of the new opportunities. And if I got promoted again, the same thing happened. Thanks to these new assignments, I acquired capabilities that others simply didn't have the opportunity to develop. Of course, had one of them been promoted instead of me, the situation would have been reversed. So it was important to always remember that achievement begins with opportunity and deserves humility.

Every new opportunity was a chance for growth. And my next assignment constituted an enormous opportunity.

In June of 1977, I was transferred from Indiana Bell to Illinois Bell to serve as general manager for Chicagoland's north suburban region. I was one of four people with similar titles, each of us handling one section of that sprawling metropolis and its environs.

In my new role, I had total responsibility from the northern edge of Chicago through Evanston, Winnetka, Wilmette, Kenilworth, Lake Bluff, and on to Lake Forest, all the way up the North Shore, and then northwest to places like Barrington, Fox Lake, and up to the Wisconsin border. Instead of just handling one particular aspect of the business, as I had in previous positions, I oversaw all phone service activity in my area. Everyone from installers to repairmen to marketing people to engineers was my responsibility. It was like running my own phone company.

Yet, according to the AT&T hierarchy chart, I was still a Level Five executive, just as I'd been at my last Indiana Bell job. In theory, my new position carried approximately the same status as my old one.

Except that it didn't.

A military analogy neatly explains the difference. In the Navy, if you hold the rank of captain, you could have either a desk job somewhere inside the Pentagon or the command of an aircraft carrier. Technically, those two positions are on the same level, but obviously they're not. Riding a desk in the bowels of an office building just doesn't carry the same status, or offer the same opportunities for career advancement, as commanding a warship.

The job I now held at Illinois Bell was an aircraft carrier job—a significant, high-responsibility, high-profile assignment that meant I was going somewhere, or certainly had the enhanced opportunity to go somewhere if I took advantage of the opportunity I'd been given.

My transfer to Illinois was my first concrete indication that the company had big plans for me. Though I didn't know it at the time, I'd been identified as somebody who, at some point, likely would become president of one of the AT&T subsidiary companies or perhaps make it all the way to AT&T's global headquarters in New Jersey. After all, Illinois Bell had for years served as sort of the lead Triple-A farm club for promising AT&T executives. In baseball terms, it was the final test before you were called up to "The Show."

The reason, I believe, was that Illinois Bell was a microcosm of the country in general. It included Chicago, lots of suburbs, vast rural areas, and the state capital in Springfield. So, perhaps not surprisingly, a disproportionate number of people in top AT&T leadership positions passed through there. My former Indiana Bell boss, Jim Olson, had recently replaced Charles "Charlie" Brown as president of Illinois Bell. Brown was later promoted to chairman and CEO of AT&T and would become one of the most significant CEOs in the company's long history. And Bob Allen, who'd been my boss when I worked in Evansville, was to become Illinois Bell's chief operating officer. From there, both he and Jim moved on, and eventually each became AT&T's chairman and CEO.

The truth of the matter, which I learned when I became a very senior person at AT&T, was that much of this was orchestrated by people who knew a lot about you because they'd watched you for years. For instance, my quick promotion certainly would not have happened without the blessing of Jim Olson. At AT&T, as in the military, to advance you had to prove yourself capable, but it also helped immensely to have someone higher up the chain of command who knew what you could do, believed in you, and looked out for your interests. Although later Charlie Brown would become my most important champion and mentor, to that point, Jim was the most senior person I knew. Bob was also very much a protégé of Jim's.

The challenges of my new position were myriad. I was, as it had become usual for me, facing something entirely novel. In addition to running all aspects of phone company operations for my area, I also oversaw people who didn't know me and who might be suspicious of an out-of-state stranger. Plus, while I had grown up in Indiana and knew the people and the geography, Illinois was a literal and metaphorical terra incognita.

It was the same for my family, of course. Marilyn, Paige (who was ten at the time), Todd (who was seven), and I traded our Carmel residence for a new home in the far northern Chicago suburb of Lake Forest.

Today it's quite common for spouses or partners to both have jobs, which means that if one of them gets a promotion that requires a move, they both have to figure out how to juggle that—or even if they want to. But not during this era. Given the time and the company for which I worked, we all pretty much understood that moves were mandatory. My higher-ups didn't say, "We'd love to offer you a job at Illinois Bell. What do you think about that?" It was more like, "Congratulations, you're going to be promoted," followed by me going home to Marilyn and saying, "Guess what, we're moving to Chicago."

The kids, for their part, didn't seem troubled by this. I remember asking Todd what he thought about pulling up stakes, and his response was, "Am I going to be able to get into the back of the moving truck?"

My first Illinois Bell office was in Skokie, Illinois, a suburb about halfway between the downtown Loop and the majority of the northern suburbs. I commuted using a company car. I also had access to a company driver if I wanted one, but I almost never used that service.

Later, when I was promoted to vice president of Illinois Bell and transferred to its downtown Chicago headquarters, I started taking the train. The commuting process began at 5:15 a.m. when I got up and got dressed. I'd drive about a mile to the station, park, and take the 6:04 train downtown. My goal was to get to the city a little after 7 a.m. and to my desk by 7:30 a.m. But it was a pretty good walk from the station to my office, and in the dead of winter, the icy winds were grueling. But I had a friend, Ray Humke, another AT&T vice president who lived in the same neighborhood in Lake Forest as me, and who had been at Illinois Bell all his life. He knew a secret route from the station to the office that got us to work without having to step outside too much. We had to go through tunnels, loading docks, a department store, and even straight through a hotel kitchen, but on the bitterest of cold days, it kept us out of the elements.

I had a demanding job and the commute was long, so on workdays I'd often be away from home for 12 hours. In spite of that, I don't think I was ever an absentee father. I tried to manage my schedule carefully to make sure I had time for Marilyn and the kids. I certainly wasn't perfect, but I think I mostly succeeded. Once, years ago, Todd, Paige, and I talked about this very thing. I remember being gone a lot during those times, and especially in later years, after I moved to AT&T headquarters and was traveling all over the world, I felt like I missed out on a lot of school events. But when I mentioned this to the kids, they looked at me kind of bewildered and said that they remembered that mostly I was always there. I think that meant that even though I still think I missed a lot, I must have been mostly there for what they remembered as the important things.

Sometimes helping out with the kids meant tackling "new assignments," just as I did at work. I remember, during the Lake Forest days, that Paige at about the age of 10 started playing team soccer on Saturday mornings—something few Americans of that era, including me, knew anything about. The coach asked if I would serve as his assistant, which basically entailed helping out with things like putting cones on the field and herding 10-year-olds. I said yes, with the caveat that I was utterly ignorant of the game.

So I came home early on weekly practice nights to help out. But about a month after I signed on, the coach told me he was being transferred for his job. Effective immediately, I was the new head coach.

That was another "deer in the headlights" moment. But I got a couple of books, read up on soccer, and developed a practice routine for the girls. Fortunately, these were young kids, so the level of play wasn't all that sophisticated. The principal challenge was trying to keep them from all immediately sprinting to where the ball was—and keeping some of the parents in their seats!

I was also around a lot on weekends, in part because I didn't play golf. Most of my friends played, but I didn't feel like I had time on the weekends. I wanted to do things around the house and be with Marilyn and the family.

Not long after getting my first Illinois job, I was promoted to another general manager position, but with more territory. Then, in September of 1978, came a real surprise. I was promoted to vice president. I think there were eight of them at Illinois Bell, and my job was to handle residential telephone service for the entire state. It was my first Level Six position.

But the biggest surprise—and undoubtedly the biggest surprise of my AT&T career—came in late 1979.

I was in my office on the executive floor of the Illinois Bell Headquarters building in the downtown Chicago Loop. Chuck Marshall, the president and CEO of Illinois Bell at the time, came in to tell me that I was to call Jim Olson at his office at AT&T headquarters in Manhattan. At that time, Jim was one of the company's most senior officers.

I called Jim, who promptly told me that John Clendenin, who was the corporate VP for residence services, was being promoted to president of Southern Bell (one of AT&T's largest operating companies), and that Charlie Brown had selected me to replace him. This meant moving to the company's East Coast headquarters.

I was absolutely floored. And truth be told, I still am. At the age of 39, I was promoted to the highest ranks of America's largest corporation—one of the top fifty officers in a one-million-employee enterprise. And I was doing so just as that corporation prepared to embark on tremendous changes that would reshape both AT&T and the entire U.S. telecommunications industry.

EARNING A SPOT IN THE AT&T BOARDROOM

Chapter Fourteen

I soon realized that I had been promoted in part to help deal with the huge realignments coming.

My new job as corporate vice president was the only promotion in my entire career that truly and completely blindsided me. I even remember thinking, "In this corporation of one million employees, if they're going to put me in this job, what does that say about the talent pool they think is available?"

I officially reported for work on the first workday of January 1980. Not surprisingly, I was a bit intimidated. At least for a while.

On my first day, I joined a meeting of CEO Charlie Brown's cabinet, of which I was now part. AT&T maintained two corporate boardrooms that doubled as conference rooms for the gatherings of the company's senior-most officers, one at the company's massive New Jersey campus and the other in its traditional headquarters at 195 Broadway in New York City. On this particular day, we met in the New Jersey sanctum. It was decked out in thick carpet and elegant wood paneling, and it featured a custom-made table that seated approximately thirty people.

I remember entering the room and having my new peers introduce themselves and congratulate me. Most of them I'd never met personally, though I'd seen their faces in the company's annual reports or other publications or listened to them speak. The people who formed the CEO's cabinet consisted of about fifty executives. Approximately twenty-five (such as myself) held the most senior headquarters jobs while a similar number were running places such as Indiana Bell, Illinois Bell, Western Electric, Bell Telephone Laboratories, and so forth.

They were almost godlike figures to me. But on that day, I learned something important about them. As I listened to them discuss the issues on the agenda, I realized that the views they expressed and their disagreements weren't all that different from what I'd heard at Illinois Bell meetings. I guess I thought that I would sit in that room and hear the AT&T equivalent of the Ten Commandments delivered. Instead, it almost felt like I'd been on the yellow brick road for years, and now I'd arrived in Oz and seen the curtain pulled back.

I don't mean any disrespect to these people, who were extraordinary at what they did. Individually, they hadn't arrived in their lofty positions by accident. It's just that I now understood that though they operated on a different level, they still struggled with the same issues my previous associates and I had faced, and they approached them in the same way. They were, to put it simply, human.

My surroundings, however, were Olympian.

Though it still maintained a New York City presence, AT&T conducted most of its business at its sprawling office complex located near the bucolic town of Basking Ridge, New Jersey. Opened in 1975, it consisted of seven large buildings connected by tunnels and walkways. It blended beautifully into the 200 acres of hilly, wooded countryside on which it sat. There was a heliport, a 15-acre underground parking garage, a cafeteria with wood-burning fireplaces, and even an indoor waterfall. It housed about 5,000 people.

My office, identical to those of each of the other senior officers, was in keeping with this grand setting. It was quite large and featured expansive windows overlooking the woods, plus an imposing desk, a separate seating area, a large walk-in closet/dressing room, and a bathroom with a shower.

Marilyn, Paige, Todd, and I took up residence in nearby Bernardsville—a community of about 6,500 just down the road from Basking Ridge. Our first home was a just-completed new property, but later we built one of our own. Interestingly, years later, actress Meryl Streep (who grew up in Bernardsville) told me that she and her high school boyfriend used to park and make out on the road in front of what would one day be the Tobias residence. Small world.

Bernardsville's population was very eclectic. Since the 19th century, it had hosted opulent country estates that served as summer residences for New York City's upper crust, plus (when we lived there) celebrities such as Jacqueline Kennedy Onassis, boxer Mike Tyson, and the King of Morocco. The area was also home to many other corporate headquarters, which brought with them large contingents of executives. And finally, there were the multigenerational residents of Bernardsville itself, many of whom were the descendants of folks who had come from Italy a century or more earlier to work on the old estates.

It made for quite a mix. Todd went to high school there and always considered himself a Jersey boy. His best friends were both the sons and daughters of corporate types, as well as the offspring of longtime residents, including the son of a senior officer in the

Bernardsville police department and the son of a postal worker. They all came from great families, and it was a wonderful mixture for the kids.

This was a good thing because as with all AT&T relocations, this one too was mandatory. Paige was 13 at the time and had lived in six homes already. Todd, who was in the fourth grade when we moved, had also been through several changes of address. However, both seemed to again take it in stride.

In retrospect, the person who took it the hardest—indeed, who very justifiably took all of our moves the hardest—was Marilyn. She was more of an introvert. And though you wouldn't have known it from the smiles she displayed in public, she also had a tough time making new friends in new places. It just wasn't her personality. My job, as always, provided me with an instant networking system that eased the transition. But she had no such automatic support. It was up to her to do everything from making new friends to figuring out where the grocery store was.

On the personal front, one of the Tobias family's biggest relocation "wins" was the important, enduring family connection we made with John and Lynn Smart, their daughter Holly, and their son Andrew. John was an AT&T executive with a background in Long Lines. We'd met and become friends a few years earlier during a six-week AT&T executive marketing program at the Wharton School of the University of Pennsylvania. The Smarts also lived in Bernardsville, and Holly and Todd were in the same class in school. In the years to come, John and I would work together in a number of important ways. He was one of the people I relied on for insights into a part of the business that was new to me. That personal relationship forged in those early days in Bernardsville remains to this day an incredibly important part of my life. Lynn and Marilyn were close friends in those days, and I've always been grateful for her efforts to help Marilyn find her new comfort zone. In the years since, the Smarts have been at every Tobias family wedding and funeral without fail—friends through both the good times and not-so-good times.

If I had been 59 instead of 39 when this transfer to headquarters happened, this likely would have been the last move the Tobias family ever made. In the years preceding it, AT&T was the picture of stability and the kind of place where you would typically spend an entire career. But as I took up my new duties, it became obvious that all of that was about to change. In fact, I soon realized that I had been promoted in part to help deal with the huge realignments coming to both the company in particular and the telecommunications industry in general.

To explain these momentous changes, I must digress for a moment to outline the company's history and its unique position in the American economy.

AT&T's roots reach back to 1876 when Alexander Graham Bell and two business associates founded the Bell Patent Association, which would morph into American Telephone & Telegraph, last for 108 years, and eventually accrue more than $150 billion in assets and serve 70 million customers. Its products and services permeated every American home and business to a degree almost unimaginable today. In 1980 the AT&T name and logo represented the most recognized brand in the world and among the most admired. No wonder that AT&T's ubiquitous phone service, officially known as the Bell System, was nicknamed Ma Bell.

At the moment when I reported to corporate headquarters to take up my new duties, AT&T was the largest corporation in the world. It was also a government-regulated monopoly—the sole provider of almost all long-distance and local telephony for the United States. Local service was furnished by 22 Bell Operating

Companies, each responsible for a specific geographic area (Indiana Bell, Illinois Bell, etc.).

But that doesn't begin to explain just how thoroughly the company dominated the American telecommunications market. One division, Bell Laboratories, handled all phone technology research and development, and its scientists had earned an astounding seven Nobel prizes. A wholly owned subsidiary, the Western Electric Company, manufactured every Bell System phone, plus other network gear, at massive factories around the country. And AT&T Long Lines processed every long-distance call within the U.S. as well as to and from the U.S. and the rest of the world.

In exchange for this very lucrative monopoly, under an existing government consent decree, AT&T agreed to stay out of other businesses, such as telegraphy (in the early days) and computers (in later years). It also confined its operations to the United States, except for connecting its network around the globe.

Not surprisingly, plenty of people were unhappy that such a sheltered market existed in America, the land of free enterprise. Over the decades, a couple of concerted efforts were made to create competition, to no avail. However, in 1969 Microwave Communications Inc. (later known as MCI) applied for permission to sell private (meaning not connected to the network) business-to-business long-distance service between Chicago and St. Louis. AT&T resisted, and in 1974 MCI filed an antitrust lawsuit against the company.

MCI won its case in 1980, getting $1.8 million in damages. But that was a minor annoyance compared to what came next. At roughly the same time MCI filed its challenge, the United States Department of Justice filed an antitrust suit against AT&T. Also at the same moment, Congress held hearings and threatened legislation to break up the company. The Justice Department suit took years to wend its way through the courts, but it became increasingly likely the case would be settled in favor of the government. In anticipation of this, various schemes were offered for preemptively reconfiguring AT&T—most of them fairly conservative. The final formula, however, would be wrenching.

After much wrangling, the divestiture plan was unveiled on December 16, 1981, by Charlie Brown for approval by AT&T's board of directors. Seventeen company directors gathered in the firm's twenty-sixth-floor, Lower Manhattan executive boardroom while Charlie presented a report that would reshape the telecommunications industry beyond all recognition. After walking his colleagues through the terms of the settlement worked out with the Justice Department, he asked for approval to, in essence, disassemble the world's most powerful corporation.

It was the company's most momentous day—and one in which I played no part, other than as a footnote. While the plan was mulled over, I sat cooling my heels outside the boardroom, accompanied by my boss, executive vice president Tom Bolger, and oblivious to the specifics of what was taking place inside. I was waiting nervously to give a marketing presentation, which (in light of emerging developments) was soon canceled. There were vastly weightier issues on the docket.

Under the circumstances, Charlie could have simply sent an aide to tell me to go away, or forgotten about me entirely. Instead, in the midst of what was likely the most high-pressure workday of his entire life, he quickly penned a personal note to me, a 39-year-old, newly minted corporate vice president, in which he apologized for blowing off our meeting. It reads:

"Randy and Tom,

I am very, very sorry to have delayed you this way. The discussion here now is exceptionally important and I cannot cut it off. I don't want to do a half job on your subject so let's postpone it.

I apologize.

CLB"

On the surface, these words might seem like nothing particularly special. Certainly nothing worthy of the high esteem in which I hold the yellowing piece of paper on which they're written. But given the circumstances, this note amounts to an almost unfathomable act of compassion and consideration. It impressed me so greatly that I hung it on my office wall, where it remains to this day, framed along with clippings from the *New York Times* and the *Wall Street Journal* describing the board meeting.

That simple gesture made a lifelong impression. It illustrated the importance of treating everyone, no matter their title and circumstances, with respect. Charlie didn't preach this sort of mindset. As his note signified, he lived it. He was truly an outstanding leader.

I'm not trying to insert myself into that day's events with this story. As I mentioned earlier, I was very much on the sidelines. I just want to emphasize how important a simple consideration can be. In this case, of all the things that happened that December morning—things that would drastically change the trajectory of both my professional and personal lives—the one I remember most vividly is that note.

As for the divestiture itself, I and the rest of the company would have to wait a bit longer for the official news.

The master plan for the breakup was unveiled on January 8, 1982 —a date called Fateful Friday by some. The negotiated settlement called for AT&T to divest itself of all 22 Bell operating units, which would be grouped into seven independent companies called Regional Bell Operating Companies or RBOCs, but known to the world as the Baby Bells. For its part, the remaining AT&T would hang onto (among other things) domestic long-distance service, international service, equipment sales, Western Electric, and Bell Laboratories. It was also free to enter new businesses, such as the nascent personal computer industry.

To say this turn of events unsettled rank-and-file employees would be an incredible understatement. AT&T had been a corporate edifice for most of their lives, and the idea of breaking it up seemed almost as inconceivable as privatizing the army. But according to the divestiture agreement, all of this was scheduled to happen in just two years, on January 1, 1984.

Needless to say, there was a lot to do to get ready. I spent my first year at headquarters helping to reorganize AT&T's residential operations, placing the company on a more market-driven footing. Then, just before Fateful Friday, I was named president of AT&T Consumer Products. This put me in the thick of our attempted transition from a monopoly to a free-market competitor.

Until this moment, AT&T hadn't had to worry about *selling* anything. For much of the company's existence, it was actually illegal to hook non-Bell phones up to the Bell System. It was believed (or at least stated) that such "outside" gear might somehow disrupt the integrity of the network and compromise the service. So, if you wanted a phone, you had to get it from AT&T. Not that you could simply buy one. You rented them from your local operating company. If you moved, Bell reclaimed your phone, refurbished it at one of its Western Electric facilities, and reissued it to someone else.

One year prior to the 1984 breakup of the Bell System, on January 1, 1983, all of that would go out the window under a separate pro-competition order from the FCC. Effective on that date, not only did AT&T lose its monopoly on telephone set rentals, but the local telephone companies it still owned, such as Indiana Bell, couldn't even tell their customers where to obtain AT&T products.

This meant that in preparation for that cataclysmic event, we (or more accurately, I, in my role as president of AT&T Consumer Products) had to lead the effort to figure out how to build a retail sales system from scratch.

Our solution was to create the precursors to today's ubiquitous cellular stores that are found in virtually every strip mall in America.

We called them AT&T Phone Centers. Standing them up was a monumental task because we started from absolute zero. Everything from mall leasing agreements to product distribution systems to the hiring of staff to store interior designs had to be created from whole cloth. And it had to be done on a huge scale because AT&T needed hundreds of locations nationally. In addition to our own free-standing stores, we negotiated agreements with major retailers for space in their stores. The first five were rolled out in Indianapolis—not because of my Hoosier connections, but in part because the city hosted the enormous Western Electric handset factory that manufactured all AT&T telephones, greatly simplifying initial logistics. Each of those first locations sat inside one of the five Indianapolis Sears stores. Sears at the time was by far the country's biggest retailer.

Interestingly, my work with Sears offered a telling insight into how mighty, market-leading corporations can stumble.

During negotiations for the AT&T/Sears retail alliance, I attended a top-level executive meeting in what used to be called the Sears Tower in downtown Chicago. As befitted an organization still at the top of its game, the luxurious conference room included a board that tracked, among other metrics, the share prices and market share data of Sears and its major competitors, principally such long-gone retailers as JCPenney and Montgomery Ward.

Though Sears watched its perceived "peers" with great interest, I noticed they didn't bother displaying information about Kmart.

It was the nation's leading discount chain at the time, and it used a similar formula to the one that would, in coming years, turn Target and Walmart into household names and gut Sears's customer base.

"Why aren't you tracking Kmart?" I remember asking a senior executive.

The guy looked at me straight-faced and said, "We don't track them because we don't compete with them. They're discounters."

That little exchange was quite insightful. Sears didn't see, or perhaps couldn't see, the threat that new technological, demographic, and retail trends posed to their tried-and-true business model. Within a decade, competitors such as Walmart (which had only a few hundred locations at that time) would eat its lunch. Sears didn't understand the threat until it was too late.

Likewise, AT&T didn't comprehend the toll that disruptive new technologies and fierce free market competition would take on its operations even though there were already plenty of signs.

Our phone stores, more than 500 of them in the first few years, rolled out reasonably smoothly. And they served their function well, becoming the template for most of the consumer electronics outlets that came after. But while this allowed AT&T to offer its wares directly to the public, it did little to address much larger issues. Primarily, these were the inability of company officials to accurately predict how new technologies might change the industry, a lack of insight into which parts of our business would be most valuable in the future, and an all-too-human failure to grasp just how harshly AT&T would be punished for not adequately addressing these questions.

The drastic changes began even before the divestiture took effect—tellingly, at the Indianapolis Western Electric plant where handsets for the first AT&T stores were manufactured.

For decades AT&T built and reconditioned its phones at this sprawling Indianapolis factory—one of many such Western Electric facilities around the country. Skeletal telephone frames would move down the assembly lines, and workers with power screwdrivers would screw one particular component onto the frame and then put it back on the line for the next person. As I recall, there were something like 46 screws in each Trimline phone, which meant a lot of workers touched every single handset.

In the 1960s this factory was the world's largest telephone producer, employing more than 9,000 workers. But by the early '80s, the workforce had shrunk to around 3,800. The reasons were obvious. When AT&T was a monopoly, it really didn't matter if we manufactured a price-competitive product, or the most technologically advanced. The Trimline phone was introduced way back in 1965, and in 1983 we were still cranking them out. But technology had left it behind. Everything you needed to make a phone could now fit comfortably on a single computer chip. This meant smaller, overseas competitors could make them just as well as, and far more cheaply than, AT&T. That's why, in the early '80s, much of our phone-making operations moved to Singapore. In September of 1983, we announced that, within a few months, the Indianapolis plant would close, along with the ones in New Jersey and Illinois, which were performing different manufacturing operations. All told, about 14,300 workers were made redundant. I well remember my painful conversations—which took place just a few hours in advance of our plans—with Senator Richard Lugar, Senator Dan Quayle, Indiana Governor Robert Orr, and Indianapolis Mayor William Hudnut. Each of them I knew reasonably well, and quite predictably none, particularly Mayor Hudnut, was happy. He tried his best to figure out how to get the decision reversed but of course there was nothing to be done. It was set in stone, not by AT&T executives, but by market forces.

I have great empathy for those people who lost their livelihoods, and signing off on that decision was far from easy. But I also knew there was no choice. At the time, it was common to blame the loss of American manufacturing jobs on foreign competition. But the truth is, in many cases, those jobs weren't exported. They simply vanished—rendered unnecessary by new technology. The functions performed by the parts inside a Trimline phone that had once required 46 screws to assemble were now performed by a few silicon chips. At that time, literally any technology producer in the world with access to the right chip designs could build a comparable product more cheaply than could be done in Indianapolis, and without an army of workers. And that's exactly what happened.

The impact of technical advances on our manufacturing operations was clear to anyone who could read a spreadsheet. But the potential repercussions of other emerging breakthroughs weren't nearly as well understood.

The most glaring example was cell phone technology, which was only starting to emerge in the early 1980s. In an era when most phones were still tethered to walls and desks by a physical cord, a portable model that could be used anywhere sounded like science fiction—or a potential financial black hole. The case for cellular service seemed far from open and shut, certainly among AT&T traditionalists and even with potential customers.

In anticipation of the breakup of the Bell System, AT&T, which stood at the forefront of cellular development, commissioned the highly respected management consulting firm McKinsey & Company to gauge the technology's potential market. We needed to understand the future value of our cellular technology as we sorted out which assets would go to the seven regional companies to be split off and which remained with a greatly downsized AT&T. The results couldn't have been more wrong. The people we surveyed really didn't much like the idea of toting a phone around, fearing they'd never be free from office calls or unwanted contacts. For many it was an answer looking for a question. I was in the room with a handful of senior executives, including Charlie Brown and the other most senior officers in the company, when McKinsey reported that they estimated a maximum U.S. market for maybe five to six million units.

It goes without saying that the demand was somewhat stronger than that. At the time of this writing, there are roughly 15 billion cell phones in the world!

Who should be blamed for this wildly inaccurate assessment? It certainly wasn't generated by an incompetent consulting firm or out-of-touch executives working in isolation. It was based on scientific polling of hundreds of actual consumers overlaid with the best available experience and judgment. But neither those consumers nor the executives involved could understand the cell phone's true future utility. Because it wasn't just an old product being replaced by a new one. It was an entirely new paradigm—a fundamental change in the way we live our lives. Only as those changes began to take hold, did it become ubiquitous to a degree that pretty much no one in the early '80s, no matter how prescient, could have foreseen. Could more effective executives have been better able to see around corners into the unknown future and better anticipate that future? Of course. But that takes an absurdly rare combination of insight, intuition, creativity, and luck. That's why Amazon continues to grow, Jeff Bezos is one of the wealthiest men in the world, and Sears is no longer around.

I think the cell phone quandary and the interlude at the Sears Tower pretty well sum up the problems the new, downsized AT&T faced. Stripped of its fundamental reason to exist—to provide universal telephone service—it had to find a way forward in an era of cutthroat competition, new markets, and new technology. It was a towering challenge—one that AT&T's most senior management (including me) would grapple with for years to come. And my colleagues were (almost entirely) men I'd had on a pedestal from afar while growing up in the business. Only in the past few years, since arriving in the company's headquarters, had I come to realize we were all just as fallible as other mortals.

A WORLD TURNED UPSIDE DOWN

Chapter Fifteen

AT&T possessed many assets, but it lacked one critical thing: a tangible strategic goal and a plan to achieve it.

On the last workday before the divestiture took effect, Charlie Brown gave parting tokens to the company's top officers. They were small, rectangular pieces of marble salvaged from the 195 Broadway building. Each carried a bronze plaque inscribed with the famous Bell logo (the most identifiable in the world, at the time), along with the words, "One Bell System—It Worked Very Well." It was followed by Charlie's signature and the date of December 31, 1983—the Bell System's last day.

Decades later, this memento still sits in a place of honor on my desk.

In retrospect, I think one of the old Bell System's greatest achievements was its final one: engineering a breakup that didn't trigger widespread telecommunications disruptions. Charlie Brown, in my view, made one of the most difficult, courageous, and farsighted decisions a business leader ever made. Then, based on the best strategic assumptions available to him at the time, he led the development of a plan to thoughtfully take this huge, million-employee company apart in a way that didn't degrade service.

Though the run-up to divestiture and the events that came afterward were incredibly dramatic, the first day of the telecom industry's New World Order—January 1, 1984—was nothing of the sort. At least for me. The heavy lifting to make it all possible had already been accomplished, which meant that when the fateful hour arrived, I was at home with my family. As a matter of fact, I don't think I marked the moment in any way.

Perhaps it held so little import because the focus had already shifted to what came next. Longtime Bell System colleagues suddenly found themselves working for the remaining AT&T or the different Baby Bells, pursuing interests often at odds with those of their former associates. The company's internal slogan had been "One Bell System." Not anymore.

The story of what happened to the post-divestiture AT&T is a complex tale that could easily fill its own book—or several. In this chapter, I intend to offer an overview of that story, which began in 1984 and ended just twenty-one years later in 2005, when the company —or at least the version that I'd always known—ceased to exist.

In the early days, we called the downsized corporation the "new" AT&T. It faced a task even more formidable than divestiture: finding a reason to exist in an era of rapid technological change and free market competition. Everybody at AT&T took this challenge seriously, but I don't think anyone understood that what we faced was truly a matter of life or death.

Our initial post-divestiture strategy seemed quite logical on paper. AT&T would stay a vertically integrated company primarily focused on domestic and international long-distance and data transmission businesses, which were formerly a monopoly but were now becoming highly competitive. The company would also have access to network equipment markets (including most prominently those of the spun-off operating telephone companies), equipment sales to residential and business customers, new opportunities now permitted in computers and international markets, and the research and development for all of this.

Management fought hard to preserve these assets in the split-up, and when the divestiture dust settled, we retained AT&T Long Lines (which provided network voice and data services), Western Electric (our manufacturing arm), R&D powerhouse Bell Laboratories, and the sales and marketing organizations focused on equipment opportunities for residential and commercial customers. The Baby Bells, which were spread out in a patchwork from coast to coast, initially focused on local service in their areas.

The idea was to position ourselves as a telecommunications research and manufacturing power and leverage those already-existing strengths to enter other markets—most prominently, personal computers. Based on our limited understanding of what sorts of corporate assets truly mattered in the fast-changing 1980s telecoms market, this seemed like a workable plan. Unfortunately, it turned out to be anything but.

Not that management—myself included—initially understood how badly we'd miscalculated. For instance, sometime in 1984, I participated in an executive tabletop planning exercise built around the outlandish-sounding premise of what would happen if the entire post-divestiture AT&T failed so miserably that it actually vanished. The event's planners even printed a fake *Fortune* magazine cover story, set perhaps fifteen years in the future, outlining the scenario. The point of the exercise was to talk about ways to keep this from happening. But we didn't take it very seriously because no one thought it was a real possibility.

It's no surprise that AT&T's senior management felt that way. It's human nature to be optimistic based on what you know—or at least to fail to grasp just how quickly and catastrophically circumstances can change.

Often it takes a real disaster to focus everyone's minds, as I learned when AT&T's senior executives spent a day with the senior leadership of Ford Motor Company. In the early 1980s, Ford had come within a hair's breadth of bankruptcy and had only been saved by the timely development of the technology platform for the Ford Taurus. We wanted to find out how they reinvented their company since that's exactly what we needed to do to ours.

One of the points the executive delivering the presentation hammered home was that Ford stayed in denial about its troubles until they snowballed to disastrous proportions. Picking up on this, I asked if they'd learned anything that might help managers recognize the signs of a crisis early, before they metastasized into an existential threat.

I remember this guy's exact words. He said, "I'm sorry to tell you that I've concluded that you aren't going to successfully get the attention of the entire organization until the ox is already in the ditch."

So it would be for AT&T. It possessed many assets, but it lacked one critical thing: a tangible strategic goal and a plan to achieve it. The company couldn't figure out what steps to take after the breakup. As a result, it didn't focus on anything that could achieve sustainable market leadership.

The company faced a scenario that was perhaps unique in American industry. It had originally been predicated on having a protected 100 percent market share, but now it had to compete in a rapidly changing cutthroat industry where the federal government's policy had changed to prevent the company from having a 100 percent market share. It was like turning a domestic dog loose in the wild and expecting it to challenge the local wolf pack. That pack, by the way, included the Baby Bells. They quickly set out to prove they didn't need their old parent to prosper, grow, and acquire more assets, and that they wouldn't be shy about going after AT&T's markets.

Meanwhile, just as government policy makers intended, the profitability of our own long-distance service suffered at the hands of new competitors such as MCI and Sprint. Nor did the other portions of the new AT&T live up to our own expectations. Western Electric's massive factories had been assumed to be quite valuable to the planners of the breakup. But they were dinosaurs. Sure, they manufactured lots of phone networking gear, but previously our only "customer" had been AT&T itself, which bought 100 percent of everything Western Electric made. Now we had to find new markets domestically and overseas. Of course, the Baby Bells remained the obvious customers, but why would they buy equipment from a supplier that was also a competitor if they could find other options?

Similar problems arose in other areas. As I mentioned earlier, AT&T developed and controlled the original cellular technology. But during the divestiture, it was hugely undervalued and dealt away primarily to keep the company's research and manufacturing assets.

It was all quite demoralizing. One can argue that the die was cast by the flawed choices made before the breakup by AT&T's leadership as to which assets would have strategic value in the new world and which would not. But even with so many disadvantages, the company didn't have to fall as hard, as fast, or as far as it eventually did. Perhaps things would have unfolded differently if the top management ranks, all of us highly successful in running the old telephone company, had been better equipped to provide vision and leadership in the drastically altered world ahead or had adjusted more quickly.

On January 1, 1984, the first day of the new AT&T, Charlie Brown organized the very top of the business into a six-person leadership team called the Office of the Chairman. Charlie continued as the chairman and CEO. Jim Olson was president, with responsibility for all of the equipment businesses including Western Electric and Bell Labs. Bob Allen was the chief financial officer. Morrie Tanenbaum, who earlier in his career had been a brilliant Bell Labs scientist, was the initial Chairman and CEO of AT&T Communications, encompassing what had been AT&T Long Lines and other assets focused on providing voice and data network services to domestic and international residential and business customers. Chuck Marshall was chairman and CEO of AT&T Information Systems, which encompassed the remaining consumer and commercial customer premises equipment businesses, including the nascent personal computer business. And finally, Howard Trienens was the brilliant and wise General Counsel.

Initially, I remained in the role of president of AT&T consumer products reporting to Jim. But very soon, Charlie called me to his office to tell me he wanted me to take on a special assignment reporting directly to him. I was to be his liaison with the Reagan White House—specifically with the White House Chief of Staff James Baker, the Counselor to the President Ed Meese, and their staff. My role was to get the White House to orchestrate actions across the government to achieve the resolution of some messy unresolved issues in order to more smoothly implement the divestiture. Ironically, and typical of Charlie's values, what I was charged with getting done (and it did get done) was of more benefit to the divested seven regional telephone companies than to the remaining AT&T.

This leadership team remained in place until early 1986 when Charlie returned from his year-end vacation at his Florida retreat. It soon became clear he'd been doing a lot more thinking and planning than vacationing. Apparently, not totally happy with the way things were evolving through the first two years in our new world, he had decided to make some changes, specifically in the leadership of the company's major operating units. Effective shortly thereafter, Morrie Tanenbaum became vice-chairman and chief financial officer, with some additional responsibilities including corporate planning. Chuck Marshall became vice-chairman, with responsibility for a number of corporate functions such as human resources and public relations. To fill the key operating roles these executives had previously held, Bob Allen became chairman and CEO of AT&T Information Systems, replacing Chuck. This part of the reorganization addressed the consumer and corporate customer premises equipment business and, perhaps most importantly, the perceived transformational opportunities in the personal computer business.

And in an enormous surprise to me and probably others, I'm guessing especially to Bob, I was named chairman and CEO of AT&T Communications, the network services businesses, domestic and international, that provided data and voice services to both residential and business customers and was AT&T's largest enterprise. The profits from that part of the business were greater than 100 percent of the corporation's total bottom line. In addition, I became a member of the Office of the Chairman.

From what I later learned, this was a little more awkward for Bob than I realized at the time. He had been my first boss out of college, was seven years older than me, and during my career he had been typically one or two levels above me on the corporate ladder. I continued to look up to him and certainly considered him my effective senior, even with these new assignments. But with these moves, I had the part of the company driving the bottom line, and Bob had the much less glamorous business and consumer equipment part—a portion of the portfolio that was shrinking rapidly. He also faced the challenge of trying to make something of the perceived opportunities in computers—a very daunting task. It meant that for the first time, and for at least a while, we were on the same corporate level and I had bigger responsibilities. But that was only temporary.

On August 1, 1986, Charlie Brown retired, triggering the next evolution in leadership. My longtime mentor, and also Bob's, Jim Olson, was elected chairman and CEO, replacing Charlie. At the same time, Bob was promoted to president and COO. I retained my responsibilities for AT&T Communications but in addition took over all of Bob's prior responsibilities for AT&T Information Systems (which included computer and telephone sales). I now had responsibility for all of the company's consumer- and business-facing entities worldwide, and also filled the seat on the AT&T board of directors vacated by Charlie.

As I was the least senior member of the Office of the Chairman, Jim Olson gave me the task of figuring out how we should honor Charlie upon his retirement. During his early years with the company, Charlie had worked in the former AT&T Long Lines part of the business, which I now oversaw. Among a great many other things, this included responsibility for the company's worldwide fleet of undersea cable-laying vessels, including the 340-foot-long CS (Cable Ship) Salernum. Charlie was a proud U.S. Navy veteran, so I came up with the idea of renaming the Salernum the CS Charles L. Brown. The ship got a fresh paint job and had its new name painted on its bow during a Hawaii stopover, then voyaged to San Francisco for a surprise presentation party for Charlie. His wife, Ann Lee, found a way to get him to the city without revealing our true plans. The members of the Office of the Chairman and their spouses surprised him at the Fairmont San Francisco hotel, where I proudly offered a video retrospective of his career. It concluded with some cinema-quality "beauty shots" we'd filmed with a helicopter-mounted camera, which zoomed in to reveal the name "CS CHARLES L. BROWN" painted in capital letters on the bow of Charlie's now namesake vessel, just as it emerged from underneath the Golden Gate Bridge. Charlie, who never ever showed any emotion, teared up. The next morning we all visited the ship in person, and Ann Lee christened her by breaking a bottle of champagne on the bow. After Charlie's retirement, which at the time was only weeks away, he and his wife actually went on a couple of short trips on the cable ship.

Then fate intervened. In 1987 Jim Olson was diagnosed with colon cancer and died in April of 1988. What made it even more tragic was the fact that Dr. Joe Warren, the AT&T physician who attended to the company's highest-level executives, had urged Jim to include a periodic colonoscopy as part of his annual physicals. He had been due for one as part of his most recent annual check-up. Unfortunately, he was always too busy and just never got around to scheduling the procedure. In his final days, Jim went to some effort to assure Dr. Warren that he accepted full responsibility for something that might have been avoidable, had he only listened.

Bob, quite logically, replaced Jim as CEO, first provisionally, then formally. His prior role was eliminated.

Over time our evolving and conflicting visions for the company's future created increasing friction between Bob and me. Even as it became clearer and clearer to me, and in fact to many in the senior leadership, that circumstances were not unfolding the way the planners had anticipated, he stuck to his "stay-the-course" view. For example, Bob was determined to retain all of the post-divestiture equipment businesses. In addition, he and a small number of confidants who now had his ear were still hell-bent on making AT&T a major power in the computer industry, with little understanding of the critical factors for success in those markets. Some saw the switching equipment we already manufactured as basically just powerful computers, and Bell Labs had invented the transistor, along with many other computer-related advances. So there was a strong belief among those advocates that we would evolve into a major force in that industry, on a par with titans such as IBM. Whatever additional data processing resources we might need we could acquire—or so the theory went.

But it wasn't to be. AT&T spent the rest of the 1980s (and a great deal of money) trying to find its footing in those markets. During the first three years of this effort, the company pursued four different strategies, often at the same time and even when they were at odds with each other. Overall, the computer effort cost us roughly $3 billion during the late '80s but produced few results. We started seeing layoffs numbering in the tens of thousands.

AT&T looked around for partners to help us, but this effort also ended badly. In December of 1983, we spent $260 million to purchase a 22 percent interest in the Italian office equipment company Olivetti, itself trying to transition from typewriters to personal computers. The idea was to sell each other's products and share resources. It was also, supposedly, our entrée into the fragmented and underserved European market. However, Olivetti was something of a small fish that soon fell out of contention in computer development, tanking sales of its products. Plus, there was an ongoing "culture clash" with its top management—one I saw firsthand because for a time I served on the board of this joint venture. I remember attending meetings in Milan, where everything was unapologetically conducted in Italian. Olivetti also balked at a provision that allowed AT&T to increase its share in the company to 40 percent. In 1989 the alliance ended. We were in way over our heads and got taken to the woodshed.

Urged on by those closest to him, mostly outside hires he'd recruited, Bob then pushed hard to purchase a company called NCR, a leading manufacturer of advanced cash registers and automatic teller machines (ATMs). They and he saw it as another chance for AT&T to buy its way into the personal computer business. I, to put it mildly, thought it was the craziest idea I'd ever heard. The effort to purchase NCR turned into a very hostile takeover that dragged on until 1991 when AT&T finally acquired it for $7.5 billion. However, NCR quickly went into a slide, with sales and innovation stagnating. AT&T spun it off in 1996, taking a $1.6 billion charge against earnings to do so.

And so it went during the final decade of my tenure with the company. Strategic missteps gradually bled away AT&T's financial resources and corporate assets. There were some terrible decisions made during this time, along with some good ones. There were decisions made that I very much agreed with that turned out to be wrong. So nobody had a corner on wisdom—certainly not me. But the fundamental strategic direction of the company seemed to me to be a disaster.

For example, I told Bob I favored breaking up the company in order to, among other things, eliminate strategic conflicts in which one of AT&T's major businesses was viewed as a major competitor to the most important customers of another of AT&T's businesses. I also believed we could enhance each remaining unit's strengths as necessary through well-conceived mergers or acquisitions. That approach seemed pretty attractive to me, but not to Bob. To him, changing course and breaking the company into pieces was unthinkable. Thus, though we always remained cordial, we found ourselves increasingly at odds. It created a difficult working relationship.

It seemed to me that there were opportunities for AT&T to stop being just an equipment and network services supplier and move into the far more promising software and content areas. During the late 1980s, with Bob's reluctant agreement, I had several substantive discussions with Gerry Levin, the COO of what was then Time Warner, about potentially combining parts of AT&T's technology with the media giant's content. Gerry was very interested. Though no one can say for sure, the result might have led to something similar to the streaming services that dominate the media landscape today.

In the end, Bob had no interest in any of this. He told me that Charlie Brown and his team hadn't fought all the battles they'd fought to both gain the freedom to pursue the computer business and hold on to the pieces of the company we had successfully retained just to have some of those businesses spun off or changed beyond all recognition. We would play the cards we were dealt, no matter what.

And so the company did, almost to the bitter end.

By the late 1990s, most of the key components of the new AT&T were gone. AT&T's mindset seemed to have been, "How can our competitors be successful when they don't have any of these incredible assets?" But often, what the pre-breakup planners had seen as assets proved to be millstones. In 1995 AT&T Technologies (the rebranded Western Electric) was renamed again as Lucent Technologies. It was spun off in 1996, merged with Alcatel, and then acquired by Nokia, a Finnish telecoms firm, in 2016. Likewise, Bell Laboratories was sold off and passed from one company to another in rapid succession. It's currently owned by Nokia.

In 2004 the world-famous business I spent decades serving was sold to an outside buyer. Not that this was the end of AT&T. At least technically. The purchaser was SBC, formerly Southwestern Bell. It had begun life as a Baby Bell, but by the early 21st century, it had grown into a strapping adult. While we wasted our resources on poor strategies and bad acquisitions, Southwestern Bell grew larger and larger, acquiring cellular assets, cable companies, and other regional telecoms. Finally, it made a play for AT&T itself, purchasing the company for $16 billion. SBC promptly renamed itself AT&T and took the old Bell System's history as its own. It even moved the Spirit of Communication or "Golden Boy," a famous golden statue that formerly stood on top of AT&T's old Manhattan headquarters, to the lobby of its Dallas headquarters.

Ironically, in 2018 this "new" new AT&T began to lose its way too. It spent $108 billion to acquire WarnerMedia, the former Time Warner. In doing so, it attempted to transform itself into the sort of software- and content-rich organization I'd thought might work for the company's previous incarnation back in the late 1980s. But subsequent events showed that the window for such a move had passed, assuming it had ever existed as I had once believed.

The passing of time has revealed some other interesting facts to me about those critical years. For instance, I now know from those who were either "in the room where it happened" or otherwise privy to those events that if just a few things had happened slightly differently back in the late 1970s, today we might live in an alternate reality in which the rapid, radical dissolution of AT&T never happened. Instead, the company (possibly under entirely different leadership) might have evolved in a much more gradual, thoughtful way.

As early as 1970, the Federal Communications Commission (FCC) started nibbling at the periphery of AT&T's monopoly status, opening up areas such as private line communication to competition. Gradually, this turned into what Charlie Brown called a "three-ring circus," with the FCC in Ring One promoting rule changes to foster telecommunications competition; committees in both the House and Senate in Ring Two developing notional legislation to accomplish similar goals; and the Department of Justice (as previously outlined) in Ring Three bringing suit against AT&T, accusing the company of illegal, monopolistic behavior.

John deButts, who served as AT&T's chairman and CEO from 1972 to 1979, spent much of his tenure resisting such challenges. He largely succeeded in maintaining the status quo, but the pressure for change kept growing. Ultimately, he decided to retire and make way for Charlie Brown in part because, after years of opposing the various government breakup plans, he recognized he was seen by public policy decision-makers as an obstructionist and would not be the right person to shape the coming battle for AT&T's future—a battle which in the end would surely require some accommodation.

When Jimmy Carter won the presidency in 1977, John Shenefield was appointed assistant attorney general in charge of the government's antitrust division. At some point, after Charlie became CEO, he asked Al Partoll, one of AT&T's most senior and insightful strategic thinkers, to approach Shenefield to discuss how the Justice Department's case might be resolved. These talks led to a negotiated deal that would have given the company pretty much everything it could have reasonably hoped for under the circumstances.

In exchange for being removed from the Justice Department's radar, AT&T would do several things. It would separate itself from its captive equipment manufacturer, Western Electric, which in turn would be divided into two manufacturing companies, each with the presumed capabilities to compete successfully with the other. It would also give up control of the Pacific Telephone Company, which provided telephone service to California. And it would sell off its minority interest in three other service providers: Bell of Canada, Cincinnati Bell, and Southern New England Telephone, which covered Connecticut.

This was an incredibly advantageous proposal for AT&T. Losing Pacific Telephone was a blessing in disguise because dealing with California regulators was always difficult, generating lots of headaches but no profit. The company's interests in Bell of Canada, Cincinnati Bell, and Southern New England Telephone barely amounted to rounding errors on AT&T's income statement. And while losing Western Electric would at the time have been seen as a major sacrifice, it wouldn't have posed a long-term hardship—as we would learn years later.

If we did these things, the Justice Department would agree to drop its antitrust suit and consider its proceedings with AT&T concluded.

The deal, hammered out by Shenefield and Partoll, was presented to Charlie Brown and Carter's Attorney General, Benjamin Civiletti, both of whom agreed to the terms. And for AT&T, why not? In exchange for giving up portions of the company that were mostly either problematic or were or would become relatively insignificant, AT&T would emerge largely unscathed.

Not that I think this would have stopped the company's eventual breakup. Industrial globalization and accelerating changes in communications technology were under way, and that would eventually have necessitated more dramatic action. But with that proposed resolution, the transition to today's telecommunications world might have been accomplished in a more gradual and orderly way.

Unfortunately, none of this came to fruition—thanks primarily to the Iranian revolution.

In early 1978, Iran's U.S.-friendly monarchy was overthrown by Islamic fundamentalists. Then, on November 4, 1979, radical college students seized the United States Embassy in the country's capital city of Tehran, taking approximately 50 Americans hostage.

President Carter and his administration became totally consumed with this extremely drawn-out crisis. The momentum to implement Partoll's negotiated agreement was lost. Over time, with Carter's reelection prospects increasingly on life support, the agreement to dismiss the AT&T case was seen by the Justice Department and the White House as both a distraction and an unnecessary political risk. Ultimately, the Carter administration, and any hope for the settlement, ended on January 20, 1981, with the inauguration of Ronald Reagan (and the near-simultaneous release, after 444 days, of the embassy hostages).

This meant, of course, the arrival of an entirely new set of players in Washington, an administration one might have assumed would be more friendly to AT&T. That was not to be. President Reagan understandably would play no personal role in the case. His newly appointed Attorney General, William French Smith, a former member of the Pacific Telephone board of directors, necessarily recused himself—as did Deputy Attorney General Edward Schmults, who had done some legal work for AT&T while in private practice. This left the matter completely in the hands of Assistant Attorney General William Baxter, the newly appointed head of the Justice Department's antitrust division. Baxter was a man on a mission and, because of the recusals above him, a man with no oversight. As AT&T General Counsel Howard Trienens once described him to me, he was a lawyer without a client. Baxter had some novel and controversial ideas about antitrust, based on his work as a law professor at Stanford University prior to joining the Justice Department. Unlike the company's agreement with the Carter Justice Department, Baxter wanted a comprehensive breakup of AT&T, based on his academic theories. He insisted on a divestiture decree based on a structural separation of the purported "monopoly local exchange businesses" from the purported "competitive network and manufacturing businesses," which is exactly what came to pass.

This isn't the only "alternate universe" scenario from those days. Were it not for a few twists of fate, the post-breakup AT&T might well have been led not by Bob Allen, but by an executive who in my opinion was far better suited in temperament, strategic instincts, and confidence in his own abilities to guide the company into a new, competitive era.

In 1977, when I moved from Indiana Bell to Illinois Bell, my new boss in Chicago was a vice president named John Clendenin. John was one of the most intelligent people I ever worked for, and I respected him greatly.

In 1979 John was promoted to AT&T's corporate headquarters as a Level Seven vice president overseeing U.S. residential telephone service. This coincided with a major strategic change at the end of deButts's tenure and the beginning of Charlie Brown's that dramatically reconfigured the company's organizational structure. For decades, the management at both AT&T headquarters and its subsidiaries was organized functionally around the various operational components of what the company did, be it customer service, sales, finance, engineering, or myriad other pursuits. A high-ranking executive was in charge of each function, both within each operating company and at corporate headquarters. With Brown's help, deButts reorganized the company around markets—primarily the residential and business telephone markets.

The corporate headquarters was similarly reorganized, with Clendenin overseeing residential service for the entire country—a job that was every bit as important as it sounds. After becoming AT&T's CEO in 1979, Charlie, who held John in very high regard, promoted him to CEO of Southern Bell, one of AT&T's largest subsidiary companies, headquartered in Atlanta. John was in his late 40s at the time. By the way, John's promotion also led to that completely unexpected 1979 phone call in which I learned I'd been picked to replace him in his AT&T headquarters position overseeing residential service.

Then, in 1982, Jim Olson, at Charlie's direction, offered John another promotion to become the chief financial officer of AT&T. Had he accepted this role, it might well have eventually led Clendenin to the CEO's office. But again, fate intervened. It turns out John Clendenin's family had a history of congenital heart disease. His father and brother both died at comparatively young ages, and based on his knowledge of his own genetics, he himself didn't expect to live beyond his 50s or, at the most, early 60s. After talking it over with his wife, Ann, he respectfully declined the CFO position, telling Jim Olson and Charlie Brown about his health concerns and his belief that staying put at Southern Bell would be less stressful and a better life-style choice for himself and his family. So Charlie told Jim to get in touch with their second choice, Bob Allen, who took the CFO job and eventually, as events unfolded, moved up to CEO and Chairman of the Board.

Bob too was reluctant to accept the CFO position, but for different reasons. He simply didn't see himself as having the requisite finance background and experience to be comfortable in the CFO role and would have preferred to stay where he was, as CEO of the Chesapeake and Potomac Telephone Company. My own view is that he became an excellent and respected CFO. But I'm sure it was that unease that led him to recruit Bob Kavner in 1984 to join the company's senior ranks. Kavner was a senior partner at the accounting firm of Coopers & Lybrand and had for some time been responsible for the firm's AT&T audit team. Kavner saw himself as a creative entrepreneur and strategic thinker with ambitions well beyond being AT&T's CFO and would later be the lead proponent of a number of the company's ill-fated decisions, including the decision to acquire NCR. Kavner left AT&T in 1995.

If John Clendenin had become CFO instead of Bob Allen, he would have likely been the obvious candidate to succeed Jim Olson at his passing. And Bob Allen probably would have stayed as CEO at the Chesapeake and Potomac Telephone Company, which after the divestiture added other former Bell System assets in Pennsylvania and Delaware and became Bell Atlantic.

Having worked for both John and Bob, respected both, and observed both over a long period, I'm willing to speculate that Bob might well have been much more comfortable as CEO of Bell Atlantic than he ever was at the helm of AT&T. And that John would have been a better fit than Bob for the role of post-divestiture CEO of AT&T. It's not a matter of one being *better* than the other, but a matter of one being a *better fit* than the other.

Bob seemed to believe that if his own experiences and instincts had not prepared him for this unexpected future, then surely his younger colleagues from the former Bell System were equally unqualified—thus, his heavy reliance on a few outside hires. John's record, on the other hand, suggests to me that he was a good judge of both talent and strategic choices. He would have been more willing than Bob to rely on the best and brightest of the next generation of key leaders from within the Bell System itself (such as those who had grown up in AT&T Long Lines and possessed a deep understanding of AT&T's core potential strengths and weaknesses), augmented with the experience and insights of strategically recruited and perhaps more carefully vetted talent from outside the company. I believe John's leadership might well have improved the post-divestiture AT&T's chances of success, and that serving as CEO of Bell Atlantic might very likely have given Bob greater satisfaction in the final years of his own career—a career that, sadly, did not end well.

But of course, that's just my opinion. Perhaps John's decisions as CEO might have been different, but just as flawed. Perhaps the stressful environment would have indeed compromised his health. Or perhaps no one could have saved the company. We'll never know.

But here's one thing I do know. John Clendenin, who was so fearful of a premature death that in his early 50s he passed on the chance to get in the queue to lead AT&T, lived to the ripe old age of 85.

Given how things turned out, you might expect me to think that divestiture was a bad idea. But a glance at America's reinvigorated, thriving information technology industry proves it was anything but. It was definitely tough on the version of AT&T I worked for and a tragedy for the hundreds of thousands of people who lost their jobs there because of it. But the hard truth is that there are many more jobs today in the resultant field than there were in the days of Ma Bell.

Back then, people didn't have personal computers or cellular phones. Fax machines were relatively new, and the Internet was in its infancy. The Bell System worked when new telecoms tech could be released in a controlled way, without becoming a negative for the consuming public. In other words, it worked when the main business (as it was for most of the 20th century) wasn't computers or information processing, but delivering voice communications on landlines. But when the 1980s ushered in new, transformative technologies, the need for a free-for-all competitive marketplace became obvious. The breakup of the Bell System helped create Silicon Valley and all the companies that sprang from that, including a company called Juniper Networks. But more about that later.

Not that the journey from monopoly to free market wasn't long and painful. In fact, I count myself among the legions who realized they could no longer soldier on with AT&T. My departure would place me and my family on an entirely new trajectory in our lives, and make me the CEO of a Fortune 500 company.

OUT OF THE BLUE   *Chapter Sixteen*

I'd given a lot of consideration to who might take over at Lilly but had never once thought of myself as a candidate.

Bob Allen was in an unimaginably difficult position, doing the best he could. The challenges he faced were as great as those faced by any other CEO I've known. I'll never know for sure how much of AT&T's course during his time in the corner office was actually based on his own personal insights, conclusions, and convictions, and how much was based on the views of the people he chose to listen to. Quite understandably, I think he found himself in such an uncomfortable role relative to his own interests, instincts, and experiences that the strategic bets he made were mostly bets on people who held views rather than on the views themselves. I didn't then and I don't now believe he was always well served by some of those vying for his attention.

As for me, by that time, I felt that the company I had worked for my entire adult life was strategically rudderless, still searching for a raison d'être and facing a very bleak future. And I had a hard time even imagining what my role within this ever-diminishing organization might be. My views about an appropriate strategic path were clearly at odds with those of the CEO so that was unlikely to end well. Yet, even as we caromed from one ill-starred acquisition or poorly thought-out initiative to the next, I didn't seriously consider looking for a new job.

As was the case with many of AT&T's lifetime employees, it simply didn't occur to me that I might want to pursue a professional life beyond Ma Bell. Instead, I discussed with Marilyn the possibility of retiring. I was still relatively young but had accumulated enough wealth to allow us to walk away and live comfortably for the rest of our days.

But retirement wasn't in the cards. Instead, I was on the cusp of a massive career change I could not have anticipated—one that would take me home to Indiana.

The seeds of this change were planted in the mid-1980s.

During my years in upper management, I served on the boards of a small number of publicly traded companies. This was a well-established practice among senior officers in corporate America, the belief being that lessons learned from helping to run other businesses could be applied to one's own. For me, any board seat I was offered had to meet at least four personal requirements. Most importantly, the nature of the company's business had to be such that I would be gaining experience and insights that would be useful to me in my own job and that my particular skill set would be of use to the company in question. Also, its gatherings (usually six to eight in-person meetings each year) couldn't conflict with my AT&T schedule. The company needed to have a policy of transporting its directors to and from meetings on their own corporate aircraft, so I could carry out my roles without being away from the office more than absolutely necessary. Last, but definitely not least, the business had to interest me.

In addition to AT&T, at various times, this placed me on the boards of a diverse group of firms, including Chemical Bank of New York; the media company Knight Ridder; Phillips Petroleum, which during my tenure merged with Conoco to become ConocoPhillips; and Kimberly-Clark, which makes paper-based consumer products ranging from Kleenex to Huggies diapers. Interestingly, my position with that company allowed me to secure a supply of some of the very first disposable Little Swimmers diapers that could be worn in pools. Two of my daughter Paige's kids, Emily and Connor, were among the first children in America to try them.

Speaking of Paige, another of my board assignments helped create lots of opportunities for father-daughter bonding time. In 1986 she enrolled at Duke University, graduating in 1990 with a double major in political science and French. She did a year of postgraduate work in Paris through a Duke-run program and in the fall of 1991 enrolled at the Duke University School of Law, graduating in 1994. This worked out well for me because shortly after she was admitted I accepted an invitation to join the university's board of trustees, intending to serve only until she graduated. I visited campus roughly three times a year, allowing us to have dinner and occasionally attend basketball games together and giving me the chance to get acquainted with her friends. Ultimately, I too fell in love with the place. I stayed on the Duke board for thirteen years, rising first to vice-chairman and eventually to chairman of the board, at which point I was on the campus about eight times annually. I'm proud of the fact that to the best of my knowledge I remain the only non-Duke graduate in modern times to have been elected to that position.

In 1986 I also became a board member of the Indianapolis-based pharmaceutical firm Eli Lilly and Company. I was invited, more or less out of the blue, by Dick Wood, its chairman and CEO. I had served for a time with Dick on the board of Chemical Bank, which was then one of the three principal New York City banks and later one of the principal merger partners that created today's JPMorgan Chase. I had resigned from that board after a couple of years because I just didn't feel my involvement met my first criteria—namely that I learned something useful and made myself useful in turn.

I didn't instantly say yes to Dick's invitation. I was flattered and interested, but I needed time to investigate. And I wanted to do some research. I didn't follow the pharmaceutical industry, and I was so out of touch with my home state that I had no idea about Lilly's current situation, what issues it faced, and how it was viewed. All I knew was that it had been a great company during my years in Indiana.

I soon discovered everything was a match with my criteria and interests, so I signed on. It was a great opportunity to get involved with a terrific company working in a vibrant industry, and also to keep in touch with my Hoosier roots. Visiting Indianapolis several times a year for board meetings offered a chance to keep some home-state connections, no matter how tenuous.

An outside director like me was known as an "independent director." In those days it was not uncommon for major, publicly traded corporations to have 12 to 14 board members, including the CEO and a small number of company officers. The rest (such as me) were from outside the organization. We independent directors had no real or perceived conflicts of interest. Our only goal was service to shareholders and the company's other constituents. We served as a counterweight to board members on the company payroll who might, understandably, hold views skewed in favor of plans and strategies favored by the top leadership. For obvious reasons, "insiders" weren't likely to be at odds with their boss, the CEO. Lilly was somewhat behind the times with corporate governance standards in that all of its most senior officers, comprising half the board, served as directors. In today's world, good governance practices would never permit that arrangement. Currently, only the Lilly CEO is also a director.

Eli Lilly and Company has been an Indianapolis landmark for nearly 120 years, and it's difficult for outsiders to understand its enormous impact on the city's development. Beyond founding the company and running it through three generations for its first 77 years, perhaps the Lilly family's biggest contribution was the creation of the Lilly Endowment. Founded in 1937, it is now one of the largest charitable foundations in the world, responsible for dispensing billions of dollars annually for programs focused on education, community development, and religion.

The Lilly company has employed tens of thousands of Hoosiers, and its personnel have given copious amounts of time and money to numberless civic projects and organizations.

The company was founded in 1876 by Colonel Eli Lilly in an era when medicines were as likely to be dispensed by door-to-door quacks as they were by actual doctors. There were few if any rules governing what claims could be made about these ridiculous concoctions, so many of the common "remedies" available at the time didn't perform as advertised. Many actually did more harm than good.

Enter the Colonel, a 38-year-old pharmaceutical chemist and Civil War veteran. Deeply frustrated by amateurish approaches to drug development, he founded his company with the then-novel goal of creating products using the most advanced scientific methods and then carefully testing them to make sure they were safe and effective. Lilly's signature breakthrough came in the early 1920s when its director of biochemical research, George Henry Alexander Clowes, collaborated with a team of scientists at the University of Toronto to develop insulin as a diabetes treatment. This fruitful meeting of minds allowed Lilly, in 1923, to bring to market the first insulin product available commercially in the U.S. for the treatment of type 1 diabetes. Before that, the disease was almost universally fatal, with no treatment options.

The importance of the drug, named Iletin, cannot be overestimated—either for the millions whose lives it saved or for Lilly itself. It was, without question, for many years, the most important drug in the company's history and turned Lilly into one of the world's major pharmaceutical manufacturers.

The breakthroughs continued in the ensuing decades, making Lilly Indianapolis's largest publicly held enterprise. By its 50th anniversary in 1926, the company generated $9 million in sales and produced more than 2,800 products. In the 1940s, it led in the development of mass-produced penicillin. During the '50s, '60s, and '70s, it created numerous antibiotics, including the top-selling oral brands, Ceclor and Keflex. And in 1982, a few years before I joined the board, the company used the then-new recombinant DNA technology to create Humulin, an insulin identical to the kind produced by the human body (earlier versions were extracted from animals).

Throughout all these decades of innovation and success, Lilly's leadership remained remarkably stable. During its first 125 years, it had only six top bosses, beginning with the Colonel and followed by his son, his son's two sons, Gene Beesley (the first non-family leader), and the man who brought me in, Dick Wood.

Dick was certainly the equal of any of the Lilly chief executives who came before him. And his career path at Lilly in many ways resembled mine at AT&T. Born in the town of Brazil, Indiana, which was only a little bit bigger than Remington, he joined Lilly in 1950, back when it was still run by the Colonel's two grandsons, Eli and Josiah Kirby Lilly, Jr. He rose through the ranks, becoming president in 1972 at age 45. Before he retired in 1991, he oversaw Lilly's transformation into a truly global enterprise, with profits that increased sevenfold during his tenure to $1.13 billion.

This combination of solid leadership and ever-improving returns meant that, during the early years of my tenure as a director, company board meetings were genial, upbeat affairs. We typically met formally about seven times a year on Mondays but got into town on Sunday nights, when we would all have dinner together. At one of those meetings, a dinner in a private dining room at the former Canterbury Hotel in early 1991, Dick made what would turn out to be a momentous announcement, both for the company and for me.

"You know, I'm going to be 65 and will be required to retire next October," he said. "I just want to let you know that my recommendation is, with your approval, that Vaughn Bryson will succeed me as CEO. It's further my recommendation that I stay on for a while as chairman of the board."

Vaughn, Dick's now designated successor, was 53 years old at the time, was a pharmacy graduate from the University of North Carolina (where he'd been a star baseball player), and had spent his entire career at Lilly. He possessed a lot of traits that had always been important for the company's top executives. And he was young enough to provide a decade or more of uninterrupted leadership.

The board accepted Dick's selection without much discussion. Vaughn seemed a logical choice, perhaps the only logical choice. Maybe Dick's recommendation that he stay on for a while as chairman should have been a warning that he had reservations about the only logical choice (if indeed he did). But the company had been so successful for so long, I don't think it occurred to anyone to seriously question Dick's judgment or propose looking further. In those times there was nothing unusual about that approach in corporate America.

Yet there was a problem. Actually, several. The pharmaceutical industry was changing rapidly. There had been some recent disappointments in Lilly's new drug pipeline. New technologies were roiling the waters, and an era of massive company consolidations had begun. It was not the time to be vulnerable. Vaughn was very keen on shaking up Lilly's staid management style and business model, but as gradually became apparent, there was a little too much ready, fire, aim in his approach. In the view of a number of senior managers who were there at the time, and ultimately the board, he moved too quickly and without enough forethought or strategic direction. In doing so, he violated what a wise AT&T colleague of mine used to call "the first rule of wing walking."

After World War I, barnstorming pilots, back from the war, went around the U.S. putting on extremely dangerous aerial shows, many of which included wing walking, in which a daring performer in a two-seat biplane would climb from the passenger seat onto the top wing and walk back and forth, clinging to the plane's wire struts. According to my AT&T associate, the first rule of wing walking was "Don't let go of the cable you're holding until you have a firm grip on another cable."

Unfortunately, Vaughn often ignored this rule.

Before becoming president and CEO, Vaughn had been an executive vice president, in recent years working outside the company's core pharmaceutical business and, as far as the board could see, doing an excellent job. His brief had included everything from the Elizabeth Arden cosmetics company (which Lilly purchased in 1971 and sold in 1987) to its accumulated portfolio of medical device businesses to the Elanco plant science and animal health businesses. When he took over day-to-day operations from Dick, one of his biggest goals was both overdue and quite laudable—to overhaul some aspects of Lilly's corporate culture, which had developed a reputation for being staid, top-down, and extremely conservative. It was perfectly summed up by the dress code, which leaned heavily toward formal business attire. Spotting a male employee outside his office or cubicle without his suit jacket was almost as startling and rare as a Bigfoot sighting.

Vaughn made a point of being seen without a jacket, to the delight of rank-and-file employees. He also launched a concerted effort to modernize Lilly's hidebound bureaucratic processes and ensure open communication between management and staff.

Unfortunately, while there was a focused commitment to reforming the company's internal processes, there was often no clear or workable vision for replacing them. At the time I arrived, his effort to implement bottom-up budgeting had resulted in a billion-dollar shortfall in the first draft of the budget for the following year. Nor was there a strategy for the future of Lilly's businesses. As one well-respected manager later told me, the sense in the organization about what was coming down from the executive suite was that the sky was falling, but we didn't know what to do about it. As the months of Vaughn's tenure rolled by, this became an ever-greater concern to the board, especially when that lack of direction contributed to a severe erosion of the company's stock price.

As I mentioned earlier, Lilly had for most of its existence grown steadily in size and profitability. Particularly under Dick Wood's leadership, when it posted a record of quarter-over-quarter earnings growth that was second in length to only one other Fortune 500 company. But in the months after Dick gave up his CEO post in 1992, Lilly's market value plummeted from $24 billion to $14 billion.

Vaughn was indeed bringing radical change to the company, but not the kind that Wall Street expected or the board desired.

This financial uncertainty came at a time when the entire pharmaceutical industry faced several existential challenges. One of the biggest was the Clinton administration's massive health care reform program. It had the potential, were it enacted, to transform the field almost beyond recognition. Also, a round of mergers and acquisitions was overtaking the market. With Lilly losing so much stock value, investment bankers were making it crystal clear that the company was increasingly a prime hostile takeover target, something with potentially dire consequences that neither the company's employees nor the Indianapolis community had yet to understand. But the board certainly did.

In addition to this, there was another problem—Vaughn's attitude. He had a hard time working both with Dick (who was still chairman of the board) and some of his associates whom he saw as either too loyal to Dick or part of the old-time business regimen he wanted to do away with. The board grew ever more concerned about all of these things, and the outside directors, along with Dick, held several conference calls to discuss the situation.

Finally, an in-person meeting of the independent directors took place at a hotel near Chicago's O'Hare Airport, something unprecedented in Lilly's long history. We talked about our concerns regarding Vaughn, but at that point always couched it in the context of, "What do we need to do to help him be successful?" After this gathering, a small group of three directors was charged with telling him, in a supportive but firm way, that at the next board meeting we must see his strategy for dealing with the challenges the company faced. The board's list of concerns had also grown to include the status of Lilly's new drug pipeline.

During the next board meeting, Vaughn duly made his presentation about how he planned to tackle Lilly's difficulties. But the board was underwhelmed and found it, to put it mildly, unsatisfactory. Even worse was the board's perception of his attitude, which, whether he intended it or not, could be summed up as, "I'm the CEO of the company, you're a bunch of outsiders, I'm now running this place, and I know what I'm doing."

After that meeting, the directors' thinking changed from "What can we do to make Vaughn successful?" to "Vaughn's not likely to be successful, and we may have to do the unthinkable, which is to replace him."

Our first instinct, which was certainly consistent with the company's history, was to identify the next insider to take the job. At the next Indianapolis board meeting in May of 1993, we hashed over some limited possibilities, but no candidates were identified as being both capable and ready.

After the meeting ended, I drove up to Rensselaer, near Remington, to visit my mother. She was quite ill at the time and in an extended-care facility.

The next day, while I was still with my mother, a nurse told me my office was asking me to call. Maureen Radigan, my long-time AT&T assistant, told me that Dick Wood had called her himself and wanted to speak with me, so I called him using a pay phone in the hallway outside my mother's room. He promptly offered a startling proposal. He said he'd spoken to most if not all of the other outside directors, and they unanimously supported the idea of asking me if I would be willing to leave AT&T and take over Lilly. If I agreed, Dick would step down from his current post and I would serve as both CEO and chairman of the board.

The proposal felt like a bolt from the blue. I'd given a lot of consideration to who might take over at Lilly but had never once thought of myself as a candidate. I told Dick that I needed to go home, think about it, talk with Marilyn, and get back to him.

While I certainly wasn't expecting to be offered the position, upon reflection, I began to see the logic that Dick had shared. I'd been on the board for several years, so I was as familiar with the issues the company faced as a director could be. And recent events at AT&T gave me experience working with an organization facing rapid, radical change. It also didn't hurt that I was born, raised, and educated in the state of Indiana. I had an understanding of Hoosier culture and values, and because of AT&T's significant presence in the state, I was acquainted with many of Indiana's important players, including the governor and its U.S. senators.

In other words, in addition to having a good deal of relevant corporate experience, I was probably the most "inside outsider" they could find.

Two days later, after a lot of discussion with Marilyn, who signed off on the plan with some enthusiasm (which, of course, would require us relocating from New Jersey back to Indiana), I called Dick and told him I was willing to do it, but with a couple of provisos. I wanted to recuse myself from the board's future discussions about Vaughn's fate. Further, I wanted the decision to remove him to be entirely separate from the alternative plan to bring me in. Replacing the company's CEO would be incredibly wrenching and painful, and I wanted the choice made independently, without any input (or even the perception of input) from me. If the board ultimately decided Vaughn had to go and then separately decided it wanted me as the new CEO, then I'd be willing to sign on.

In retrospect, it may seem a bit like counting the angels on the head of a pin. But it was important to me that I not be perceived as playing a role in all of this, which might perhaps give the impression of a conflict of interest. So that's the way it unfolded.

On Monday, June 21, 1993, the board met to deal with this complicated, emotional change of leadership. The proceedings officially dragged on because once Vaughn was told of the position of the independent directors, he (with the support of several but not all of the "inside" board members who worked directly for him) didn't go quietly, confirming his "imperial" attitude about his role versus that of the board. I attended the initial part of the meeting that day but stepped out of the room when it came time for the discussion and vote on his formal removal. But the matter dragged on for four more days as Vaughn tried to pressure the officer-directors who reported to him to resist the decision of the independent directors. I immediately summoned Maureen and my longtime AT&T speech writer, Ed Bligh, to join me in Indianapolis to provide administrative and communications support when it came time to conclude this. I knew it was going to be a mess and there was no one in the company prepared to handle what would be required. Not until Friday, June 25, was I formally elected chairman, president, and CEO. After doing what I could to begin a transition, I returned to New Jersey late Friday with Maureen and Ed to tie up some loose ends.

Vaughn vacated his office over the weekend, but there was a behind-the-scenes standoff for several more weeks before his resignation from the board was finally consummated. In fact, the board was incredulous when he actually showed up for its July meeting. As a negotiating tactic over the size and terms of a severance package, he took the position that the board might dismiss him as CEO, but only the shareholders who had elected him could remove him as a director. The more this played out the more the board was convinced it had made the only decision it could. In the end, Jim Cozad, the former CEO of AMOCO, who had taken over from me as chair of the board's compensation committee, skillfully negotiated a package with the attorney Vaughn had retained, allowing us to finally move on.

My appointment was just one of a rapid-fire succession of company firsts—few of which could be described as propitious. Over one long weekend, Lilly, whose CEOs typically reigned for decades and were either actual members of the Lilly family or at least lifelong Lilly employees, turned a new page and plunged into the unknown. They dismissed their CEO after just 20 months and replaced him, not with the familiar face of a lifer, but a stranger. A new guy. An unknown quantity (at least to the rank-and-file employees) from the world outside of Lilly.

Even in the best of times, establishing my leadership under such circumstances would have been a complex process. But these times were far from the best. And they were about to get even tougher.

A FAST START

Chapter Seventeen

*My first hours on the job were
going to be very eventful.*

After I accepted my new position, I believed (erroneously) that I might have at least a brief period during which I could wrap things up at AT&T before fully transitioning to Indianapolis. At the time, in my additional role as chairman and CEO of AT&T International, I was in the final stages of helping some very talented and tenacious AT&T people conclude a high-profile, long-gestating proposal to the Chinese Ministry of Telecommunications to use AT&T equipment and technology to bring China's telecommunications network up to modern standards. It's hard to overstate the importance of that arrangement, both to the company and to U.S.-China bilateral relations. On my final trip to Beijing to close the deal, I met personally with China's premier (and soon-to-be president) Jiang Zemin. The negotiations were followed closely in the U.S. and international press. It was a potential $5 billion deal—one that I hoped to wrap up personally and then hand off to someone else at

AT&T to implement. During the negotiations, I was responsible for the *New York Times* editors' choice for their quote of the day. There was a small effort in Congress, led by the future Speaker of the House, Nancy Pelosi, to negatively impact the terms of the deal by lobbying for the Executive Branch to withhold "most favored nation" trade status over legitimate concerns about China's human rights record. In response, I told a *Times* reporter that we all know that the pen is mightier than the sword. By facilitating these improvements and thus the ability of the Chinese people to communicate more freely, I believed we were going to learn that the fax machine was mightier than the rifle.

But a pause before departing from AT&T wasn't to be. A long list of issues demanded my immediate attention. A list that grew longer by the hour.

I was elevated to my new position at Lilly on Friday, June 25, 1993. While in this case it was obviously not planned, Friday is typically the day that public companies announce problematic developments. You wait until the end of the workweek so that interested parties can have the weekend to digest the news, instead of (theoretically) running straight to their computers and dumping your stock. And in Lilly's case, announcing that they'd fired their still wet-behind-the-ears CEO and replaced him with an unknown quantity from outside the company—in fact, from outside the pharmaceutical industry—sounded very problematic indeed.

The day after the announcement, I learned just how rapidly my transition from AT&T to Lilly would happen.

On the morning of Saturday the 26th, I received a steady stream of phone calls from Lilly execs about a rapidly developing crisis. The company was deep into clinical trials of a treatment for hepatitis B called FIAU, which was an abbreviation for the chemical compound fialuridine. The trials, done in collaboration with the National

Institutes of Health (NIH), had gone on for months without incident. But early that morning the NIH's principal investigator told Lilly that one of the patients in the trial had been hospitalized for profound liver failure.

Shortly thereafter, the NIH and Lilly made a joint decision to end the trial, and the other 14 test patients were instructed to stop taking the medication and report to the NIH as quickly as possible. Soon several of them showed early signs of liver toxicity.

I was in a tough spot. I had to immediately address this extremely important issue, about which I was still learning, while also soothing the nerves of Lilly employees and winning the confidence of the executive staff.

Monday found me in Indianapolis for my first management meeting as CEO. Over the weekend the press had characterized my appointment as a "boardroom coup." Company employees at the Lilly campus gathered in the halls and around building entrances, talking among themselves. TV vans were camped outside, waiting for news.

The uncertainty in the air was palpable and understandable, given the lack of solid information provided by the company—an approach still connected to the old culture of not saying much. Some thought I'd been brought in as a "hatchet man" to prune the payroll. After all, wasn't that what I'd been involved in doing at AT&T for years?

It also didn't help that, to the rank and file at least, I was an unknown quantity. In a less-than-appropriately-worded press release, Vaughn was said to have "… announced his retirement due to differences with the board over management philosophy … ." He had been quite popular with the rank and file during his 20 months as CEO. In many ways the lower-level employees actually saw the need for change, particularly regarding Lilly's top-down hierarchical culture. They saw Vaughn as a potential agent of change, but of course without comprehending the shortcomings that were so apparent to the board. While his inability to produce value for shareholders alarmed the board and many of his senior management colleagues, his push for a more open, less hidebound corporate culture endeared him, quite appropriately, I thought, to the broad base of Lilly employees. Not surprisingly, and fed by the wording in the statement, his departure was interpreted in some circles as a push by upper management to return to the button-down "good old days."

My first hours on the job were going to be very eventful.

When I walked into the Lilly executive conference room that first morning for a meeting scheduled to review the clinical trial events of the weekend, I found it packed with most of the top management. All conversation ceased as I took my spot at the head of the table and said, I'm sure quite unnecessarily, "Good morning. For those who don't yet know me, I'm Randy Tobias."

After brief introductions from some of the research scientists and physicians who I hadn't met during my days as a board member, we got down to business with a briefing on the FIAU situation. It was unprecedented for something like this to happen in a clinical trial. The experts gathered around the table that morning spent some time going over the scientific and medical details, and our legal counsel and public relations staff also chimed in. Once their presentations ended, all eyes once again turned to me. What did the "telephone guy" think of all this?

I started by thanking everybody who'd made presentations and expressing my confidence in their ability to address the issue. And then I gave what, in retrospect, was probably my first speech as Lilly's boss. One that set the tone for the leadership style I planned to pursue.

"I know that you all know what needs to be done, and I want you to proceed accordingly. But from my perspective I also want to be sure we are focused on doing the most we can for these patients and their families," I said. "Certainly, I want to understand the potential legal and financial exposure that could result from this situation, but let's not be driven by those considerations. I don't want that to be our priority. The patients and their families are our top priority. I want their well-being to be the driver of our decisions, first and foremost."

I further instructed that we needed to pick up any medical expenses incurred by the families of the patients and fly the families to the NIH immediately, on our dime, if that's what they wanted.

"We need to communicate, in short, our desire to help in any way we can," I said. "Not only because we have a responsibility to do those things, but more importantly, because it's the right thing to do."

I learned later that several people decided at that moment, with great relief, that maybe the telephone guy actually had the values of a Lilly guy.

In the next few weeks, 5 of the 15 patients in the trial study died of severe liver toxicity. It was a tragedy, but it didn't metastasize into a public outcry or damage our financial position. This was at least in part because we approached the debacle in a compassionate, open way. Two years later, the Institute of Medicine of the National Academy of Sciences issued a report exonerating Lilly and calling the deaths "uniquely and totally unpredictably unavoidable."

I think that putting the welfare of the patients in our study first, which came naturally to me, set the proper tone for how I intended to lead. Don't cover anything up. Don't sweep anything under the rug. Tell the truth and work hard to communicate clearly with all stakeholders.

Good communication would be vital for almost everything I needed to do. For instance, getting the word out that I wasn't there to make arbitrary, draconian staff cuts, or to reinstitute the company's old social mores. And so, among a great many other things, I started eating lunch in the employee cafeteria. Historically, Lilly execs didn't take meals there, but when I could, I would go through the line with a tray, pick out a group of people at a table, and ask if I could join them. Sure, admittedly, it was an orchestrated effort. But it was a great chance to answer questions and put forth my ideas about what to do going forward—ideas that, thanks in part to these lunchtime conversations, were promptly circulated far and wide through the company grapevine.

I also spent as much time as practicable visiting various parts of the company in person—on campus, around the U.S., and around the world. I wanted to meet the key players as well as rank-and-file employees, hear their thoughts, and alleviate any fears as to what I might have in store. I'm sure to this day there are a lot of plaques in far-flung Lilly facilities around the world commemorating the first-ever visit of the CEO.

Of course, making a good impression wasn't the only thing on my to-do list. Fortunately, my time at AT&T gave me an almost instinctive understanding of the major priorities on which I needed to focus. One of my first acts was to develop and articulate a manageable list. They were:

- Get the company operationally under control.
- Restore confidence in Lilly, its leadership, and its future—beginning with our own employees, our shareholders, and the financial community.
- Move quickly to increase shareholder value.
- Make important and needed strategic choices.
- Rekindle and refocus the company's core values.

- Strengthen and deepen the company's leadership capabilities—at the top as well as in other key parts of the business—with the skills and experiences required for the road ahead.

It was an ambitious list, but I wasn't exactly starting from scratch. I'd spent more than half a decade on Lilly's board, so while I wasn't intimately familiar with the drugs in the pipeline and every research effort, I possessed a meaningful overview of the issues facing the company. And I knew what was required of any organization facing the need for drastic changes. Indeed, I've often said that at least 80 percent of what I did at Lilly was no different from 80 percent of what I had done as CEO of AT&T Communications. I've also said that being the CEO was really the only job at Lilly for which I felt totally qualified. I couldn't run the research labs; I wouldn't have been the best person to oversee the sales force; and I wouldn't have been an appropriate choice to run the manufacturing operations. But I had experience doing the things that a CEO needs to do. And that's what I proceeded to do.

A CEO needs to make sure the company has a strategy, that the strategy is clearly articulated and understood, and that senior management understands, supports, and forwards it. And as I've already emphasized, it's important to communicate, communicate, and communicate. It's the only way to get everybody on board with your plans and pulling in the same direction.

It doesn't matter if you're publishing newspapers, helping to lead a major research university, making Kleenex, drilling oil wells in the North Sea, selling telephones, or developing drugs—all areas where I'd had some experience. Across all industries, those fundamental leadership concepts apply.

One of my very first moves was holding one-on-one meetings to determine which of the current senior management staff had the right mindset to continue in their roles. To put it simply, anyone with the primary attitude of, "Let me explain to you how we do it here," didn't last long.

In some cases, this meant identifying and promoting a new generation of senior managers. It certainly wasn't that the current leaders who needed to go were ineffective. Many of them in fact had run one of the most effective and successful companies in the country. But in many cases, they were so wedded to the way they'd always done things that they couldn't possibly drive the changes we needed. They had to lead by looking through their windshields, not at their rear-view mirrors. In several key roles, I identified and promoted a new generation that could rally around the strategy I selected.

This isn't to say that I "cleaned house." One of the things of which I'm very proud is that I didn't do what other "outside" CEOs often did: bring in an entirely new team to turn the company around. Instead, I brought in a small number of people with skill sets that the company either didn't have or hadn't historically valued. For instance, Jim Cornelius, who served 28 years at Lilly, had been an incredibly effective CFO and a very supportive and valued advisor to me. When Jim took a new and even more important job as the chairman of our medical device businesses, he left big shoes to fill. Rather than replace him with someone from within, I recruited Charlie Golden, whose entire career had been as a finance executive with General Motors. It was an opportunity to bring a different perspective and a different model of what a CFO does.

In the main, however, it was Lilly people who did the revamping.

In my first months, I also examined staffing levels throughout the company. Though I had no plans for wholesale firings, it seemed apparent to me that the headcount needed to be reduced. The old Lilly culture, by default, encouraged a bloated payroll, because it wasn't unusual, when someone proved ineffective at their job, for them to simply be moved to another one. This is a pretty convincing sign that you have more people than necessary.

I asked my management team if they thought we had an overstaffing problem, and most reluctantly agreed. So I tasked them with assessing how many jobs they thought could be eliminated from their portions of the businesses, and they came back with a number totaling about 2,500.

Based on my AT&T experience, I knew that this number would be a bit light. As I mentioned earlier, I wasn't brought in to be a "hatchet man," and I never ever relished the idea of downsizing lots of people. Nonetheless, I wanted this workforce reduction to be large enough to be a one-time occurrence.

"Trust me, we're going to double that number because we are not going to cut off this dog's tail an inch at a time," I told my team. "If we ever have to do this a second time, nobody is ever again going to retire from this company. They're just going to continue working in anticipation that we're going to announce the next incentive retirement program. So this has to be a one-time effort."

The number quickly rose to between 4,000 and 5,000. But we didn't go around sacking specific people we didn't think were pulling their weight. Instead, we offered voluntary early retirement plans. Federal regulations require companies to make the downsizing packages available to everyone in a particular employee category. In other words, we couldn't and didn't look at a group of 100 people who all did the same thing, pick out the 30 worst performers, and tell them, "I'm offering you an early retirement program but the rest of you can't go."

So we made the enhanced retirement plan available to all who met the criteria. However, I have to admit that in very private one-on-one conversations either with myself or other trusted members of the company, we approached some very senior people and said, "You know, this would be a really good time for you to declare victory on what has been a wonderful career and take advantage of this early retirement program and move on." It was a face-saving opportunity for individuals who'd made extraordinary contributions but weren't cut out for the dramatic changes ahead. This allowed us to introduce some fresh air into Lilly's senior ranks.

While fine-tuning the management structure and trimming the payroll, I also examined and revamped the company's efforts to discover and develop new medicines. I felt that our research approach suffered from a lack of strategic focus. It reminded me too much of the baseball movie *Field of Dreams*. "If we build it they will come!" It seemed to be very much an environment in which many of the scientists worked on the things that interested them, whether or not these were efforts strategically focused to lead to marketable products in priority areas. It seemed logical to me that we should find ways to provide greater resources to our research enterprise to invest in drug discovery—inside and outside our own laboratories—and then focus that increased research spending in fewer strategically selected areas, without at the same time stifling closely related efforts that might lead to unexpected, serendipitous breakthroughs.

It seemed to me that a better approach would be to try to target selected unmet medical needs in areas where we had matching capabilities, with the intent of developing products most likely to have attractive margins in those targeted therapeutic areas. So one of the initiatives I put in place during my first few months on the job was an effort to focus our research. I shared my thoughts with Dr. Gus Watanabe, who I'd recently installed as head of Lilly Research Laboratories and who agreed with my conclusions. I asked Gus to take a few of his key people off-site for however long it took and determine how we could better focus our efforts. They came back with a recommendation that we should focus our research on about five therapeutic areas instead of the dozens that were then absorbing scarce resources.

Gus and his colleagues also initiated approaches to bring products to market faster and more efficiently. Fortunately, the next few years saw the introduction of a bounty of popular new drugs. In 1996 alone, Lilly debuted the schizophrenia drug Zyprexa, along with Evista for osteoporosis and Gemzar for pancreatic cancer.

Though it would be nice to say that my initiatives made this possible, all those drugs started development long before I became CEO. The truth is that it takes a decade or more for a new compound to progress from a gleam in a researcher's eye to a product a doctor can prescribe. So any pharmaceutical company CEO who takes credit for all the products that reach the market during his tenure is kidding himself. It's a long-term effort involving lots of people.

Nevertheless, I did what I could to provide more resources for research, bring greater focus to that research, and encourage the efforts of those who understood what was needed to speed the process. I also learned that the price "assigned" by the market for pharmaceutical stocks is based not just on what the company is doing now or in the near future, as is more the case in other industries, but also on what it is *capable* of doing in the future.

Here's where Lilly's old culture became a problem. Traditionally, it was viewed as almost unseemly to tell the financial community about items that were still under development. In fact, the company's unofficial slogan was, "The Lilly brand will speak for itself."

That may sound great and reflect admirable humility, but if you're in a position where you need to implement totally legitimate initiatives to elevate a company's stock price—which we certainly were, if for no other reason than to discourage hostile takeover bids—it's counterproductive. So instead, almost immediately after my arrival and at the urging of Jim Cornelius and others, we started talking to the investment community about what we were working on. When we spoke to securities analysts in New York, we took along not just the relevant senior executives but also key scientists, who were more knowledgeable about and could better articulate what we were doing in our research efforts.

And it worked. I believe we actually raised our stock price by just opening up to the investment community about our plans and capabilities. So, while I didn't preside over the development of any of the drugs that debuted during my tenure, I can confidently say that we were able to realize more value for those products in the pipeline and to enhance the research capabilities and emphasis going forward. I'm hopeful that the research focus we revitalized in those days strengthened the foundation for the work that has gone on since.

I also tackled another issue that had brewed for quite a while. At the time of my arrival, Lilly owned just shy of 20 medical device businesses, which operated quite separately from Lilly's pharmaceutical business. For a period of time, they were quite successful and provided something of a growth engine for the company. But then some began to have issues with the FDA, in some cases by at least appearing to officials there to be operating too close to the edge of the agency's rules and regulations. It seemed apparent to me that the culture required to be successful in those businesses was more like cultures found in Silicon Valley than in the pharmaceutical business. Whether or not they should be retained or sold off had been a raging debate within the company for some time. Intuitively, in my judgment, they didn't seem to be a good fit because they didn't mesh well with the culture of a pharmaceutical company. If you're developing and bringing to market, say, implantable defibrillators, that seemed to me to require the skills and mindset of a Silicon Valley business. It certainly wasn't a good match for the skills and mindset required for success in pharmaceuticals. The presence of this stepchild in our portfolio caused a lot of internal debate as to whether to keep the companies or spin them off. But while there'd been lots of talk, no one had actually done anything. One of my earliest decisions was to end all the pondering and decide to decide!

In late 1994, we finally settled the issue. We concluded that the device business wasn't a good fit and that we were not the best owner to advance its interests. Also, a very enlightening analysis revealed that the price of Lilly stock was no higher as a result of owning those entities than it would have been had we stuck solely to the pharmaceutical business—an amazing revelation.

In an effort to streamline and refocus Lilly, as well as to better deploy our resources, our medical device interests were gathered together and, in a uniquely structured transaction, "split off" as Guidant Corporation under the capable leadership of Ron Dollens as its CEO and Jim Cornelius as its chairman. The money we were able to retain within Lilly because of the way we structured that transaction was then plowed into our core pharmaceutical research. After a decade of operation as an independent and very successful firm, Guidant was acquired by Boston Scientific in 2006 for $27 billion, nearly twice the value of the entire Lilly company when I became CEO.

In those early days, I also began traveling from Japan to Germany to Brazil, touching bases with our Lilly entities around the world. Interestingly, for a company that's headquartered in the American Midwest, Lilly's senior management was quite cosmopolitan. Some were born outside the U.S., and almost all had done at least one stint outside the country—perhaps as an officer or even president of a Lilly subsidiary in Canada, Japan, Germany, or someplace else.

Those overseas offices were built around teams of people who were laser-focused on handling Lilly's interests in that country.

Oddly, we lacked a structure focused in that same way on the U.S. market. While we certainly had a strong U.S. sales force, the people at the global headquarters in Indianapolis who made the overarching, worldwide decisions also largely ran things strategically in the U.S. So I strongly supported going even further with the creation of what was essentially a subsidiary that mirrored what we had in Australia, Brazil, or France. Called Lilly USA, it exclusively ran our United States business operations. And to make sure it could operate as independently as our more far-flung entities, I moved it into a building entirely separate from corporate headquarters. It was capably led by Mitch Daniels, who had been appointed to lead the U.S. sales force as Vaughn Bryson's final and perhaps most inspired decision.

Unfortunately, Vaughn did himself no favors thanks to the manner in which he made this important senior-level appointment. Mitch's selection was made and announced without first informing the board and seeking its endorsement. It was yet another perceived poke-in-the-eye from him to his bosses, at the exact moment when his future as CEO teetered on the brink. It was in fact probably the final straw.

Beyond his many important contributions to Lilly, Mitch went on to become a member of President George W. Bush's cabinet and then perhaps Indiana's best-ever Governor, serving two terms. Following his governorship, he served for 10 years with great distinction as the president of Purdue University. Today we're blessed to have Mitch and Cheri as close and valued friends. From my experience with him at Lilly and beyond, I view him as one of the most effective strategic thinkers and leaders I've ever known. His contributions to Lilly during my time and beyond were stellar.

Putting Lilly's house in order of course necessitated some very long days and nights. But while I worked through an ample list of internal issues, there was also one very, very large external problem with which to contend. One that was far beyond my personal control. It was called the Health Security Act of 1993.

In hindsight, it's hard to comprehend just how world-shaking I and the entire pharmaceutical industry expected it to be. It was a 1,342-page bill written by President Bill Clinton's administration that, in a nutshell, proposed to give prescription drug insurance coverage to every American, either through Medicare (if you were over 65) or through government-sponsored buying groups called regional health alliances.

The widespread use of low-priced generic drugs would be encouraged, and doctors could only prescribe drugs on an approved government list, called a formulary. If your drug didn't make that list, it was likely as good as dead. This meant that whoever generated the formulary would be the absolute master of the U.S. pharmaceuticals market. Indeed, for all intents and purposes, they would become the pharmaceuticals market. The government could also blacklist drugs it deemed too expensive.

Though the Clinton administration said their plan would not include price controls, it was obvious that this scheme would create them in everything but name. In 1993 it seemed highly probable that this plan would become law in some form, bringing seismic changes to Lilly's business. Instead of competing in an open market, the federal government would become the one and only buyer, able to dictate whatever terms it saw fit.

As CEO, I was actively engaged in lobbying against the proposal. The effort was coordinated by an organization called the Pharmaceutical Research and Manufacturers of America (PhRMA). PhRMA was our industry's trade association and the place where Sidney Taurel, the executive vice president heading sales and marketing, continued to lead Lilly's efforts as he had prior to my arrival. PhRMA's leaders crafted a political strategy, and under the organization's guidance, myself, and other pharmaceutical companies' CEOs met with senators, congressmen, and others and helped fund advertising programs and so forth.

I expended a great deal of time and effort on the issue and participated in making important decisions with an eye toward the changes it might bring. One thing that seemed certain was that companies known as pharmacy benefit managers (PBMs) would play a key role. Created to control costs for private providers of drug benefit programs, they arranged volume purchases with manufacturers, negotiated prescription prices with pharmacies, dictated the substitution of generic drugs for brand-name compounds where practicable, and created formularies of drugs for which they provided full reimbursement. In other words, they already did, on a smaller scale, what the government proposed to do on a grand scale.

This made it seem like a good idea for any pharmaceutical company that wanted some sort of say in how their drugs were treated to own a PBM. Two of our competitors, Merck and SmithKlineBeecham, had already snapped up PBMs. There was only one of any real size, PCS Health Systems, still available for purchase, which meant that Lilly had a decision to make—an expensive one. We could purchase PCS and use it to (perhaps) increase our influence in the brave new pharmaceutical world that was (perhaps) about to dawn. But there were so many uncertainties. Was a PBM truly a good fit for a company that had just spent a great deal of time refocusing on its core business? And what if the bill didn't become law? At the time, it seemed like a shoo-in, but still … .

In the end, we purchased PCS for $4.1 billion in 1994. And not long afterward, the dreaded Health Security Act quietly died in

Congress. Suddenly, we were stuck with a company that didn't really fit our portfolio. It also attracted unwanted attention from the federal government, which worried that PBMs owned by pharmaceutical companies might be used to keep competitors' drugs off the market.

In 1997 Lilly wrote off $2.5 billion on the investment and then sold PCS to the drugstore chain Rite Aid for $1.5 billion in 1998. In hindsight, it was the biggest misstep of my tenure at Lilly. And maybe or maybe not only in hindsight. We were struggling to chart a path forward for the company in a turbulent time, based on a woefully imperfect understanding of what the next few years might bring. In the end, I'm comfortable saying that I made the best decision I knew how to make with the foggy information at hand. But it wasn't good enough. As I said at the time, if I could get back that decision or even just the $2.5 billion write-off, I'd take it. The acquisition was a flawed choice, and I own it.

Nevertheless, I think the slightly less than six years I spent as CEO and chairman of the board at Lilly were viewed by most observers as a resounding success. When I took the job, the company's market value stood at about $14 billion. When I departed it was more than $70 billion. Our stock price had risen more than 400 percent, delighting shareholders and ending the threat of a hostile takeover. We also shed numerous sideshow businesses, from medical devices to plant sciences, allowing us to spend more time and resources doing what we'd always done best—addressing unmet medical needs by developing drugs. And we were able to bring those drugs to market approximately 18 months faster than previously.

We streamlined staff and made our operations more efficient, while at the same time making Lilly a better, more forward-thinking place to work. Lilly introduced on-site daycare and flextime programs, earning us a spot on the *Working Mother* magazine's list of 100 best

U.S. Companies. In 1996 the magazine named me its CEO Family Champion of the Year.

From a purely business perspective, my return to Indianapolis and leadership at Lilly went very, very well. Yet when I look back at that time, the memories are bittersweet. While my career hummed along, my personal life was checkered with loss, tragedy, and change. Those travails would play a huge role in my decision to leave Lilly after just over half a decade on the job.

TRAGEDY STRIKES

Chapter Eighteen

The last thing I want is for Marilyn's life to be defined by the way it ended.

The darkest day of my life was May 16, 1994, when Marilyn, my wife of 28 years, took her own life.

To say we were stunned would be an understatement. Paige, Todd, and I knew she was struggling with clinical depression, which had been diagnosed some months before. But the idea that she might harm herself never crossed our minds. Even her psychiatrist was blindsided. His pager used a special code to alert him if one of his patients attempted or succeeded in committing suicide. When he saw that code on May 16, he automatically ticked through his patient roster in his mind, trying to guess who it might be.

Marilyn, he told me later, was the last person on his list that he'd considered as a possibility.

But even though the experts couldn't foresee this tragedy, over the years I've spent a great deal of time wondering why I didn't. What could I have done differently? Could I have helped her?

Could I have stopped her? Why didn't I grasp the true depth of her pain and how far she would go to end it?

I've been told that this sort of second-guessing is a fool's errand. Yet even thirty years later I can't help endlessly dissecting the events that led to that fateful day.

As I think back over the years, I wonder when the first hints of trouble began to surface. For instance, I remember that sometimes Marilyn would talk wistfully of our days in the mid-1960s in bucolic Lebanon, Indiana, which was the first place we lived after marrying. She looked back very fondly on our happy, low-stress days living that small-town life. She had a lot of friends there, and she taught second grade. "Wouldn't it have been great if we could have just lived in Lebanon?" she would sometimes say.

Of course, that's not how things worked out. Far from it. Because of my career, we were destined to move more than most. Each relocation was in response to a significant and unexpected promotion, which certainly created a better economic situation for the family, though not without consequences. But back in the 1960s and '70s, if you were on the way up in a major corporation such moves were just part of life. It wasn't anything the two of us ever questioned. Or at least, questioned out loud. At least I didn't. But maybe "on the way up" was not a life Marilyn ever wanted.

Though she never said anything about it, in retrospect, I think being uprooted so many times had to have affected her long-term mental state. I'm now convinced I just didn't understand the impact on Marilyn. And that makes me sad.

Our nomadic lifestyle didn't seem to take a toll on either me, Paige, or Todd. In my case, I had a built-in support network at the office. But I think there was more to it than that. I just naturally approached life with more of an eagerness to embrace change.

Maybe it's also why I never stopped to appreciate how much it might have bothered Marilyn.

Though honestly, for the first couple of decades of our marriage, it certainly didn't seem to trouble her either. During my AT&T days, when the kids were old enough to stay with Marilyn's mother, who would come from Oklahoma to visit us, she accompanied me all over the world on business trips, her sparkling personality routinely turning strangers into friends. At home she stayed busy, taking several teaching jobs, but mostly devoting herself to the kids.

She would spend hours on homework, school projects, or homemade costumes for Paige and Todd. She drove them everywhere for their various activities. When it came to the kids, there was really no limit to her care and concern. For instance, when Todd was around seven or eight, he started running competitively in road races, and Marilyn and I would take him all over the place on Saturdays for amateur meets against other kids his age. He often did quite well. In one case, however, and I believe it was a race that was very important to him, he didn't place in the top three. Yet he got a trophy anyway, which he displayed for years in his room. Turns out Marilyn actually had it made for him because he felt so strongly about that race. It wasn't until years later that he learned the full story.

Her illness may have begun to assert itself five or six years before we moved to Indianapolis. First, she complained of being more tired than usual and started taking an occasional nap. Only in retrospect do I now think that maybe, beginning at about that time, she slowly started to shy away from some optional events and business trips she might previously have enjoyed.

Thinking it was some sort of physical ailment, we sought the help of numerous physicians. But their opinions were all over the map. At one time or another, her problems were speculatively attributed to everything from Lyme disease to lupus to a liver disorder to chronic fatigue syndrome. But that was the way the heavily compartmentalized medical system worked at the time. If a possible ailment was outside the wheelhouse of a given specialist (as mental illness was for almost all of them), it simply wasn't considered.

Even though she was fully involved in the decision and had expressed enthusiasm about moving, her troubles worsened dramatically after I took over at Lilly. I couldn't help but wonder whether she'd actually been enthusiastic or not.

On the surface at least, returning to Indiana seemed like a good move for both of us. It was clearly an exciting career move for me, and the prospect of living in Indianapolis and more easily becoming involved in the community and connecting with new friends seemed exciting to Marilyn. Upon our arrival, we found a house right away, but Marilyn stayed mostly in New Jersey, joining me part-time in the hotel where I lived while renovations to our new place were made. During this time her medical issues, including fatigue, sadness, and I now know, rising alcohol consumption, became ever more difficult for her to control or conceal.

We were both social drinkers, but not heavy drinkers. If we went to a restaurant, she'd have a glass of wine, but we wouldn't order a bottle. And by ourselves in the evening, we might each have a cocktail, but not three. Again, in retrospect, I wonder if perhaps she was always drinking more than I realized. In Indianapolis, she tried to do it in secret—sometimes while locked in a guest room at the house. I now assume she must have been drinking when I was traveling internationally, and I wouldn't have known. But after the move to Lilly, either her consumption increased so much or her defense mechanisms diminished so much that hiding it proved impossible.

Finally, approximately eight months into my Lilly tenure, her depression was properly diagnosed. Ironically, it was Marilyn's

Indianapolis OB-GYN and Gus Watanabe's wife, Dr. Margaret "Peg" Watanabe, who first recognized the problem. She in fact diagnosed Marilyn during their very first interview. That finally triggered the proper medical attention. Were it not for my position at Lilly, with so much medical expertise literally at my fingertips, I don't think she ever would have found the answer.

I should take a moment to clarify the difference between clinical depression and feeling a bit "blue." Because even today there's a widespread misunderstanding of the difference between the two.

Everybody occasionally feels sad, anxious, or perhaps overly tired or run-down by life. But for most people, the feeling passes after a couple of hours or days, and they return to a more balanced state of mind. This is common and quite normal. But it's different for people suffering from clinical depression. Their feelings of debilitating sadness and hopelessness can be very severe and last for weeks, leaving them unable to function properly.

The disease can be caused by anything from differences in brain chemistry to genetics and can be exacerbated by environmental factors. It also manifests a dizzying array of physical and mental symptoms, including alcohol or substance abuse (which can be seen as a form of self-medication), sleeping problems (either insomnia or too much sleep), and a grab bag of physical complaints such as joint pain and digestive issues.

Some people are born with a predisposition toward clinical depression. Though it may not become a debilitating issue for decades, at some point, anyone who suffers from it will likely need medical intervention. Though there's no cure, it can often be treated with a combination of therapy and drugs. In most cases, the patient can live a normal life.

Traumatic events can cause clinical depression to rapidly worsen. The list of possible triggers is quite long and includes losing a job, losing a child, getting divorced, moving, or having a child go off to college. Of course, we had just moved (again), and both of our kids were now away at university.

Over the years, I've wondered if the root of Marilyn's problem might have been more genetic. Her mother was a very nice, even-keeled person. Her father, who was an electrician, died before I met Marilyn. As I mentioned earlier in this book, Salyer family lore says that although he was hit by a truck while crossing a road in what was characterized as a pedestrian accident, it seems entirely possible, from the circumstances, that he may have intentionally stepped into traffic. No one will ever know.

After Marilyn died, her psychiatrist told me that in all likelihood she had suffered from some aspects of clinical depression for a very long time and that she'd gotten to a point where she just couldn't cover it up anymore. And if you're wondering why she tried to cover it up at all, it's because in those days, even more than now, a great deal of stigma was attached to mental illness. If someone had a broken bone or heart disease, they'd seek appropriate treatment and wouldn't worry about what other people thought. But depression was too often seen not as a health issue, but as some sort of personal failing. Which meant that its sufferers often felt they had to hide it and pretend everything was fine. Even today I'm not sure how much progress has been made in reducing that stigma.

After Marilyn's diagnosis, we immediately did two things. We arranged for her to see a psychiatrist, and she was put on one of Lilly's star products, Prozac. Its chemical name is Fluoxetine, and it's an extremely effective antidepressant that was discovered at Lilly in 1972 and brought to market in 1986.

At the time of Marilyn's diagnosis, Prozac had become widely known and occupied a prominent spot in the popular consciousness. Books were written about it, comedians riffed on it, and it was mentioned in films and TV shows. It was (erroneously) seen by the public as something of a wonder drug for curing depression, maybe even a happy pill. Would that it were. It did nothing to make one happier. It only made one less unhappy. But for about 30 percent of patients, Prozac simply had no effect at all.

Unfortunately, that was the case for Marilyn.

I've often wondered if this somehow contributed to her decision to end her life. She knew she was getting the best treatment, the best medications, and the best care from some of the most skilled, knowledgeable practitioners available. Yet none of it helped. Perhaps that knowledge caused her to give up.

All of this happened at the same time I was implementing my plans to turn Lilly around. Honestly, if Marilyn's problems had worsened sooner, I never would have accepted the position. But as things stood, I felt an obligation to lots of people to continue doing what I'd agreed to do. When Marilyn's symptoms became more severe, I informed the four or five people who worked closely with me daily (though not in great detail) that Marilyn was dealing with some health issues. I wanted them to understand the problem and not speculate when I turned up late for work or had to leave early. However, at Marilyn's behest, I kept the true state of affairs from everyone else, including Paige and Todd.

Every morning, I would try to make sure Marilyn was out of bed and ready for the day before I departed for work. And I would occasionally vanish from the office at odd times if I was needed at home or thought I might be. For the first time in my life, I started clocking out many days by 5:30 p.m. because Marilyn's spirits seemed to flag if she was home alone in the evening. Of course, business trips all but ceased.

I think she worried that she'd become a burden. Once, to ease her mind, I remember showing her a newspaper story about how well Lilly was doing. I tried to do my best at work. Likewise, I tried to do my best for Marilyn. And even though it's hard to accept on an emotional level, objectively, I know that even if I'd devoted myself full-time to helping her, I don't think things would have ended differently. The time and place might have changed, but not the final outcome.

Her last few months were very rough. She resorted more and more to alcohol to the point where she couldn't hide her addiction. Yet even then, she could still pull herself together, to a degree, when the kids came home. True to the stigma surrounding her ailment, she didn't want them to know. And she made me swear that I wouldn't tell them.

But in the end, I violated that confidence. I believed they had a need, indeed a right, to know what was going on. So, while they were home over the 1993 Christmas holiday season, I told them. I would say they were surprised, but not shocked. I know they had sensed that everything didn't seem quite right with their mother. They certainly did what they could to support her. Todd, who'd just completed an undergraduate degree at the University of West Virginia, moved to Indianapolis and started working in a bookstore in anticipation of going to graduate school at IU the following fall. Paige, who was completing her last semester at Duke University School of Law, came home when she could, both to visit her mom and to discuss with her the details of her wedding, which was to take place that August.

I'm thankful I told them. It made it a bit easier for Paige and Todd to accept and understand what happened next. If they hadn't known, I'm sure it would have come as an even more overwhelming shock.

Not that it wasn't still a terrible blow.

The last time we were together as a family was on May 8, 1994, for Paige's graduation from Duke University School of Law. Marilyn seemed quite happy and centered during the ceremony. But perhaps for a very dark reason. I've heard that when people decide to commit suicide, they often become less anxious because they finally have a definite plan for ending their suffering. I was told, after the fact, that the graduation might also have been a symbolic moment for her. It was a sign that her work as a parent was finished. Both of her kids were out of the nest, and she was free to put her suicide plan in motion.

She did it eight days later, on a Monday. We'd had a particularly rocky weekend because of her drinking. For much of that time, she had locked herself in a guest room and wouldn't come out or even answer me at the door. Sometime during that Sunday night, she'd come to our bedroom and gotten in bed. On Monday morning, with Marilyn awake but still in bed as I got dressed for work, and in one of those increasingly rare totally sober moments, I asked her, as I had occasionally before, how she might feel about going someplace as an in-patient to get the best possible treatment for her depression as well as for her alcohol issues. She nodded her head in agreement and said, more convincingly than in a long time, that she knew she needed help and that she wanted to talk about the options. So I left for work at 7:30 a.m., as usual, figuring we might actually have a start toward a plan and that we would talk about it more when I came home and see if she was still interested. Based on past experience, however, I wasn't highly confident she would still be willing to take that step.

Sometime in the midafternoon, the meeting I was in was interrupted by an urgent call from Todd, which had never happened before. He'd stopped by the house and let himself in. He immediately smelled exhaust fumes and followed them to the garage where he found his mother lying on a blanket on the floor next to the exhaust pipe of her still-running car.

Marilyn was rushed to the intensive care unit at nearby St. Vincent Hospital and immediately placed on a ventilator. Tests revealed she'd suffered extensive brain damage due to lack of oxygen.

Todd felt (and would continue to feel) terribly guilty. Later I learned that he was torturing himself with his own thicket of "what ifs." What if he'd come over just a bit sooner? He would have caught her before she had a chance to start her plan. And if he hadn't gone at all, she would have died immediately, not wound up lying in a hospital bed with brain damage that assured she had no chance of resuming a normal life, but with the possibility she might linger in a vegetative state.

He, like me, would be haunted by such thoughts for years.

It was Marilyn's first suicide attempt, and as the experts told us, the way she planned it made clear she meant it to be her last. This wasn't a cry for help, in which someone with a bottle full of pills only takes a third of them. It was a carefully planned operation with only one possible outcome. She had no idea Todd would stop by, and she didn't expect me home until 6 or 7 p.m., which was many hours after she closed herself up in the garage and started the car.

Of course, Todd's visit tossed a wrench into her careful plans. Medics were able to get her to the hospital while she still had vital signs. Almost immediately after I arrived at the hospital, I asked Dr. Gus Watanabe to join us to provide medical advice. After about 36 hours, he told us it was clear there was no chance she could recover. He told us with great compassion that it was time to have her taken off life support. By then Paige, who returned to Indianapolis on the first available flight, had the opportunity to join her brother and me in making that decision and in saying goodbye—and to begin, along with Todd and me, the long process of absorbing the reality of what was happening. Life support was terminated late on Tuesday evening, May 17, and she passed away in the early morning hours of May 18.

As I've said again and again, hardly a day goes by that I don't think about her in one way or another. When someone takes their own life, the tragedy leaves behind a lot of questions in the minds of loved ones about what they could have done to prevent it or, worse, whether they in some way contributed to it. From a rational perspective, it was obvious that Marilyn had made a firm, carefully premeditated plan to kill herself. Maybe at best, we might have unknowingly delayed it, but there probably wasn't anything we could have done to stop her.

That's the rational perspective. But the emotional parts of our minds couldn't stop dwelling on the "what ifs." So it was then, and so it is now.

Nevertheless, the last thing I want is for Marilyn's life to be defined by the way it ended. Or by its last few months, when her depression finally overwhelmed her. The person we'd known for decades was brave and strong, probably privately struggling for years with a debilitating ailment, fighting it to a standstill for most of her life. She was energetic, intelligent, well-loved, and devoted to her family and career. She was a great wife, mother, and friend.

Though her life had ended at 55, life for the rest of us mostly went on. And thank God it did because I can't imagine how I would have dealt with this tragedy if I'd had the time to do little more than endlessly dwell on it. But I didn't. In spite of everything, I still had a company to run. And soon, I would have a wedding to help plan.

PAIN, JOY, AND NEW BEGINNINGS

Chapter Nineteen

My days were filled with my work at Lilly and my evenings with helping to organize Paige's wedding.

I remember, sometime after Marilyn's death, having a conversation with Gus. In retrospect, it was more like an intervention.

As I've mentioned before, I don't seem constitutionally prone to clinical depression. Yet if ever there was a time in my life when my mood should have approached those black depths, it was then. Gus, who'd watched me during the worst of Marilyn's troubles and in the months since her passing, wanted me to understand that even though I seemed to be handling things as well as could be expected, I still should look after myself and reach out for help if I needed it.

During our conversation, he ticked off that infamous list of life dislocations that can trigger or exacerbate clinical depression—loss of a parent, children moving away, loss of a spouse, a new job, etc. Then he noted that, out of this roster of (I believe) ten life-changing crises, I'd recently suffered roughly eight.

"It's amazing that Randy was able to not fall apart, because most people would not have been able to get through all that," he said in an interview for *Put the Moose on the Table*.

Marilyn's death was, of course, the biggest blow by far. But Gus went over some of the others.

For instance, for years I had suffered from type 2 diabetes, which ran in our family. My brother, Roger, had it too. For a long time, I was able to manage it with diet, exercise, and oral medication. But when I came to Lilly, keeping my numbers where they needed to be got much harder.

I attribute it to my chaotic personal regimen. One of the best ways to keep diabetes under control is to watch your diet and take your medication on a regular schedule. But try doing that when your job includes constant travel. My typical work week might find me staying in Indianapolis until Tuesday, then traveling to London, then Spain, and then perhaps Colorado. It's tough to determine when to take your medication if you're a half dozen time zones from home. And regulating food intake can be equally problematic when you're attending a banquet in Europe.

On the other side of the coin, I worked for a company where diabetes treatment was a major part of the business. I was around some of the top diabetes experts in the world, and they told me I should begin using Humalog because it would help me better control my blood glucose levels. It did indeed, but I also had to start giving myself shots. And as any diabetes patient can tell you, the day one moves from controlling the disease with diet and oral meds to injections can be quite jarring.

And that wasn't my only health concern. Around this time, I was also diagnosed with a significant melanoma that had to be surgically removed. Obviously, I was also still working at a challenging job, and the long hours I put in at Lilly hadn't (indeed, couldn't) change all that much unless I decided to quit.

Also, my mother passed away on February 22, 1994, at age 90.

She spent her last days in the same nursing home that I had visited when I was first approached about becoming Lilly's CEO. It was a small place in the town of Rensselaer, about 12 miles down the road from Remington. At the time, my dad was still living independently in their home. Each morning, he would get up, have a bowl of cereal, get the mail at the post office, and maybe have a cup of coffee with some of his old cronies at Woody's, the little downtown coffee shop. Then, around 10 a.m., he got in his car and drove to the nursing home to stay with my mother in her room.

Typically, they'd have lunch together. Then, in the early afternoon, when she usually took a nap, he'd go home. He followed that routine seven days a week.

After my mom passed away, he continued living in their house, but it was obvious he was in declining health. My father enjoyed gardening, and in his younger days, he always planted a significant amount of corn, tomatoes, and other crops in his ample backyard garden. But as the years passed, one could almost chart his physical decline by the dwindling size of the plot he tended.

Each fall a neighbor with a garden tiller would come over to plow everything under and then again in the spring to turn the soil for planting. Well, as my father's stamina faded, the space he wanted tilled started to shrink. Finally, one fall not long before his passing, he told the neighbor with the tiller that, come spring, he wanted to plant the garden area with grass. He just physically couldn't manage it anymore, and maybe more significantly, was losing interest. He passed away on March 24, 1996, at the age of 89. For me, it was incredibly wrenching. It was the end of an era.

I'd imagine that, given all these crises and dislocations, some might wonder how I could bear to go into the office at all. I can understand that view and sympathize with anyone who has trouble attending to mundane but necessary tasks under such circumstances. But my case was different—for me, having a long, long list of issues to tackle was actually therapeutic. I couldn't dwell as much on the tragedies my family had endured, which meant that they never had a chance to overwhelm me.

For the moment, my days in the summer of 1994 were filled with my work at Lilly and my evenings with helping to organize Paige's wedding.

My daughter's fiancé, Tim Button, grew up in Summit, New Jersey, roughly 15 to 20 miles from Bernardsville, where we lived while Paige was in high school. At that time, however, the two of them had never met. After high school, she attended Duke University, graduated, and then spent a year in Paris before returning to Duke for law school. During her time in Paris, she was visited by a friend from home and Tim was with him. Paige picked them up at the Orly Airport in Paris and spent the next week showing them around the city. That was the first time she met Tim, which makes for a fantastic "meet cute" story. They grew up just down the road from each other in New Jersey but met for the first time in Paris.

In the aftermath of Marilyn's death, Paige and Tim decided to reevaluate their personal plans. Both were just relocating to work in New Jersey, and Paige was studying for the New Jersey bar exam and had a job lined up at a law firm where she had previously worked as a summer intern. Originally, they'd planned to start their working lives there. But with the drastically changed circumstances, they decided to move to Indianapolis.

I couldn't have been happier to have them there. Todd had already relocated, which gave the three of us a mutual support network for dealing with our family tragedy. We'd sit together night after night, sometimes saying little, other times crying together, and sometimes just reminiscing.

After much family discussion, it was decided that Paige and Tim would continue with their original plan for their wedding that August. And since, traditionally, the father of the bride isn't exactly covered up in pre-wedding obligations, I volunteered to help with the arrangements. I told Paige I would now be the mother of the bride too, and I quickly threw myself into such unfamiliar issues as floral arrangements and guest lists. I personally arranged seating charts and created contingency schemes for every possible emergency.

And so it was that, on August 27, 1994, about three months after Marilyn's death, I gave Paige away at her wedding. It took place at the Second Presbyterian Church in Indianapolis, the same church that had been the site of Marilyn's funeral and where I am now an Elder. When the minister, the Rev. Dr. William G. Enright, asked "Who gives this woman in holy matrimony?" I answered "Her mother and I do."

There wasn't a dry eye in the church, including my own.

Afterward, I got an unexpected chance to rest and take stock of my situation. Shortly after the wedding, I was approached by a good friend, Gene McDonald, who was executive vice president of Duke University. He and his wife, Barbara, had purchased a property in northwestern Ireland that included the remains of a 200-year-old house which they were restoring and turning into a vacation getaway. Gene called me with an offer I couldn't refuse.

"Barbara and I are going to go fly fishing for salmon in Ireland, and you're going to go with us."

I'm not sure he expected me to say yes, but I did. He was dead right about me needing a break, and Ireland sounded like a great place to take one.

Shortly afterward, we departed for our September trip. The salmon were indeed running, and we spent a great deal of time in waders, fishing our assigned "beats" on the local river. Gene, Barbara, and I all stayed at the Ballynahinch Castle Hotel, not too far from the cottage they were restoring. In the evenings, we'd decamp to the castle's pub, with its dark interior and a peat fireplace that seemingly had a fire burning at all times, regardless of the weather outside. We'd listen to fishing stories and other tales in fireside conversations with the hotel's Gilly. Lodging in elegant surroundings and enjoying the bracing Irish landscape and atmosphere proved to be tonic. It was my first opportunity to catch my breath. Both Gene and Barbara are gone now, but I'll always be grateful for their thoughtfulness and friendship.

Yet it would be wrong to say that I'd somehow "weathered the storm" or put the worst of the last few months behind me. As the years have passed, I've realized that in the case of a loss as terrible as that of Marilyn, it's never really over. During my time in Ireland, not one day passed that I didn't think about her and what I might have done differently to help her. It would continue like that for years. Even today, in quiet moments, my mind drifts back to the same old patterns. I don't think either Todd, Paige, or myself ever truly got over it. As the experts told us, when someone close to you commits suicide, the survivors deal with it for years to come.

When I returned, I found myself once again immersed in work. It's hard to believe, but when all these life-shaking trials began, I'd only been at Lilly for less than a year. The company was still in the midst of great transitions, and though I had devised a plan for turning things around, we were by no means finished executing it.

As the months passed, I started to feel very much adrift when not working—a mood that wasn't helped by the fact that well-meaning friends kept inviting me to social events. The ulterior motive was that they had someone they wanted me to meet. I typically refused because I found the whole concept of "dinner with an agenda" upsetting.

Yet there was one acquaintance with whom I had a great deal in common. Shortly after Marilyn and I returned to Indianapolis in 1993, we met Marianne McKinney. We continued to run into her regularly at civic functions, and both of us considered her a new friend.

Marianne was a musical prodigy with degrees from Radcliffe College at Harvard and the Longy School of Music, plus a doctorate in musicology from the University of Minnesota. She worked with the Indianapolis Symphony Orchestra as the resident musicologist and had been married to Frank McKinney Jr., chairman of Bank One, Indiana.

On September 11, 1992, Marianne had been at home, working, when she got word of a collision between two small planes over the Indianapolis south side. Realizing that her husband and three other Indianapolis civic leaders were departing from an airport in the same area that day, she turned on her television to find out more. Her worst fears were quickly confirmed. Frank and all the other passengers on his flight had been killed.

This wasn't the first such tragedy in her life. When she was 16, her father also died in the crash of his company's small plane. She'd faced many other crises but through it all demonstrated a gritty ability to recover from pretty much anything fate threw at her.

After Marilyn's passing, Marianne visited the funeral home to pay her respects. I remember she brought along two copies of Thornton Wilder's classic novel, *The Bridge of San Luis Rey*. It tells the story of five people who died when an 18th-century Peruvian bridge suddenly collapsed and a monk's efforts to find a satisfactory reason why those particular five, out of the thousands who crossed the span every day, were taken.

She gave the book to Paige and Todd, telling them that it had given her some insight as she struggled with her husband's death. She hoped it might do the same for them.

Months passed before I ran into her again at an annual dinner for a local board on which we both served. It goes without saying that we had a lot in common, awful though much of it was. But as time passed, we started to realize that we had other things in common besides tragedy. We had a very good relationship and enjoyed doing a lot of things together. Finally, in July of 1995, at Second Presbyterian Church, we married.

One of the things we very much enjoyed about each other's company was that we didn't have to explain to each other how we felt about what we'd been through. We had each suffered a terrible loss, and in retrospect, it's clear we bonded mostly over our feelings of grief and our empathy toward each other.

At the same time, the rest of the world (or at least the world's journalists) seemed to want to know how I, as the head of a pharmaceutical company that made the world's most famous antidepressant, felt about what I had endured.

I was somewhat conflicted as to what to do about the numerous interview requests I received. On the one hand, it was a deeply private matter that still felt very, very raw. On the other, speaking about it seemed to align with something very important to me, both in my business and personal life. Years earlier I'd borrowed a favorite saying from a friend of mine named Dr. David Nadler—"put the moose on the table." In essence, it meant that when faced with a major issue, you shouldn't ignore it. David was one of the world's foremost authorities on organizational effectiveness. As David described it, a group of people in a meeting often can't solve a problem they face because even though they are all aware of some uncomfortable truth that needs to be confronted, everyone is reluctant to put it on the table and face it directly. Try to imagine, he said, that there was a moose in the conference room. People wouldn't just ignore it. They would acknowledge it and get it back to the woods from which it must have escaped. So, using the moose as a metaphor, one needs to speak clearly, truthfully, and accurately about a major issue and about how one plans to remedy it. In other words, you need to figuratively "put the moose on the table."

During my time at Lilly, I used that phrase a lot because I wanted employees, at every level, to be able to speak openly and transparently about the problems and issues we faced, without fear of getting in trouble. Now, as I was asked again and again by the national media to speak about my loss, I found myself in a similar position. There was simply no denying the fact that the story of a national pharmaceutical company's CEO struggling to help his own wife get help with depression might be useful to people either suffering from the ailment or trying to aid someone who was.

I turned down offers from various national outlets, including *The Wall Street Journal*, in favor of a local publication, *Indianapolis Monthly* magazine, because I wanted to have total and complete trust in the writer. The story, by Donna Heimansohn, came out in the publication's February 1995 issue. It triggered an immediate, unexpected flood of notes to my office—many of them thank-you messages from families suffering in similar ways as mine.

One of those roughly 900 messages was a lengthy email from a Lilly employee. She expressed her condolences over Marilyn's death and ended with a poem she wrote that attempted to explain what it felt like to suffer as my wife had. It was a truly enlightening look at just how terrible depression can be.

As a matter of fact, her knowledge of the suffering seemed a bit too intimate.

I had enough sense to recognize a suicide note when I saw one. I quickly sent the author a thank-you email and then called Lilly's top staff doctor, who stepped in to assist her. There was nothing I could do for Marilyn, but I felt I could certainly step in now. In this case, putting the moose on the table perhaps saved a life.

As I wrote in earlier chapters, applying the "moose" philosophy to Lilly also bore fruit. As the months and years passed, its position grew ever stronger. Our stock price reached new heights; our drug pipeline was filled with promising products; and the future seemed bright.

This is why, less than half a decade after becoming CEO, I decided it was time for another big change. I wanted to do something that almost no boss of a large, successful company ever does—quit while I was ahead.

MOVING ON

Chapter Twenty

Succession planning is one of the most important tasks that any leader addresses.

By 1997, Eli Lilly and Company was in excellent shape. I got much of the credit, I'm sure, even though the turnaround was, in every sense of the word, a team effort. I knew what my role had been as the leader, and I was proud of that. But I also knew that it was Lilly people, from senior executives to people manufacturing pills, who took the clear sense of direction and the leadership they were given and turned the company around. But that's how such things usually go. If our plans hadn't borne fruit, I would have taken the brunt of the blame. Instead, I was hailed as a successful, effective CEO who executed a brilliant turnaround.

Typically, someone in my position would take a victory lap in the media and then settle down for a long residency at the top of the company's organization chart. But my circumstances were far from typical.

I was only 56 years old, but the personal, emotional, and professional challenges I'd faced during the last few years made me feel at the time about ten years older and left me physically and emotionally exhausted. I didn't want to keep doing the same thing. I wanted to spend more time with my family, pursue other opportunities outside of business, and maybe occasionally just go fly fishing or pheasant hunting. As Peter Lynch, the spectacularly successful manager of the Fidelity Magellan Fund from 1977 to 1990, stated at the time of his own retirement, "Nobody on his deathbed ever said, 'Gee, I wish I'd spent more time at the office.'"

Actually, had it not been for the more-or-less "out of the blue" chance to lead Lilly, I might have left the corporate world to pursue a market basket of side projects years earlier. Lilly, however, offered me a chance to apply my skills to a company that I'd come to care about. Plus, it was an opportunity to return to my Indiana roots. Yet I never thought of it as a long-term assignment. Once that task of righting the ship was complete, I didn't foresee hanging around.

Plus, I've always deeply believed that succession planning is one of the most important tasks that any leader addresses. I wouldn't say this is a common view because, if you look around the highest ranks of industry, most CEOs tend to leave when it suits them, rather than the company. I, however, felt that grooming and training the person who would replace me was of the utmost importance. After all, the only reason I was given leadership at Lilly was because the previous plan to bring in a new CEO went so badly awry.

Almost as soon as I took up my new duties there, I instituted a comprehensive succession-planning strategy for senior leadership posts, with the CEO's office foremost in my mind, but also identifying candidates for other important positions. As I detailed in *Put the Moose on the Table*, I met regularly with our senior vice president of human resources, Pedro Granadillo, along with Lilly president and

COO Sidney Taurel. With their help, I put in place a finely tuned system for both planning for future retirements and then identifying candidates for advancement to senior levels and providing developmental opportunities to get them ready to fill those positions.

Including, of course, identifying someone who could one day replace me.

After half a decade as CEO, retiring seemed like the best move not just for me, but for the company as well. Lilly was about to go through a very contentious period, when some of our most valuable drug patents, including the one for Prozac, expired. That meant generic drug makers would be free to create and sell cheap copies, massively impacting our sales and profits. We would need new offerings, from our research pipeline as well as from acquisitions, to make up the slack. That would require a great deal of effort for an extended time. If I'd committed to stay on in the near term, I felt I had to be willing to commit myself to a further five years or more to see this issue through. I just wasn't prepared to do that.

I came aboard to help turn the company around. In my mind, and I think everybody else's, that goal had been achieved. Now I felt it was a good time to leave so that an energetic successor could tackle this next set of challenges.

For quite a while, I kept my own counsel about exactly how this would happen. I finally revealed my views during a Lilly board meeting on December 15, 1997. As I took my place at the head of the table, I had in hand a speech I'd composed that offered a detailed road map for stepping away from the company. Interestingly, I felt very little trepidation about the metaphorical bomb I was about to drop. I'd developed my succession strategy with great care and was actually looking forward to putting this particular moose on the table.

The board meeting offered an excellent opportunity to get the ball rolling. For years I'd made a habit, toward the end of each such gathering, of excusing from the room all the "inside" board members who held positions with Lilly. This gave outside directors a chance to speak with me privately about whatever was on their minds. And at least once a year, I spent almost an entire session with the outside members alone talking about succession planning. This was just such a gathering, so no one who was actually a part of the company was in the room to hear what I had to say, nor did they find it mysterious that they were not.

I began my speech by recapping the challenges we'd faced together, the victories we'd achieved, and the many changes I'd endured in my personal life. Then I made the big announcement.

"… in thinking about the more specific timing of my own departure, I've been mindful of my long-held observation that all too often, leaders in virtually all fields step down mostly when it's convenient for them, without much regard to whether or not their own timing corresponds with what's in the best interests of sustaining the vitality of the organization they are leading," I said. "I've been determined not to follow that path. I have wanted to choose a time to leave that not only suits my own objectives but also fits well into the rhythm of the company's continued progress—not too soon, but certainly not too late.

"As you know, from the time I've spent with you in previous board meetings addressing these issues, I believe that succession planning—in all its ramifications—is one of the most important responsibilities of the leader of any institution, including this one. I want the success of my stewardship of Eli Lilly and Company to be measured not only by the results we achieve while I am here, but also by the results we achieve after I'm gone. And having given all of these issues a great deal of thought for a number of months, I want you to know today that I believe an appropriate time for a leadership transition here at Lilly is on the horizon, and I'd like to begin that process. Therefore, I'd like to propose for your consideration the following actions."

The room grew very quiet as I read these words. One board member and friend, Dr. Steven Beering, the president of Purdue University, even left abruptly and stayed gone for several minutes. Later he told me he was so overcome by emotion that he had to step out in order to gather himself.

"After I took this job," I continued, "and after I had some time to think about longer-term considerations, I made a commitment to myself that at the pleasure of the board, I would remain at Lilly until the six initial goals that I outlined here a few moments ago had been appropriately addressed—and certainly for no less than five years."

I presented my carefully mapped plan for the future. In about six months, I intended to publicly announce my retirement from the board, effective on December 31, 1998. At the same time, I would announce and start to implement the leadership transition. To begin the process, I would ask the board to elect Sidney Taurel to the additional post of CEO, effective July 1, 1998. I would retain my position as chairman of the board through the end of that year. Then, at a December 1998 board meeting (in 12 months), I wanted the board to elect Sidney as chairman, effective upon my immediate retirement.

"Finally," I continued, "in looking at our progress, I believe we've put a first-rate leadership team in place—starting with the board and extending through the senior officers and into the organization. Among the officer-directors, Gus Watanabe has made extraordinary contributions to our progress—indeed I'd be hard-pressed to name a single individual who has contributed more during my time here. He's fundamentally reinvented the way we do R&D. Charlie Golden has brought a fresh perspective and new skills to our financial disciplines as well as to our broader deliberations and has been a strong addition to our team. The other members of the policy committee, Pedro Granadillo, Becky Goss, and Mitch Daniels, are each making a very strong contribution in their own right. And the list goes on, through this generation of leaders, and well into the next. Finally—and most importantly—from the succession planning we've done together, I know you share my view that Sidney Taurel has grown to be capable of leading this company. I've been very pleased as he's demonstrated his ability to take on more and more responsibility, and, if you conclude he's the best choice to succeed me, I'm hopeful he will continue the strategic and cultural changes we've put in place during my tenure. When it comes time for him to fully take charge, I believe the transition will have been made in a way that will not cause any major waves with our employees or with Wall Street. And I expect Sidney will continue to grow every day he is in the job."

I mentioned that I planned to begin the transition process by going around the country and visiting each outside board member, one-on-one in their own offices, to get their views about where they thought the company stood and what they thought of Sidney as well as any other potential CEO candidates. Although, of course, we'd pretty much settled on Sidney. He was in so many ways the rational inside choice. Other candidates in his generation or maybe the next, including future CEO John Lechleiter (who was certainly very much on my radar), had just not yet been sufficiently prepared. Sidney was 49 years old, was born in Morocco, raised in Spain, received his undergraduate education in France, and earned an MBA from Columbia University. He had worked for Lilly his entire professional life, including in our overseas operations for 15 years with stops in Brazil, France, Eastern Europe, and the United Kingdom. He'd become executive vice president of Lilly's pharmaceutical division in 1991. But there were many reasons, beyond his resume, why I was confident in Sidney as my successor, including the high regard in which he was held within the company and throughout the pharmaceutical industry. With those experiences and the emphasis that both Sidney and I had placed on the need for the company to grow outside the United States, one could argue that no CEO in Lilly's history had ever been better prepared for the challenges he would face.

It had been quiet when I started talking, and as I wrapped up my remarks, it remained so. I told the board members that, other than Marianne, Paige, and Todd, no one knew about my departure plans, and that I wanted to keep it that way—at least for a while. It was very important to not expand the circle until we were ready to make a final decision and a public announcement, lest the news be broken via unintended rumors or speculation.

And that's pretty much how things unfolded. After I made my announcement, the inside board members (my heir apparent, Sidney, among them) filed back into the room, none the wiser. A few months later, at the end of Lilly's February board meeting when we finalized his selection, I took Sidney aside to tell him about his upcoming promotion. He needed to organize his own succession plans, and it wouldn't do for him to find out about such a major promotion at the last minute. I was gratified to see the surprise on his face. No one privy to the news had leaked it to him.

The rest of the world learned of my departure at a press conference on May 6, 1998. The announcement, I'm happy to say, was greeted with surprise but not panic. Wall Street reacted with a comparative yawn. Lilly stock lost a grand total of 25 cents that day. It was all quite anticlimactic, which is exactly what I'd hoped for.

My last months on the job as chairman of the board were equally quiet. I'd told Sidney that I would start fading into the sunset as soon as I stepped down as CEO. Then, until I officially relinquished the chairman of the board post and left the headquarters building for good, he should see me as the "fire department"—available if needed, but only for emergencies.

But as the days ticked by, no such emergencies surfaced. The last few months I spent at Lilly were anticlimactic, but in the best sort of way. In fact, one of the most memorable things that happened during my final days had very little to do with Lilly.

In the spring of 1998, George H. W. Bush was to be an honorary degree recipient at Duke University's graduation ceremony. I was, at the time, chair of the Duke University Board of Trustees and, of course, planned to participate in the graduation. I happened to see him at an event about a month before the commencement. Since he knew I would have a Lilly jet at my disposal, he asked if I could both drop him off at his summer home in Kennebunkport, Maine, after the proceedings and then stay on for dinner with himself and his wife, Barbara.

I was pleased to accept. Though I didn't know him well, we'd met several times over the years. He had actually been a Lilly board member long before my own tenure. Following the graduation ceremony and our flight from North Carolina, accompanied by three Secret Service agents, we landed at a private Maine airport and were met by two Secret Service SUVs and more agents. They took us out to the Walker's Point Estate, a spit of land surrounded by water on three sides where the Bush family lives in the summer. It's likely familiar to many because numerous television reports originated from there during Bush Sr.'s time in office.

The location was ideal for the president because one of his favorite activities was taking out the powerboat he kept there. It was called *Fidelity* (Bush 41 gave all the fast boats he owned over the years the name *Fidelity*) and was equipped with three 300-horsepower

Mercury Verado outboard engines. It's worth mentioning that the original *Fidelity*, a cigarette boat Bush 41 purchased in 1973, now resides in the George H. W. Bush Presidential Library and Museum. It was the location for a number of significant conversations and decisions by Bush, Brent Scowcroft, Dick Cheney, Colin Powell, and other senior aides during the First Gulf War. The old Fidelity's departure for the museum was the reason the manufacturer gave him a replacement boat, which had just arrived. President Bush had yet to see or drive it and was anxious to do so.

He sometimes used his boat for fishing, but he also liked to take it out for hair-raising speed runs. Something I was about to experience firsthand.

As soon as we arrived, he asked me to go for a ride. He furnished me with some casual clothes to wear instead of my suit, and in no time, he was piloting *Fidelity* out to sea, with me standing behind him. Or perhaps I should say, barely standing. The moment we reached open water, he opened the throttle all the way, so every time we hit a wave, the entire boat went airborne and then slammed back down with a bone-rattling thump.

The president was having the time of his life. Meanwhile, I had trouble simply keeping my feet under me. And I wasn't the only one. The two Secret Service agents accompanying us were hanging on for dear life, and the small pursuit boat following us, which was also filled with Secret Service agents, bounced along in our wake, trying to keep up. It was an open secret that they didn't particularly enjoy the president's boat trips, but there was nothing they could do about it. When Bush 41 went out to sea, there was never an argument about who was at the controls.

This went on for about 20 minutes before the president slowed down so he could pass slowly under a bridge in the town of Kennebunkport and give me a tour there. We were going so slow that tourists onshore recognized him and started waving—probably what he had in mind. Afterward, we cruised back to Walker's Point, where Barbara Bush had just arrived. I'm not sure she knew I was coming, but I also don't think it was all that unusual for the president to bring home strays, unannounced, to join them for dinner.

We all sat down together and had fresh lobsters, along with all the usual New England fare that accompanies such a meal. It was a lovely dinner and lovely conversation, and you would have thought we'd known each other forever. But that was just their personalities. Afterward, we said our goodbyes, and the Secret Service loaded me up in one of their SUVs and took me to the airport, where the Lilly plane flew me home. Even today, I consider that experience as one of my most fun and memorable evenings.

On December 31, 1998, I duly handed over my chairmanship of the Lilly board, marking the end of my tenure. I must report that I don't remember much of what happened on my last day at the office. There was no drama, no last-minute issues—just a smooth, seamless transition from me to Sidney. I count that among my proudest achievements.

The years that followed were among some of the most challenging in the company's history. Because of an unexpected court ruling, the expiration of our Prozac patent came two years earlier than expected, causing a huge and almost immediate impact on the company's revenues. That change in fortunes caused a big hit to the company's share price. But Sidney's calm and steady leadership was exactly what was needed to guide the company through that challenge—and others. As I observed his leadership throughout his time in the corner office, my confidence in my decision to recommend him to the board as my successor was continually reinforced.

My departure from Lilly would mark the end of 34 years spent in the corporate world. My office was packed with mementos from a very eventful half-decade—photos with four U.S. presidents, pictures of me at the Taj Mahal and Red Square, and mementos from visits to Lilly offices around the world, including a Japanese katana and a marble bust from Greece. A cross-section of those souvenirs, along with choice remembrances from my AT&T days, would soon migrate to a new, private office on the north side of Indianapolis.

I would spend the next few years doing just what I'd hoped—taking more time with my family while also attending to a grab bag of professional and public pursuits. I'd honed my multitasking skills during my Lilly days, when (among other projects) I played an important role in Indianapolis's successful effort to get the National Collegiate Athletic Association (NCAA), the nation's governing body for college sports, to move there. I co-chaired the effort to raise $15 million to defray the costs of building a new NCAA headquarters.

Shortly after my retirement, I still had one remaining Lilly duty to tackle. At the time, one or another of the large Indianapolis-based corporations annually offered their CEO to serve as chairman of the local United Way fund drive. I told Sidney that I would do this after my retirement because it was Lilly's turn, even though I wouldn't assume the post until after I stepped down. This meant that, while the city would see the work done by a "Lilly leader," the new CEO, who obviously had a lot of other things on his plate, wouldn't have to.

And that was by no means the end of my leadership responsibilities. In July of 1997, I was elected chair of the Duke University Board of Trustees—a position I would hold until June of 2000. The school was starting a major fundraising campaign, as was Colonial Williamsburg, on whose board I also served. And if that wasn't enough, I also still held my corporate board positions, including with ConocoPhillips, Kimberly-Clark, and Knight Ridder. I also planned to do more community work, conduct some side business projects, and develop a book with my son, Todd.

This, I felt, was plenty to keep me busy, but not enough to constitute a full-time job. I would, as I had wanted for some time, be more or less in control of my schedule and able to spend more time with my family. I also wouldn't have to jet halfway across the world on short notice for meetings. If I went somewhere, it would be because I wanted to.

It would be a welcome change from my corporate career. From about 1980 to 1999, either for AT&T or Lilly or for some other organization, it seemed that I was always going somewhere. In fact, as I departed from AT&T for Lilly, the pilots who flew the company's corporate jet fleet gave me a plaque. It stated that, based on their flight logs, I'd flown enough miles with them to take me to the moon and part of the way back.

I didn't doubt their math. I typically took numerous national trips for meetings or to visit major customers around the country. I also did as many as a half dozen weeklong or longer international excursions annually. Such journeys, whether for AT&T or later for Lilly, could take me to several different nations on a single jaunt for meetings with top business and political leaders. Most were as carefully planned as military campaigns, with each day's activities locked in weeks in advance.

Such journeys were of course an important part of my job. And they also offered chances to mix business with pleasure. Marilyn, for instance, would sometimes accompany me on trips to interesting locales. But as the years passed, the travel regime grew more wearing. At least, because I flew on company jets, I never had to worry about losing luggage, getting up at 4 a.m. to make a flight, or battling through crowded concourses. We left when we needed to leave and typically landed at smaller facilities that were much easier to get into and out of.

I got my best tip for making these trips more manageable from George H. W. Bush's White House schedulers. In late February or early March of 1991, just days after the Iraqi army was driven out of Kuwait during the First Gulf War, I was asked on the president's behalf to join other business leaders for a tour of the country to assess redevelopment needs. I represented AT&T, which was expected to have a role in rebuilding the country's telecommunications infrastructure.

The trip, led by Secretary of Commerce Bob Mosbacher, was even more carefully organized than my usual, private business travels. But the thing that impressed me most was a White House scheduling trick I learned about. If President Bush or members of his cabinet had an opening in their public itinerary in which nothing was specifically scheduled, it was labeled "private time/office work." Because if there was any spot on the presidential itinerary that either said "free time" or, God forbid, was left blank, it invited endless requests from people seeking the president's time. Plugging in the "private time/office work" phrase left the impression that the chief executive was meeting privately, making phone calls, or reading emails, and so was unavailable to meet. In fact, he may have just needed to close his eyes for 20 minutes.

All of this was a revelation to me. I'd always left blank spaces in my travel itinerary, and since nature abhors a vacuum, if someone noticed I had a free hour they would often ask for an in-person meeting to lobby for something or personally brief me about this or that. Usually, these were things that could have been handled in a memo. But it was difficult to put them off.

I began blocking much of that with the "private time/office work" ploy. Of course, sometimes I actually did use those interludes to catch up on work. But other times I just needed a break. And now, with retirement approaching, I desired a much longer one.

Years later when I worked in the government, Andy Card, who served as George W. Bush's chief of staff, gave me another important insight about scheduling. He told me that one of the important parts of his job was to make the distinction between people who needed to see the president and people the president actually needed to see. I've used that filter in making my own scheduling decisions by asking myself whether I needed to see that person at their convenience or they needed to see me at mine (or at all).

"For much of my adult life, the phone would ring on Tuesday and a voice from some corner of the world would say, 'We've got an appointment with the prime minister of Thailand for Thursday and it would make all the difference if you could come with us.' And I'd get on a plane and fly to Bangkok," I told the *Chicago Tribune* in a story about my retirement. "That's part of the job. But I don't have the zeal to do it like I once did."

After Lilly, I would indeed get to enjoy a bit of downtime and a far less intense travel schedule. But only for a little while because, in retrospect, the years following my resignation can be seen as a sort of intermission—a chance to catch my breath before I took up the most demanding and critically important task of my life.

PHOTOS

A lifetime's worth of photos could fill this entire book. Hopefully, these few images presented here can provide insight into some cherished and valued moments.

(Top left) Tobias Mill on the Muscatatuck River on the Jennings-Scott county line in southern Indiana. Built in 1849 by David Tobias, my great-great-grandfather, and operated by David Tobias and his son Theopolis and grandson Harry until about 1900.

(Bottom left) Theopolis Tobias, David's son and my great-grandfather, his wife Elizabeth (front row), and their children (back row, left to right) Pearl (Tobias) Sage, John, Charles, Harry (my grandfather), and Millie (Tobias) Green.

RANDALL L. TOBIAS

(Top) My mother's family. Front row: Her mother, Grace (Moore) Harwood, her brother, Raymond, and her father, Mark Harwood. Back row: My mother, Fern (Harwood) Tobias, and her brothers, Tom and Glenn.

(Bottom) My parents, Roy and Fern Tobias, on their wedding day, July 21, 1934.

Never Daunted

(Top) Harry and Leva (Sparks) Tobias, my grandparents, at about the time of their 50th wedding anniversary in 1954.

(Bottom left) Roy Tobias, my father, plowing with horses in Benton County, Indiana, sometime in the early 1930s, after losing his job at the Northern Indiana Public Service Company during the Great Depression.

(Bottom right) The State Bank of Remington where my father worked from about 1934 until his retirement in 1976.

(Top) Remington High School in the 1950s.

(Center right) Remington Elementary School in the 1950s.

(Bottom right) Me in my Remington High School track uniform in the spring of 1960.

Never Daunted

(Top left) My good friend and high school classmate Mike Merkel and me at Camp Potawatomi in the Tippecanoe River State Park near Winamac, Indiana.

(Center left) The house on Brown Street in Remington where I grew up, pictured in the 1950s.

(Bottom left) The same house in 2024 looking nearly unchanged.

(Bottom right) My parents, Fern and Roy Tobias, on their 50th wedding anniversary, July 21, 1984.

(Top) My lifelong Remington friends Bill and Janet (Bellows) Biddle at our Lake Wawasee home.

(Center left) My lifelong Remington friend Ronnie Q. Gillam on the porch of our farmhouse near Remington.

(Center right) My mother's piano, fully restored and still in my former home, which is now owned by Tommy and Darcy Allegrini.

(Bottom right) My mother and me at the same piano in the early 1950s.

(Top) As my mother noted in her distinctive handwriting, this picture commemorates my first day of first grade at Remington Elementary School in 1948.

(Bottom) With a number of my surviving classmates from the Remington High School Class of 1960 at our 60th reunion, delayed for two years to 2022 because of COVID. Left to right: Me, Linda (Thurston) Longest, Bill Biddle, Carol (Tyler) Roberts, Marvin Baxter, Sharon (Shaw) Nelson, Ronnie Q. Gillam, and Jynell (Woodruff) Jackson.

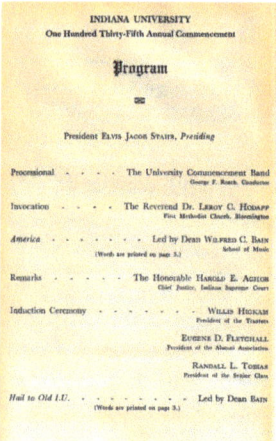

(Top left) The cover of the 1964 IU Commencement program.

(Top right) With OX at an IU–Purdue football game.

(Center left) The inside of the commencement program.

(Center right) Fall Carnival at the IU student union building in 1962.

(Bottom right) With the legendary Herman B Wells, IU's president (1938 to 1962) and chancellor (1962 to 2000).

(Top left) Speaking at the 2004 announcement of the founding of IU's Tobias Center for Leadership Excellence.

(Center left) Speaking at IU's Tobias Center for Innovation in International Development.

(Center right) As chair of the IU Board of Trustees with IU's 18th President Michael McRobbie at IU's commencement.

(Lower left) My wife, Deborah, and me with Scott Dolson, IU vice president and director of intercollegiate athletics, at the dedication of IU's field hockey facility, Deborah Tobias Field ("The Deb").

(Lower right) Coach Kayla Bashore and Deborah at the "Protect the Deb" sign that the IU field hockey team members touch before exiting their locker room.

(Bottom right) Deborah at the Deborah Tobias Field.

(Top) Me as a U.S. Army Artillery School instructor with a 155 mm Howitzer at Fort Sill, Oklahoma, in 1965.

(Bottom) The "Piper Cub" aircraft at Fort Sill with the horizontal doors that came open during my first solo flight.

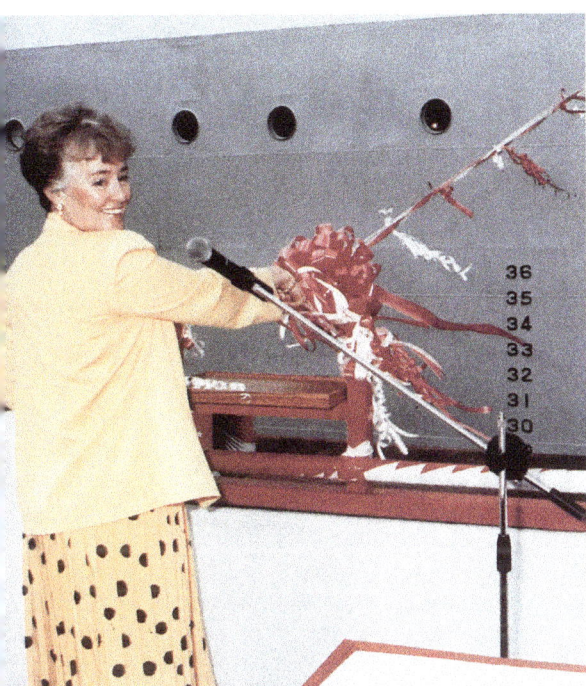

(Top left) Marilyn christening the 479-foot-long AT&T CS Global Link in the FELS Shipyard in Singapore in 1991.

(Top right) Our 1967 Christmas card photo. Marilyn was pregnant with Paige, who was born on December 14.

(Bottom left) Our last family photo together, at Paige's graduation from Duke Law School on May 8, 1994. Marilyn died eight days later, on May 16, 1994.

(Bottom right) Indianapolis Monthly's February 1995 issue interviewed me about Marilyn's battle with clinical depression.

(*Top left*) AT&T's 1986 senior executive body, the "Office of the Chairman" (left to right): Chuck Marshall, vice-chairman and chief administrative officer; Howard Trienens, General Counsel; Bob Allen, chairman and CEO, AT&T Information Systems; Charlie Brown, AT&T chairman and CEO; me, chairman and CEO, AT&T Communications; Morris Tanenbaum, CFO; and Jim Olson, president.

(*Top right*) CEO Charlie Brown's note to me during the 1981 board meeting about settling the Department of Justice's antitrust suit.

(*Center left*) With Chinese Premier Jiang Zemin, finalizing a potential $5 billion deal for AT&T.

(*Lower left*) AT&T CEO Bob Allen (bottom center), me (to his left), and the 1993 board of directors. I soon left to be Lilly's chairman, president, and CEO.

(*Bottom left*) CEO Charlie Brown gave this memento to senior officers on AT&T's last day before its divestiture.

Never Daunted

(Top right) With former Lilly CEOs Sidney Taurel, who succeeded me (left), and John Lechleiter, who followed Sidney (right).

(Center left) The 1998 press conference where I announced my retirement from Lilly and Sidney Taurel as my successor.

(Center right) With former Lilly CEO Dick Wood at the dedication of a statue of Colonel Eli Lilly, the company's founder.

(Bottom right) A chart prepared by Morgan Stanley investment bankers showing the growth in value of the S&P 500, all pharmaceutical stocks, and Lilly stock during my time as Lilly chairman.

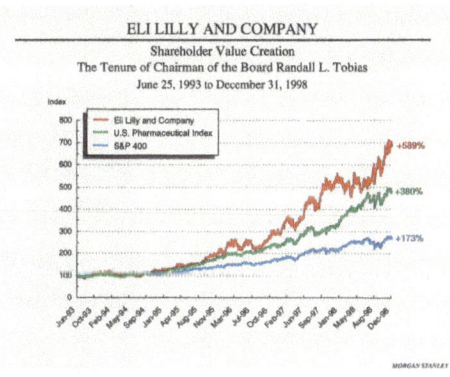

(Top) My first introduction to Tom Brokaw at the 1990 Duke commencement, when he was the speaker and received an honorary degree.

(Center) A partial panoramic view of Twelve Springs Ranch, south of Livingston, Montana.

(Bottom) On horseback at the ranch.

(Facing page, bottom) My fire trucks at Twelve Springs Ranch.

(Top right) Paige's marriage to Tim Button in August 1994. With Marilyn's family (left to right): Marilyn's nephew Derek Salyer, Todd, Tim and Paige, Marilyn's mother Ruth Salyer, me, and Marilyn's brother Jerry.

(Center left) The father of the bride and the bride.

(Center right) With the Tobias family (left to right): me, Roger, Karen, Eric, Paige and Tim, my father Roy, and Todd.

(Top) President George W. Bush's July 2003 White House Roosevelt Room announcement of his intention to formally nominate me to be the first United States Global AIDS Coordinator with the rank of Ambassador.

(Bottom) A bilateral meeting on international development matters in the cabinet room at 10 Downing Street, London, in November 2003 (left to right): British Prime Minister Tony Blair, President Bush, Secretary of State Colin Powell, and me.

Never Daunted

(Top) The Oval Office meeting when President Bush empowered my role as Global AIDS Coordinator. Clockwise from bottom left: White House Deputy Director of Domestic Policy Jay Lefkowitz (back to camera); USAID Administrator Andrew Natsios; White House Director of Domestic AIDS Policy Dr. Joe O'Neil; Secretary of Health and Human Services Tommy Thompson (partially hidden); me; the President; Secretary of State Colin Powell; National Security Advisor Condoleezza Rice; White House Press Secretary Ari Fleischer; and White House Chief of Staff Andy Card.

(Center) In the Oval Office with the President, Colin Powell, and Andy Card.

(Bottom) Deborah, me, and President Bush at Mitch Daniels's retirement as Purdue University president in 2023.

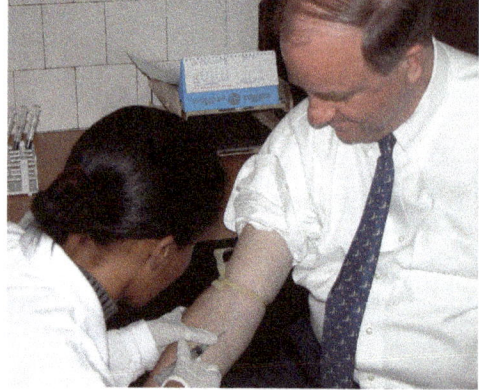

(Top) Wearing body armor with Nazanin Ash, my chief of staff at PEPFAR, USAID, and Director of US Foreign Assistance, for a Blackhawk helicopter flight over a hostile area in Afghanistan to a U.S.-funded project eradicating poppies used to produce heroin. I can't imagine why we look so fearless!

(Center left) Reconnecting with Dr. Lilian Bolt, a Kenyan physician, years after our first encounter.

(Center right) Being tested for AIDS on television in Addis Ababa, Ethiopia, to help reduce the stigma associated with AIDS testing.

(Bottom right) Meeting with His Holiness Abuna Paulos, fifth Patriarch of the Orthodox Tewahedo Church of Ethiopia.

(Top left) With Ambassador Richard Holbrook, admiring the cow an African village offered as a gift to Health and Human Services Secretary Tommy Thompson.

(Top right) With U.S. Ambassador to Uganda Jimmy Kolker (right) and John Robert Engole (center), a Ugandan who was the very first recipient of antiretroviral drug therapy supplied by PEPFAR.

(Bottom left) With the chief sangoma (traditional healer) in KwaZulu-Natal, South Africa.

(Bottom right) Inspecting a warehouse in Namibia filled with hundreds of thousands of condoms purchased by PEPFAR.

(Top) Waiting to speak after being interrupted by protesters at the 2004 International AIDS Conference in Bangkok, Thailand.

(Bottom) Listening to IU's Dr. Joe Mamlin, field director for clinical care at AMPATH, the IU-led healthcare program in Eldoret, Kenya. This program is the gold standard AIDS program in sub-Saharan Africa.

Never Daunted

(Top) Visiting Peru to see a USAID-funded program to eradicate coca plants, the source of cocaine. Upon departing, our helicopter came under fire from drug cartel security forces, unhappy with our eradication efforts.

(Bottom left) Seeing the coca plant eradication effort in person.

(Bottom right) Participating in a conference in Washington DC with Secretary of State Condoleezza Rice.

(Top left) General George C. Marshall, at his desk in the State Department where he served as Secretary of State from 1947 to 1949.

(Top right) One of several meetings with Bono (Paul David Henson), lead singer of the Irish rock band U2 and by far the most genuine and effective AIDS activist I know.

(Bottom left) The Marshall office during the time I occupied it as Director of U.S. Foreign Assistance and Administrator of USAID.

(Bottom right) Meeting with Bolivian President Evo Morales, who rose to power from his role as the head of a labor union representing coca workers. Not surprisingly, he was unhappy with our efforts to eradicate coca plants in order to reduce cocaine supplies to the U.S.

(Top left) Indiana Governor Mitch Daniels presiding at my and Deborah's wedding at our partially completed home in Carmel, Indiana, on June 19, 2010.

(Center left) Our wedding party. Front row (left to right): my great nieces Elizabeth, Abbie Grace, and Anna Tobias; grandsons Jack Button and Randall Samuel Tobias; Deborah's great nephews Andrew and Matthew Okon; grandson Connor Button. Back row (left to right): granddaughters Ella Tobias and Emily Button; Deborah's best friend Cathy Conners; Deborah and me; my brother Roger; and Deborah's great nephew Michael Okon.

(Lower left) Deborah, with her new ring on our engagement day, on the stern of my Grand Banks Trawler, Meant to Be, at our home on Captiva Island, Florida.

(Lower right) Deborah with her brother, David Flanagan.

(Bottom right) Deborah and my brother Roger at Sargent House on Lake Wawasee on the day they first met.

RANDALL L. TOBIAS

(Top) My brother Roger and me in the late 1940s.

(Center left) Roger and me in the late 1950s.

(Center right) Roger and me at an IU basketball game.

(Bottom right) Pat Day, one of the greatest thoroughbred jockeys of all time, wearing the silks of our Double R Stables at Keeneland in Lexington, Kentucky.

(Top) With my son Todd at Twelve Springs Ranch.

(Center left) With Todd prior to his wedding to Amy Brim.

(Center right) Todd at Lake Wawasee.

(Bottom right) With Paige and Todd at the Tobias Family Office.

(Top) Grandsons Jack Button, Randall Samuel Tobias, and Connor Button.

(Bottom left) Preparing for the December 26, 2021, celebration of Deborah's 70th birthday at 35,000 feet, organized by Emily and Paige.

(Bottom right) Granddaughters Emily Button and Ella Tobias with grandson Connor Button.

(Top) One of my favorite family photos—Christmas vacation 2024 on the beach at Longboat Key (left to right): Randall Samual Tobias, Ella Tobias, Ava Button, Tim Button, Paige Tobias Button, me, Deborah, Connor Button, Emily Button and her fiancé Jack Morris, and Jack Button.

(Bottom left) Deborah, Emily, Ella, and Paige, ready to fly from Indianapolis to Toronto to see Beyoncé in concert in 2013.

(Bottom right) My great nieces, Roger's granddaughters, (left to right): Elizabeth, Anna, and Abbie Grace Tobias. The day Roger died I told them that even though their Paw Paw could never be replaced, I would always do my best to be there for them, representing him.

(Top left) In front of Duke Chapel on Emily's 2021 graduation day with some of her very best friends—both then and now. Left to right: Fernanda Herrera, Caitlin Carter, me, Emily, Grace O'Leary, and Carley Lerner.

(Top right) With Emily. As a Duke University trustee emeritus, I was privileged to participate in her graduation ceremony.

(Bottom right) Me, Emily, Jack Morris, and Deborah at Emily and Jack's engagement party at our Carmel home.

Never Daunted

(Top left) With Connor at a Vanderbilt lacrosse game.

(Top right) With Ella in front of DePauw's iconic East College building, a central feature of the campus since Ella's great-grandfather, Roy Tobias, was a student there in the 1920s.

(Bottom left) With Connor at his 2022 graduation from Vanderbilt.

(Bottom right) Ella at her 2022 graduation from DePauw.

(Top left) Fishing with grandson Randall Samuel at Lake Wawasee.

(Top right) Randall Samuel on the UCLA campus with the UCLA Bruin statue.

(Bottom left) Jack and Deborah at the water park in Rapid City, South Dakota, near Mount Rushmore.

(Bottom middle) Deborah, Jack, and me with Mount Rushmore in the background.

(Bottom right) Deborah, Jack, and me.

(Top) Deborah holding granddaughter Ava a few moments after her birth in 2010.

(Bottom left) Deborah, Ava, and me at the Park Tudor School Grandparents Day.

(Bottom right) Deborah, Ava, and Paige at Lake Wawasee.

(Top) Left to right: Laura Tobias, me, Deborah, and Eric Tobias at an IU football game at the University of Nebraska Memorial Stadium in Lincoln.

(Bottom) Left to right: Me, Deborah, Paige, and Tim cheering for grandson Jack's Oregon Ducks in the 2024 B1G Championship football game against Penn State at Lucas Oil Stadium in Indianapolis.

(Top) The farmhouse and garage at Tobias Farms near Remington.

(Bottom) Shooting clays at the farm as a tune-up for our annual fall family quail hunt at Rio Piedra Plantation near Camilla, Georgia. Left to right: Me, Deborah, Paige, Laura, Eric, and Tim.

(Top left) Quail hunting at Rio Piedra Plantation near Camilla, Georgia. Left to right: Deborah, me, Paige, Tim, Eric, Laura, Emily, and Jack Morris.

(Top right) Pheasant hunting with Deborah in the snow at Paul Nelson Farm near Gettysburg, South Dakota.

(Bottom) In my Peter Breen gentleman's racer, *Theopolis*, in front of our Lake Wawasee home, Sargent House.

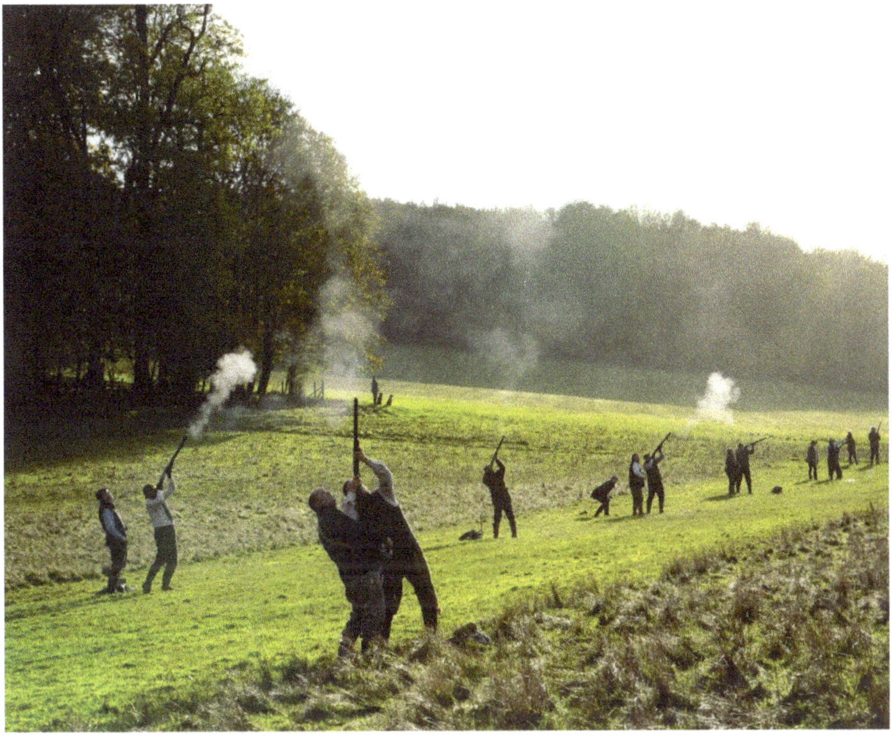

Terry Allen

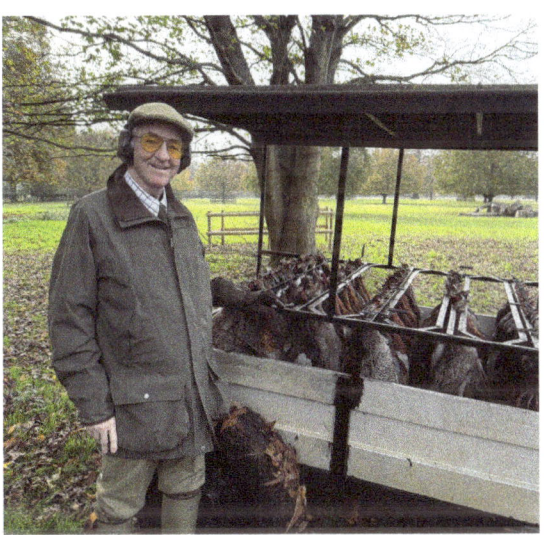

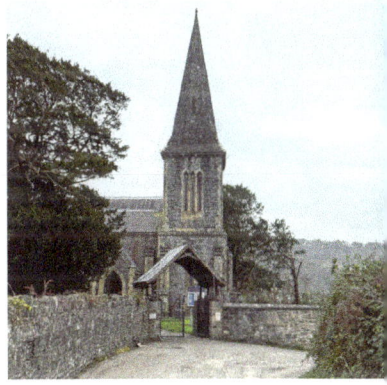

(Top) A driven shoot in Hertfordshire, United Kingdom, with the Anglo American Shooting Society.

(Bottom left) Pheasants in the game wagon.

(Bottom right) St. David's Church in the village of Abergwili in Carmarthenshire, Wales. My fifth great-grandparents, Thomas Tobias and Catherine Richards, were married here on November 2, 1736, and are buried in the church cemetery.

(Top) Standing by the River Tywi in Carmarthenshire, Wales, the area of my Tobias ancestral roots.

(Bottom left) Remembrance Sunday services, November 10, 2024, at St. Tybie's Church in the village of Llandybie, Carmarthenshire, Wales. To my right is the stone baptismal font where my great-grandfather, David Tobias, was baptized on June 30, 1816.

(Bottom right) Examining a Tobias family gravestone in the village church cemetery in Llanarthney, Carmarthenshire, Wales. Our genealogist is exploring how we might be related to the Tobiases buried there.

KEEPING BUSY

Chapter Twenty-One

12 Springs Ranch was one of my most enjoyable investments ever.

Though I was technically a "retiree" after I left Lilly, I still had plenty on my plate. During the next few years, I kept myself occupied both by traveling with my family and by tending to an eclectic grab bag of assignments. I did a lot, but mostly at my own pace and my own pleasure.

Not long after relinquishing the CEO position in May of 1998, I got to start spending some of my newfound free time with Paige, her husband Tim Button, and my soon-to-be first grandchild, Emily. At that time, Tim worked for Lilly as a pharmaceutical representative in Pasadena, California, where he and Paige lived. A few days before Emily's birth on August 19th, I headed out to visit and then just sort of hung out for a couple of weeks. I told Paige that since I'd figured out a way in 1994 to be the substitute "Mother of the Bride" I saw no reason why I couldn't also figure out how to be the substitute "Mother of the Mother!"

Obviously, "hanging out" hadn't been possible during most of my Lilly tenure. Being able to take the time to hold my granddaughter in my arms and to help out with her day-to-day care offered a wonderful preview of the less hectic, much more family-focused interlude I was about to enjoy.

My main residence remained in Indianapolis, but before leaving Lilly, I'd begun construction of a new house at Lake Wawasee. Located in northern Indiana's Kosciusko County, the lake is, at roughly 3,000 acres, the state's largest natural body of water (with the exception of Lake Michigan). For the better part of two centuries, its banks have been lined with summer homes, in many cases owned by expats from Indianapolis and other northern Indiana towns and cities as well as a few from Chicago, southern Michigan, and eastern Ohio.

It wasn't my first piece of Hoosier waterfront property. When I first moved back to Indianapolis, I purchased a house fronting a much smaller body of water called Grandview Lake in Brown County, Indiana. This worked out perfectly for me because it was so close to the city that I could spend weekends there and then get up on Monday mornings and drive to work, which was only about an hour distant on the highway. But when I married Marianne, who had spent nearly every summer of her life at Wawasee, we instead started visiting a property she owned there.

I eventually sold the Grandview house, and in 1999 we decided to build a new Wawasee place. Standard lakefront lots were often 50 feet wide, but we managed to find an elderly couple selling a small house set on two lots totaling 100 feet. By coincidence, those lots sat adjacent to the Lilly estate—a large portion of shoreline acquired by Colonel Eli Lilly himself in the late 1800s and held by various family members ever since. Before we broke ground, I inquired of my good friends Peter Nicholas and Ginny Lilly Nicholas, the

Colonel's great-great-granddaughter, about whether the family might be interested in selling their adjacent lot. Along with Ginny's siblings, Rennie Lilly McCutcheon and Ted Lilly, they were happy to sell another 75 feet of shorefront next to our lot, giving us 175 feet in total. The actual construction of our lake house took place during my final year at Lilly, and I was so busy with work that I simply wasn't that involved. Indeed, I only made it to Wawasee for a single weekend during the summer before I retired.

After retirement, we also set up housekeeping on Captiva, an island off Florida's Gulf Coast. We acquired a large house, a guest house, and a dock that could accommodate the boat I purchased. I'd become interested in boating during my early days at AT&T when I worked in southern Indiana. In 1968 Marilyn and I purchased a small ski boat and tooled up and down the Ohio River with it—which in retrospect probably wasn't the greatest introduction to the hobby. The boat was secondhand and only 18 feet long, and the deep, wide Ohio was full of swift currents and enormous, lumbering strings of barges moving coal and other goods.

My Captiva craft was quite a bit more accommodating. Built in Singapore by Grand Banks Yachts, she was 48 feet long, with two staterooms and other amenities that could comfortably accommodate eight to ten people. Ironically, even though I owned her for about a decade, I think I spent exactly one night aboard. Most of my Gulf of Mexico excursions were day trips, such as fishing, lunch, cocktail cruises, or occasionally a trip to Naples or Key West for a few days. But it was a great deal of fun, and I loved that boat.

Wawasee and Captiva were both wonderful places to relax. But neither meant as much to me as an acquisition I made in Montana. I had always enjoyed the western U.S., having owned ski condos at Steamboat Springs and later Beaver Creek. But for a long time, I'd hoped one day to own a ranch. I was able to acquire an incredible

3,000-acre Montana spread called 12 Springs Ranch, which I purchased in the summer of 1998, about six months before leaving Lilly. I have to say it was one of my most enjoyable investments ever.

The ranch was the culmination of a dream. And now was the time, I decided, to fully immerse myself in this mythic land.

12 Springs became my family's favorite retreat. I rode and took care of horses, and branded cattle. When not on horseback, I got around on a four-wheel-drive all-terrain vehicle, in an open Jeep, or a restored 1953 Chevrolet pickup truck. I had a room at the ranch house that was filled with hunting and fly-fishing gear. The property included two trout-filled ponds, where I fished anytime the spirit moved me.

I loved everything about the place. It was such an authentic slice of the Old West that it had been used as the backdrop for part of the filming of the Robert Redford movie *The Horse Whisperer*, and Redford himself lived in one of the ranch's houses during filming. My next-door neighbor was NBC News anchor Tom Brokaw, who owned a ranch roughly the same size as mine. We had met some years earlier when he received an honorary degree from Duke but did not really know each other. When he learned of my purchase, he called to welcome me to the neighborhood. At some point during the conversation, he said he wanted to warn me about readying myself for unanticipated, self-identified guests.

"When your friends hear you own a Montana ranch," he said, "be prepared to hear, 'Gee, I've never been to Montana!'"

Over our time as neighbors, we became good friends. We entered into a business partnership shortly after we got acquainted, using some of our adjoining pasturelands to raise buffalo. We kept a joint herd of around fifty for seven or eight years.

I had large numbers of elk and black bear on the property and would even see the occasional wolf—likely a refugee from

Yellowstone National Park, which was only about 50 miles away. I employed a full-time ranch manager and his wife, who, among other things, were responsible for overseeing a hundred or so head of cattle, about a dozen horses, and all the property and buildings. The division of labor was simple. I owned the land, but they ran the place.

Even though none of us ranch owners lived within shouting distance of each other, this stretch of Montana was a very close-knit area. If a ranch manager needed assistance moving cattle from one pasture to another, he could just phone ranchers on surrounding spreads and ask for their help. Fighting fires was also a community effort. It had to be. Obviously, with everyone so spread out, putting out a blaze could be tough. If you found a fire somewhere on your property and called the U.S. Forest Service, it might be several hours before they got there with equipment.

So I bought a firetruck. It was old but fully equipped with a big water tank and all the necessary hoses and pumps. As a way to be a good neighbor instead of an uncaring outsider, I made it available to the whole neighborhood—and by that, I mean ranches within a 15- to 20-mile radius of mine. There were a couple of occasions when people called my ranch manager to ask for help because lightning had started a grass fire on their property. The help was greatly appreciated.

The fires were typically caused by something called dry lightning. You'd think there was going to be a thunderstorm, but in late summer it was so hot and arid that the rain would evaporate before reaching the ground. However, the storm's accompanying lightning struck as usual, igniting dry grass and dead trees. You'd have an acre or two burning before you knew it, and maybe another 50 before you could do anything about it. So that firetruck, because it was so handy, helped save a lot of acreage. One neighboring rancher sent me a check for a couple of hundred dollars for its use, which I sent back to him. This was just not the way neighbors should treat each other.

Tom Brokaw and I both tried to do things like this to ingratiate ourselves with the locals because we were absentee owners surrounded by people who often went back several generations in the area. Not surprisingly, they often looked askance at outsiders, assuming the worst. We wanted to be good neighbors, so we tried to be as helpful as possible.

Tom came up with a very creative community project that he and I joined forces on. Back in the old days, before Montana ranches became popular with outsiders, the local kids could go elk hunting pretty much anywhere they wanted. But once folks like Tom and I started buying property, we wanted to protect the wildlife and were worried about insurance liability. So neither of us permitted hunting on our land. Nor did most people like us, which meant that kids grew up without having a place to hunt. So the two of us created something called "Bugling for Books."

During the fall, which is the elk mating season, the herds come down from the highlands to the valleys, and the males make loud bugling noises to attract mates. Hence the name of the program. We got a couple of sporting goods stores in two neighboring towns to sell $25 tickets for a drawing, with all the proceeds going to the local library. Two teenage winners were then drawn from the tickets, with one getting to go elk hunting on my ranch with my manager as the guide and the other on Tom's with his manager. They hunted while accompanied by an adult, and they could keep at it until they bagged an elk. Some got one on their first Saturday while others needed a couple of weekends. But every kid got to shoot an elk.

One of the greatest things about the ranch, at least from my perspective, was the splendid isolation. I built a new ranch house during my tenure, and when I sat on the front porch, I could see the mountains 50 miles away. I also could look in any direction and not see another manmade structure. Talk about privacy. There just aren't many places where it's possible to experience that, and not very many people have the privilege of enjoying it.

Yet even though I owned the ranch, I always thought of myself as just a temporary caretaker of that extraordinary land. The locals nailed it when they called Montana The Last Best Place.

We would visit several times each year, without fail. But home was still Indianapolis, where I maintained an administrative center that came to be called the Tobias Family Office.

At the time of my retirement, it was standard practice for ex-CEOs at many companies to continue to enjoy perks furnished by their former employers, such as (depending on the firm) access to paid office space, assistants whose salaries were covered by the company, or even the use of corporate planes and cars. One distinctive, decades-old Lilly tradition was to allow former CEOs to maintain their offices at the company's headquarters. In other words, if you were the new CEO, you had to contend with the fact that the former CEO was still there, sitting in his office pretty much every day, doing God knows what and how it might relate to interacting with people in the company.

I thought this was an absolutely terrible idea, and I had no intention of following the precedent. Instead, I arranged for some office space far from the corporate campus—to my knowledge the first retired CEO in the company's history to do so. At the time, our animal health business, Elanco, was consolidating its headquarters operations in a new complex on the Indianapolis north side, and I found a space that fit my needs in another part of their building but as part of that lease.

Effective January 1, 1999, I moved into the Office of the Chairman Emeritus, which later evolved into the Tobias Family Office. There was space for myself and an assistant, a small reception area, and enough room for files and storage. My legal and financial advisors told me I needed to hire a financial person to help with money matters, so at my own expense, we included room for her. And when Paige, Todd, and I decided to start a family foundation with an executive director, we acquired additional space for that, too, also at my expense.

While the Lilly-provided support was quite modest, the excessive business-funded largess toward former chief executives that was once common among other large companies isn't a "thing" anymore. And I think that's a good idea. Mostly thanks to former General Electric CEO Jack Welch, it gradually all came to an end. During divorce proceedings, the extremely lavish post-retirement perks he enjoyed (including corporate planes and use of a New York City apartment) were revealed. The reaction of stockholders and the general public was less than favorable, and such arrangements rapidly fell out of fashion. Shortly after that I terminated Lilly's support.

I must admit that even though I didn't know what a "family office" was when it was first broached to me, it has certainly proved useful. And the quarters occupied by the Tobias Family Office provide a far more relaxing environment than my former corporate digs. Unlike at AT&T or Lilly, I only wore a suit to work if I had a meeting—a really important meeting. And for the first time in my adult life, I started each workday not by reviewing emails or making phone calls, but by closing my office door, enjoying a cup of coffee, and reading the newspaper.

Not that there wasn't plenty of actual work to do. For one thing, I still sat on numerous corporate boards, including Phillips Petroleum, where I was deeply involved in an effort to find a new CEO. Later, in

2002, along with my friend and board colleague, Norm Augustine, the CEO of Lockheed Martin, I served on a small board committee to help engineer a merger between the firm and another oil company called Conoco. The combined organization was named ConocoPhillips, and I took a seat on the new, blended board.

The merger negotiations were interesting and quite instructive—mostly for what they revealed about human character. And human folly. While we spent a great deal of time on substantive issues such as finances and corporate strategy, in the end, the biggest struggles were over what in the merger world are called the "social issues." Though deals like this are called mergers, they rarely result in a marriage of equals. Someone is always perceived as the dominant player. If one company is mentioned first in the new name, retains its headquarters, and furnishes the new CEO, it is seen—at least within the organization—as the "winner." Typically, in so-called "mergers of equals," those three social issues are divided in some way between the two merging companies. This sort of thinking has been around for a very long time. Indeed, it's often said that companies that are weak and need a merger partner almost always end up on the "right side of the hyphen." In other words, if Smith Industries is weak and Jones Industries stronger, the new company will be called Jones-Smith Industries. And if Jones happens to be the weak sister, the opposite occurs.

We on the Phillips board were well aware of this sort of thinking, and during the merger talks, we used it to our advantage. We agreed to name the company ConocoPhillips; abandoned our headquarters in Bartlesville, Oklahoma, and consolidated at Conoco's Houston headquarters; and picked Conoco's CEO as the new company's chairman of the board, with Phillips's boss as CEO.

This sounds like a sweeping social issues "win" for Conoco, and their CEO certainly saw it that way. Unfortunately for them, it was much less of a pragmatic victory. At Phillips, we'd long contemplated moving the headquarters to Houston anyway because it's the epicenter of the U.S. oil industry. And while, in theory, the ConocoPhillips CEO (the former Phillips CEO) would report to the chairman of the board (the former Conoco leader), the reality was quite different.

I don't think the ConocoPhillips chairman understood the true state of affairs until the first meeting of the new, blended board of directors. I distinctly remember him calling the meeting to order, uttering a few pleasantries, and then turning over the proceedings to "his" CEO, the former Phillips boss, who had been placed in direct charge of everything else in the company, from finances to operating issues. In other words, he ran the company.

It likely wasn't until that exact moment that the chairman realized something vital. Out of the thousands of employees theoretically under his control, only one of them reported to him—the CEO. He figured it out eventually, and not too long after, the chairman retired.

During our lengthy merger negotiations, we at Phillips focused on the hard, nuts-and-bolts question of whose strategy would prevail and who actually was going to run things. And in order to gain wins in these vitally important areas, we were more than willing to "lose" on the social issues, such as whose name came first and where the headquarters was located. As I've seen again and again, feeling too strongly about such emotionally charged items often gets in the way of rational thinking.

There is another interesting thing about those Phillips (and later, ConocoPhillips) board meetings. A couple of times a year, the company liked to have off-site gatherings of the board at some important location where it had operations. On two different occasions, those meetings were held off the coast of Norway, on gigantic oil rigs in the storm-tossed North Sea.

It's hard to give even an inkling of how immense these platforms are. One of the units we visited was basically two adjacent complexes connected by a long bridge, spanning almost a mile in total, from the far corner of one platform to the far corner of the other. One of them was for the actual drilling and extraction operations, while the other was a support structure that included, among a great many other facilities, a seven-story hotel. We helicoptered in, dressed in heavy thermal survival suits that made you look like the Michelin Man. That was necessary because, if the helicopter went down in the North Sea, an unprotected human would last only a few minutes in the freezing water.

Even on relatively calm days, massive waves still constantly collided with the platforms' legs. It's really spooky to look over the side and see this and contemplate just how strong those structures have to be to withstand the 24-hour assault. Yet, for the most part, it didn't bother me. When you're sitting on top of an oil platform, and it's so sturdily built that you can't feel the slightest vibration from the wave impacts, you just kind of forget where you are.

My work as chairman of the Duke University Board of Trustees also necessitated numerous (though far less arduous) trips to the school's Durham, North Carolina campus. Holding such a role at a major university isn't a day-to-day job, but it was a rare week that didn't find me on the phone about it at least once. All told, I probably visited Duke around 10 times each year for board meetings and school functions.

The Tobias Family Office also saw the genesis of a couple of interesting family projects. For instance, I started a horse-racing stable with my brother, Roger.

Roger was four and a half years older than me. He was born on August 23, 1937, one of two male twins. The other twin was named Gordon, but unfortunately, he only lived for about two weeks. Of course, we both grew up in Remington, but he always ran around with a different, slightly older group of kids. We were part of a very close family that took summer vacations together and those types of things, but it wasn't until I came back to Indianapolis in 1993 that we had the opportunity to become truly close.

During those days, I made a point of including Roger and his wife, Karen, in everything that I was involved with in the community, when practicable. If Lilly had a table for ten at a social event, I often invited them. Or, if I had a group of people I was entertaining at, say, the Indianapolis 500, he was always on the guest list. Roger and his wife were always very popular because Roger was the most positive guy in the world.

He graduated from Indiana University in 1959 with a business degree, just as I would a few years later. He was also in ROTC and served as an active-duty army officer. He was stationed just outside of Chicago, where he had responsibility for a Nike missile battery, which back in those days encircled many major American cities to act as a defense against Soviet nuclear missiles and bombers. After discharge, he took a job at Sears and worked for the retailer for his entire career. His last position was as general manager of one of the company's Indianapolis area regional shopping mall stores.

After retiring from Sears, he spent several years in a very successful second career as a Morgan Stanley stock broker. His longtime personal interest in managing his own investments, combined with his outgoing personality, made him a natural.

During his days in the military, when he was stationed in Chicago, he and some of the other young army officers got into the habit of visiting the nearby Arlington International Racecourse, a famous horse-racing track that closed in 2021. From this experience, Roger developed a lifetime interest in horse racing. About the time I was preparing to retire from Lilly, I asked him if he'd like to buy a horse or two for a racing stable. I told him that if he would take care of running the project I would put up the money. He was extremely excited about doing this, so we launched Double R Stables—after our names, Roger and Randall.

We had our own yellow and white Double R Stables racing silks and used Pat Payne of Taylor Made Farm in Lexington as our advisor. Over the years, Pat became a close and trusted friend. I think we eventually owned something like 20 horses and raced at all the great tracks, from Belmont Park in New York to Churchill Downs Racetrack (the home of the Kentucky Derby) to the historic Keeneland in Lexington. It was great fun. Roger actually spent quite a lot of time at it, so it was something we could do together. When he died in 2016, I did not have the inclination to take over the administrative work he'd done to run the operation, so I liquidated our remaining ownership.

One of my other favorite assignments was serving on the Colonial Williamsburg Foundation Board of Trustees. I joined in the late 1980s while I still worked for AT&T, at the behest of Charlie Brown, who'd just retired as chairman and CEO and was then serving as the Williamsburg board's chairman. The organization presides over a roughly 300-acre living history museum that's part of the town of Williamsburg, Virginia's historic district. It features a selection of immaculately restored colonial-era buildings, plus highly accurate reconstructions of early 18th-century homes, public structures, and restaurants. A large complement of historical reenactors, dressed in period costumes, adds to the ambience.

After a preliminary meeting with Charlie to gauge my interest in joining the board, Marilyn and I flew down for a weekend with

Charlie and his wife Ann Lee at Colonial Williamsburg itself so that we could get the lay of the land. We stayed in a period-accurate home, which looked like something straight out of a movie. I wound up serving on the board for more than a decade, until a new assignment forced me to retire.

Interestingly, my board position at Colonial Williamsburg would soon play a role in an odd confluence of events that would propel me into a high-profile, high-stakes public service job. More about that in a bit.

Before leaving Lilly, I'd decided along with Paige and Todd that I wanted to organize our family philanthropic efforts around a more coherent strategy. I was very interested in giving money away because, when I started out in life, I didn't have any. I've been very fortunate to make more than I could ever have imagined, so it seemed appropriate to use it to do positive things for other people and institutions.

I've also learned from those with experience that, if you want your philanthropy to have a real impact, it has to be focused. Before setting up the foundation, there'd been no rhyme or reason to the causes I'd championed. Also, there were all sorts of tax implications when it came to giving away money. All in all, it made more sense to me to contribute through a foundation rather than do it personally with no strategic focus.

So we brought in Susie Hazelett, who was a part-time professional in the fundraising and philanthropy world for most of her adult life. I hired Susie to help set up the foundation and its processes and to let the not-for-profit world know that we were open for business and that we would focus primarily on education and the arts. We made grants twice a year. Individually, most of them weren't huge—typically, between $5,000 and $100,000 each. But, cumulatively, it was a meaningful sum.

We also engaged an Indiana Teacher of the Year recipient, Barbara Pederson, to develop a program we called Literacy for Life. The idea was to take all of the first- and second-grade teachers in a particular school and put them through a one-week training program that summarized the current best practices for teaching kids to read. We rolled this out at several schools and hoped to take it statewide. If things had proceeded as originally envisioned, I would have traveled around the state, speaking to Rotary Clubs and other such organizations about the project. The idea was that they would raise the money to fund it in their communities and we'd give them the necessary materials. If fate hadn't intervened, that's what I would have done.

Admittedly, this is a long list of projects for someone who was allegedly retired, but it wasn't everything. There were a couple of others on my to-do list, including one that deserves its own chapter: collaborating on both a new book and a new business endeavor with my son, Todd.

COLLABORATING WITH TODD ON A MAGAZINE AND A MOOSE

Chapter Twenty-Two

The odds of us collaborating on something meaningful seemed very slim. Yet we managed to do it twice.

One of my most cherished post-Lilly accomplishments had nothing to do with corporate boards or vacation homes. It was the opportunity to work professionally with my son Todd—not once, but twice. We collaborated on the book *Put the Moose on the Table*, and I assisted with the launch of his passion project, *Indy Men's Magazine*.

While I, of course, spent most of my adult life as a business executive, Todd went in an entirely different direction. He became a writer of considerable skill, earning an undergraduate degree from West Virginia University and a Master's in English from Indiana University. One of his most gripping stories, at least to me, was an essay he wrote in 1994 called "The Prodigal Son Diaries," about the death of his mother. It appeared in a book called *Before Their Time*, which was a collection of essays by people who unexpectedly lost a parent.

Obviously, I was very proud of his achievements. Given the huge difference between my background and his, the odds of us collaborating on something meaningful seemed very slim. Yet we managed to do it twice. I'll always be grateful for that.

First came *Moose*. It took us a while to decide exactly what it would be. At the time, the commercial market was already crowded with business books—or rather, business books that followed a certain formula. They even had similar titles—typically, something like "Turn Your Career Around in Six Easy Steps" or "Build a Successful Business in Five Steps." Though this "by the numbers" formula certainly sold well, I didn't subscribe to it. I don't think there are *any* hard-and-fast rules that guarantee success. Writing a book of that type smacked of crass commercialism, which didn't interest me.

I told Todd that we needed a fresh idea. After much thought and discussion, we developed a hybrid concept that was a cross between a business tome and a memoir. I think its subtitle, *Lessons in Leadership from a CEO's Journey Through Business and Life*, encapsulates the central idea I wanted to put forward: There's no one-size-fits-all formula for achievement. Often, as I learned through years of personal experience, it's about who adapts most quickly and efficiently to change.

With that in mind, we decided to create a book that shared some of the pivotal experiences from my personal and professional lives and the lessons they taught me. It wasn't a list of surefire success tips, but rather a meditation on how to learn and profit from change. I hoped that our potential readership would find such tales not just interesting and entertaining but also applicable to their own circumstances. Or, as I wrote in the introduction:

"The fact is, my leadership role in corporate America has, by and large, centered on the issue of striving to turn change—in all of its varied manifestations—into competitive advantage while always trying to do what's right. And that's the essence of this book."

After selecting our premise, we struggled (as I'm sure most first-time collaborators do) with how to approach the nuts and bolts of the writing. Most importantly, the division of labor. To put it simply, my son was the one with the writing expertise, and I was the one with the necessary information, although I will say I thought I too could write!

Before putting pen to paper, we did a lot of talking and planning —usually, while sitting on a sofa in the family office. First, we developed a chronological outline, starting with my youth, moving through my days at AT&T and Lilly, and finishing with my retirement (which at the time was more or less the "end" of my life story).

Todd conducted numerous interviews with me—interviews that, to an outsider, might have sounded like a normal father-and-son conversation. After we'd covered a particular topic or time period, he would turn the material into a chapter draft, which I would then look over and edit.

Early in this process, I noticed that Todd liked to occasionally add fun details to my life story that I didn't necessarily remember happening! For instance, earlier in this book, I talked about a horse my father rode to school when he was very young. Todd also mentioned this in *Put the Moose on the Table* and stated that the horse's name was Chester. Well, truth be told, I have no idea what its name was, or even if it had one. Todd just made one up. In his view, it was simply a fun, inconsequential detail. And, of course, there's no one on the face of this earth who remembers (or cares) whether the horse actually had a name or not. So it stayed in.

We had a few small disagreements over this sort of thing, but the research and writing process was fun. As mentioned earlier, however, the nature of the project made it not so amenable to the classic biography format, in which the writer interviews the subject and then writes the book. Out of necessity, there were some chapters in which I did the bulk of the writing (with Todd editing). The process was pretty seamless. So seamless that I doubt anyone could read Moose today and say, "Okay, Todd must have written that chapter." We worked very hard to make sure that was the case.

The book was published by Indiana University Press in 2003, to a generally favorable critical reception. It wasn't until a couple of years later, however, that I realized its list of fans included the prime minister of Thailand and his cabinet.

The prime minister in question was named Thaksin Shinawatra and he served from 2001 until 2006, when he was ousted in a coup. Years earlier, when I was still at AT&T and he was a well-connected businessman, he'd been engaged by the company as a consultant. The Thai government wanted to privatize its telecommunications industry, and AT&T wanted the contract. And to do that, you absolutely had to have local and well-connected representation.

We got to know each other quite well during my many trips to Bangkok. Fast forward to July of 2004, when I was once again in Thailand for the XV International AIDS Conference. This biannual function was a very big deal. On this occasion, I found myself in a ballroom for a reception before the opening dinner. I was talking to some folks I knew when I suddenly heard a booming voice from across the room. It was Shinawatra yelling, "Randy, Randy!"

He was now Thailand's prime minister, and he had most of his cabinet in tow. He introduced them one by one, and each of these high-ranking government officials, when they met me, offered some version of, "Oh, are you Randy Tobias? We've read your book."

It turns out Shinawatra ran a sort of targeted book club for his senior staff. Every month he'd assign a new volume on leadership, which they would read and discuss. Because he knew me, one of those books was *Put the Moose on the Table*.

At roughly the same time Todd and I worked on *Moose*, he was also putting together another, larger project. It was called *Indy Men's Magazine*, and it became our first business collaboration. It was to be published under the auspices of Table Moose Media LLC, a company consisting of Todd (who provided the leadership) and myself (who provided advice, plus a large infusion of seed money).

At the time, there were a lot of popular young men's magazines on the national market, such as *GQ* and *Men's Journal*. They offered everything from fashion tips to sports stories to how-to columns for everything from relationships to home electronics. Todd wanted to take that national concept "local" by creating a publication with the same target audience as the national venues but focused on Indianapolis—sort of like a city magazine (popular lifestyle publications that concentrated on just one metro area or region) exclusively for younger men.

Indy Men's Magazine debuted in 2002. It was glossy, published monthly, and free of charge. It enjoyed a readership of perhaps 100,000 per month.

It was a first-rate product. Todd and his editor, Lou Harry, enlisted an impressive array of heavy hitters to write for it. The May 2003 cover featured an original painting by artist Peter Max. Fiction writers such as Dan Barden and science fiction great David Gerrold contributed, and everyone from basketball legend Larry Bird to actor Karl Malden sat down for interviews.

Editorially, the magazine was an unqualified success. Honestly, if the only thing that mattered was the quality of the articles and the photos, Todd and his crew would have hit it out of the park. But a major problem soon surfaced: Plenty of people read and praised

Indy Men's Magazine, but not enough potential advertisers stepped forward to place ads in its pages.

This lack of advertising revenue was a very big deal because advertising was and remains the chief revenue source for print publications. It decides how many pages you can afford to print each month—or whether you can even stay in business at all.

Problems with attracting advertisers bedeviled the magazine throughout its run. To be frank, I don't think Todd ever got a handle on how to deal with this part of the business. I've always suspected that at least to some degree the content was often a bit too "edgy" and the language too "colorful" for many mainstream advertisers. But Todd had no interest in compromising on his vision by toning it down. Ultimately, however, some of the issues he faced were beyond his control. When the magazine debuted, print publications were beginning a long decline triggered by the rise of the Internet and its abundance of free online content. I remember, during the publication's run, reading a number of articles that listed the types of business startups that failed most often. Magazines were number one on the list.

Slowly, the cash reserves we'd targeted to commit drained away, and after half a decade, Todd decided it was pointless to continue. *Indy Men's Magazine*'s final issue came out in May of 2007. Towards the end, Todd, who didn't want to approach me for any more money, struck a deal with an Indianapolis businessman named Tim Durham, who invested at least $25,000 in the magazine. I mention this because that fairly trivial amount became a thorn in my side.

To put it simply, Durham was a conman. He ran an investment firm called Obsidian Enterprises that purchased shares in a number of national companies. But as the FBI would discover, his real business was running a massive Ponzi scheme that defrauded some

5,400 investors—many of them elderly—of around $206 million. In 2012 he was sentenced to 50 years in prison.

The reason I know he invested in *Indy Men's Magazine* is because, after he went to prison, the court-appointed receiver aggressively tried to recover the money he'd swindled from his investors. Because there was a record of his investment in the magazine, I was approached by the receiver, who demanded that I repay the $25,000 Durham gave the magazine.

After studying the issue with counsel, it became abundantly clear that I was under no legal obligation to do any such thing. But in the end, I wrote a check for the full amount, just to avoid the hassle of engaging a legal team to litigate the issue—a process that might well have cost more than the $25,000 in question. So not only did I lose my original investment in *Indy Men's Magazine*, I also had to cover Durham's.

Not that I'm complaining. Because the experience of seeing my son enthusiastically pursue his dream project was worth every dime.

Though the publication wasn't financially a success, it was certainly a noble effort. And it was something Todd and I got to enjoy together. I think that *Indy Men's Magazine* was in many ways his soul, his identity, and the centerpiece of his life. And when it closed, he was the one who made the decision. I think he ran out of patience before I ran out of willingness to help him. But in his view, which I think has been borne out over time, there was simply no way to make it financially successful.

On the bright side, both the magazine and our time with *Moose* gave us opportunities to work together in what was essentially a family business. Because this was really a partnership. Todd learned about me, and I learned about him. It was one of the highlights of my life, and toward the top of the list of wonderful, memorable experiences as a parent.

One fond memory sums up those times for me. Because of the jobs and titles I've held, I often got noticed at restaurants. I was used to waiters whom I'd never laid eyes on knowing who I was. A couple of years into *Indy Men's* run, a waiter took my credit card after a meal and went away to process it.

When he returned to my table, he said, "Are you related to Todd Tobias?" That was quite a thrill.

THE CHALLENGE OF A LIFETIME

Chapter Twenty-Three

I had absolutely no interest in accepting any full-time job, and especially not in the government.

During this time of my life, I thought of myself as retired. But not everybody shared this view. For instance, in the early spring of 2000, not long after I left Lilly, Steve Hilbert, chairman and chief executive of the high-flying, wildly successful, Carmel, Indiana-based insurance company Conseco, was ousted from office due to a liquidity crisis and a precipitous fall in its stock price. Shortly thereafter, I was approached by one of the company's directors and one of its significant investors to gauge my interest in becoming its next CEO.

The inquiry was a complete shock. Certainly, I knew something about turning around a company in trouble, but I knew nothing about the insurance business. And if I still wanted to be a CEO, why would I have left Lilly?

Nonetheless, and somewhat to my own surprise, I agreed to consider it. At Conseco's expense, I engaged both a law firm and an accounting firm to assess the legal and financial issues facing the company. I also engaged another attorney with a national reputation in executive compensation matters to begin to sketch out what an employment contract might need to look like, given the very unusual circumstances.

Without going into great detail, after reviewing the professional advice and talking to a couple of people I knew and trusted in the investment banking community from my AT&T days, I concluded that within the company there were likely some solid assets that could return Conseco to viability. There were also some things that would need to be jettisoned, along with a number of necessary structural and cultural changes, but there was light at the end of the tunnel.

That meant the bigger obstacle for me was the significant corporate governance issue presented by the enormous loans that a number of the directors had taken out to buy Conseco stock. Those loans from outside banks were, in the end, backed by Conseco itself, creating enormous conflicts of interest for those directors.

Discussions proceeded on three parallel tracks: my interest and willingness to join the company and the Conseco board's willingness to have me; my own terms and conditions for doing so; and finally, the company's willingness to accept those conditions.

Discussions progressed to the point where a draft announcement of my appointment was produced. But in the end we all walked away. I wasn't willing to sign on without an agreement to adopt generally accepted good governance practices—which, in my view, meant that unless they could pay off their loans, a number of directors needed to step down. That was enough of a non-starter with enough of the directors to make it unlikely we could reach an agreement. In addition, I suspect (but don't know) that some of the directors surely must have wondered if I was really the best match anyway.

As things unfolded, the company subsequently hired Gary Wendt, the former head of GE Capital—clearly a more conventional fit. The biggest thing I learned during all of this (but didn't recognize until some years later) was that, after having some time away from the fray, I might actually be ready and willing to take another significant managerial role.

That opportunity would present itself a couple of years later.

Ironically, it was my inability to continue serving on one of the not-for-profit boards in my collection that finally led me into a brand-new full-time (actually, more than full-time) job—one that would prove the most difficult, all-consuming, and frustrating of my entire life but would also be the most consequential, both for me and millions of others.

It all began in early 2003. I'd served for twelve years on the board of the Colonial Williamsburg Foundation, which I greatly enjoyed. My fellow board members included television journalist David Brinkley, Supreme Court Justice Sandra Day O'Connor, and PBS TV journalist Jim Lehrer, who was kind enough to write a dustcover blurb for *Moose*.

I would have happily remained at my post, but board members were only allowed to serve for twelve years—and by 2003 I was well into my final year. With the end of my service rapidly approaching, I started casting around for another culture-related national board to join.

I had a chance conversation with Mitch Daniels about this matter. He was at the time head of the Office of Management and Budget in the George W. Bush cabinet. I asked him about the possibility of a presidential appointment to join the board of the John F. Kennedy Center for the Performing Arts. The Kennedy Center's sprawling

Washington, D.C. campus is America's busiest performing arts center, hosting more than 2,000 events annually. I wasn't exactly sure how one became a candidate for its board, but I knew they were appointed by the president. So I asked how I might be considered.

Mitch spoke with Dina Powell, assistant to the president for presidential personnel, about my inquiry. She thought about it and then called Mitch back with a very provocative statement and query. It was something to the effect of, "Why does he want to waste his time on something mostly ceremonial like the Kennedy Center board with his recent background? I've got a couple of things that the President really cares about, if he's interested. They would be places where he could really contribute and we could really use him."

One of those options was running a freshly commissioned government organization called the Millennium Challenge—a new kind of quasi corporation that would deliver foreign assistance in a new, experimental way. The other turned out to be a much more momentous, high-profile task—overseeing the Bush administration's response to the HIV/AIDS crisis in Africa.

HIV/AIDS (short for Human Immunodeficiency Virus/Acquired Immunodeficiency Syndrome) first surfaced in the United States in the early 1980s. The virus was primarily transferred by the exchange of bodily fluids, such as via unprotected sex, transfusions of infected blood, and shared hypodermic needles. Patients who contracted it might not show symptoms for years. But eventually, the virus severely damaged the immune system, leaving the body open to opportunistic infections ranging from tuberculosis to obscure, exotic forms of cancer. Sufferers also faced precipitous weight loss, further decreasing their stamina and resistance. AIDS patients typically died not from the disease but from the infections that accompanied it.

By 2003, as many as 42 million people around the world were infected with HIV, and some 20 million had died of AIDS. But though there was still no cure (indeed, there still isn't at the time of this writing), a battery of precautions, including "safe sex" techniques and needle exchange programs, had greatly slowed the infection rate in the U.S. and much of the developed world. Plus, new medicines were extending the lives and improving the health of HIV/AIDS patients.

But this wasn't the case in the Third World—especially in Africa, where HIV/AIDS raged largely unchecked among the general populations of numerous countries. While only around 6,000 people died of AIDS in Western Europe in all of 2003, 2.2 million died in sub-Saharan Africa (76 percent of the world's fatalities). Across the continent, AIDS had reversed years of hard-won life expectancy gains and decreases in child mortality. Also in 2003, some 12.1 million sub-Saharan children were orphaned when their parents died of AIDS—up from 2.5 million in 2001.

Of the nine countries with the largest HIV-infected populations, eight were in sub-Saharan Africa: South Africa, Nigeria, Zimbabwe, the United Republic of Tanzania, the Democratic Republic of Congo, Ethiopia, Kenya, and Mozambique. And in Botswana, a tiny nation with fewer than 2 million residents, a staggering 37.3 percent of adults had HIV/AIDS. These numbers were terrible, but it was feared that, bad as things already were, the African outbreak was just getting started. Without some sort of intervention, the continent could see political destabilization, many millions more orphaned children, and of course massive fatalities. It was an apocalypse, and it was unfolding before our eyes.

In many quarters, this growing emergency fell on deaf ears—but not everywhere. President Bush took an intense interest in the matter and sought out someone to spearhead America's response. Little did I realize that by innocently enquiring about joining the Kennedy Center board, I'd thrown my hat in the ring.

Sometime in early February of 2003, while I was having breakfast at my home in Captiva, I learned what I'd gotten myself into. Mitch emailed me, saying, "The White House wants to know whether you would be interested in talking about a position in the government. However, unlike the one you had in mind at the Kennedy Center, this would involve going to work full-time. Would you be willing to come to Washington to talk about it?"

I must admit that at that moment in my life, I had absolutely no interest in accepting any full-time job, and especially not in the government. But even though it was literally the last thing I wanted to do, I felt that when the White House asked you to consider something, you couldn't reject the request out of hand. So, shortly thereafter, I went to Washington, D.C., where I met with the head of the Office of Presidential Personnel Dina Powell, Secretary of State Colin Powell, National Security Advisor Condoleezza Rice, Gary Edson (who worked for Rice), Dr. Joe O'Neil, and several other officials who were instrumental in helping the president develop his AIDS program.

I also spoke with Dina about the Millennium Challenge project. Mitch may have thought I'd be more interested in going in that direction, and as I recall he initially was surprised I had an interest in the AIDS program. For one thing, Lilly hadn't done any work in the AIDS field. Even as the former CEO of a pharmaceutical company, I possessed little more than a passing knowledge of the disease, in part because I had signed off on terminating what little research Lilly had been doing in the area. And it had never touched me in a personal way. To that point I never had a friend, family member, or business associate suffer from it. And until I spoke with the White House, I wasn't aware of the scope of the problem in Africa. On the other hand, its advocates, including Mitch, thought the Millennium Challenge had the potential to transform foreign aid. And they were right about that.

But the HIV/AIDS initiative was clearly enormously important, and I didn't think that lacking an intimate knowledge of AIDS would exclude me from being of use. As I said earlier in this book, about 80 percent of the work of running any organization, from a telecommunications firm to a global relief effort, is the same. It's all about organization, defining goals, and motivation. As for the other 20 percent, I didn't doubt my ability to bring myself up to speed on the AIDS epidemic, from a sufficient understanding of the medical facts to the politics.

Had I been better informed, however, the politics of the situation would have concerned me much more deeply. The focus of PEPFAR (the United States President's Emergency Plan for AIDS Relief) meant that many "stakeholders," ranging from private companies to politicians to numerous other government agencies, often competing for scarce funds, would want to have a say in what got done. Unless some sort of special arrangement was made, the person "in charge" of giving people their marching orders and working to accomplish things as efficiently as possible would find themselves negotiating with other groups and government agencies, pleading and cajoling them to align their goals with the program's decisions. It would be like herding cats—or, in this case, considering the power of some of the entities interested in the program, being herded by cats.

I just didn't see how such a setup could accomplish PEPFAR's goals. And so, a few days after I returned home from the meeting, I emailed Mitch and asked if he could gracefully cause my name to be removed from consideration so I wouldn't be in a position to have to decline.

"I think it's a very noble cause, but I don't think they have it structured in a way that could make it work," I told him.

But that wasn't the end of it. A couple of weeks later, I got a call from Dina Powell. "Would you be willing to come back to Washington to have a further discussion about this, including a discussion with the president?" she asked.

What could I do? Of course, I agreed to go back, and this time faced what I can only describe as a full-court press about the importance of the program, from Powell, Rice, and other administration members interested in the subject. At the conclusion of those meetings, I spent perhaps 30 minutes, privately, in the Oval Office with President Bush himself, listening to his enthusiastic commitment to his strategy and answering his questions about why I didn't think the current plan, as envisioned, would work. Clearly, he wanted to know what I thought. Given the opportunity to do so, I told him that there was too much "coordinator" in it and not enough CEO. There was to be someone empowered with the responsibility for the program, but that person would not be empowered with the authority to act decisively. Thinking about the likely impending initiative in Iraq, I used the example of General Tommy Franks, pointing out that he was the commander of U.S. forces, not the "coordinator."

The President said he felt the same. He said that if PEPFAR was to succeed, its leadership needed to have teeth. The authority given to the person in charge needed to be sufficient for the task. It couldn't follow the schematic of typical government programs, in which everybody was empowered to say no, but nobody was empowered to say yes. That's the sort of arrangement you see happening in Congress and Washington, D.C. today. A lot of people can get in the way of something, but very few (including, often, the president) can say, "Here's what we're going to do."

That would not be the case in this situation. President Bush made it clear to me that I would have full authority, backed by him; and while it was indeed still Washington and I would have to manage the various constituencies, in the end, I could make the decisions that needed to be made; and that other organizations and members of his cabinet would know it.

I still wasn't in love with the idea of returning to work, but my uncertainties had been addressed by the highest possible authority. It was a chance to potentially save millions of lives. And also, after being pressed by so many high-ranking officials, my hesitancy about returning to a full-time position had been both worn down and won over. So I said yes.

Later, on my way out of town, I wrote a quick note to Dina Powell to memorialize a set of guiding principles for the position. "Based on my discussions this morning, yesterday and Monday, I believe we're in agreement that there needs to be clarity up front with the principals about how this will all work, (the President, the Secretary of State and, at some point, with other cabinet officers and agency heads) as well as with the person selected for this role. I believe the following reflects what the President has in mind in order to give this effort a good chance of success."

In bullet points, I offered the following list of what I saw as the agreed-to governing principles for the coordinator for international HIV/AIDS assistance. First, he would be appointed by the President of the United States with the advice and consent of the United States Senate, receive the personal rank of ambassador, and for administrative support would be based in the Department of State as head of a newly created independent entity.

In addition, he would:
- Report directly to the Secretary of State in a manner reflected on the Department's organization chart in the same way as the

United States Agency for International Development (USAID) administrator and the United States Permanent Representative to the United Nations (USUN).
- Be simultaneously accountable directly to the President of the United States through the Assistant to the President for National Security Affairs.
- Be granted authority to oversee, coordinate, and directly approve all resources and international activities of the United States Government (including funding) relating to combating HIV/AIDS in the target countries of Africa and the Caribbean and other countries as may be designated by the President.
- Be granted the authority to administer, allocate, and transfer funds to and from relevant executive branch agencies, including the Department of State, the United States Agency for International Development, the Department of Health and Human Services (including the Public Health Service), and any other department or agency of the United States that participates in international HIV/AIDS activities.
- Be granted the authority to provide grants to, and enter into contracts with, nongovernmental organizations (including faith-based and community-based organizations).

Sometime in June 2003, I got a call from Dina concerning the announcement of my nomination. I'd assumed it would be done via a press release, so what came next was a huge surprise. My nomination would be announced at a White House press conference, by the president himself, with the appropriate senior administration officials in attendance.

On July 2, 2003, the President announced my nomination to be the first United States Global AIDS Coordinator, with the rank of ambassador. My family and I attended the event, which took place at the White House. The President himself gave my family a tour of the Oval Office. I couldn't have been made to feel more special. Then my family was escorted to the adjoining Roosevelt Room, where the formal announcement would be made.

Before moving to the Roosevelt Room, the President asked me to stay behind for a short meeting that included Secretary Powell, National Security Advisor Rice, Press Secretary Ari Fleischer, Secretary of Health and Human Services Tommy Thompson, and Administrator of USAID Andrew Natsios. We gathered in the seating area at the opposite end of the Oval Office from the President's desk—the spot in front of the fireplace with two armchairs and two sofas facing each other in front of them. You've probably seen the armchairs, because whenever a foreign dignitary visits the Oval Office, they're typically photographed with the president sitting in the right-hand chair and the VIP in the left-hand chair.

On this occasion, with several of the most senior cabinet secretaries from his administration in attendance, he asked me to take the left chair while everyone else sat on the couches. Then the president said, in effect, the following: "I want to say to all of you here together, in the same place at the same time, that I recognize there's been a lot of debate about the reporting arrangements for Randy's new job as the United States Global AIDS Coordinator. I know that the State Department thinks it should be there, USAID thinks it should be part of their mandate, and Health and Human Services thinks it should be there. But I've made the decision that while he's going to report for administrative purposes to Secretary Powell, he's going to be empowered by me. And I want to be sure that you and all of your people understand that when he speaks, he's speaking for me. And that's the only way that this is going to work. Randy agreed to come into the government to take this on and I've assured him that he's going to have the support he needs to make this a success. I want you to be sure that all of your people understand that he's in charge, he has my full and complete support, and will speak for me on what we're about to do here. Are there any questions?"

I was dumbfounded to have my position validated in such a dramatic way. This no-holds-barred presidential endorsement, along with the fact that I hadn't gone looking for the PEPFAR job, hadn't expected to be offered it, and had been quite ambivalent about taking it, greatly empowered me to take more risks and speak with more confidence than other people in my position might. Because my backing came from the president, I couldn't easily be pushed into a corner. And because I got the job not because I lobbied for it, but because I understood its importance and volunteered, I couldn't be intimidated by threats of being fired.

As it turned out, I would need every bit of that presidential support, and personal patience, to deal with the long, long list of problems that lay ahead—problems that reared their heads as soon as I was nominated.

THE LONG, VEXING ROAD TO SENATE CONFIRMATION

Chapter Twenty-Four

I remember thinking, somewhat naively, that this wouldn't be a big deal.

President Bush's remarks in the Roosevelt Room during the nomination ceremony succinctly outlined the powers and objectives of PEPFAR. I've elected to include the following passages, verbatim.

"As Global AIDS Coordinator, Randy will have the rank of Ambassador, and will report directly to Secretary of State Powell. He will coordinate all of our international HIV/AIDS activities for all of our government departments and agencies. He will oversee all resources of this program. And he will work with the faith-based and community groups to get the job done. He will report regularly to Congress on the progress and effectiveness of our efforts.

"Randy Tobias has a mandate directly from me to get our AIDS initiative up and running as soon as possible. We'll work quickly to get help to the people who need it most by purchasing low-cost, antiretroviral medications and other drugs that are needed to save lives. We will set up a broad and efficient network to deliver drugs to the farthest reaches of Africa, even by motorcycle or bicycle.

"We will train doctors and nurses and other health care professionals so they can treat HIV/AIDS patients. Our efforts will ensure that clinics and laboratories will be built or renovated and then equipped. Child care workers will be hired and trained to care for AIDS orphans, and people living with AIDS will get home-based care to ease their suffering.

"Throughout all regions of the targeted countries we will provide HIV testing. We will support abstinence-based prevention education. Faith-based and community organizations will have our help as they provide treatment and prevention and support services in communities affected by HIV/AIDS. And we're developing a system to monitor and evaluate this entire program, so we can be sure we're getting the job done.

"Next week I will go to Africa to meet with leaders of African countries and with some of the heroic men and women who are caring for the sick and are saving lives. They deserve our praise. They deserve our help, without delay. And they will have our help.

"When I visit Africa I will reaffirm our nation's commitment to helping Africans fight this disease. America makes this commitment for a clear reason, directly rooted at our founding: we believe in the value and dignity of every human life. We're putting that belief into practice.

"We have a lot of work ahead of us, and we're eager to get started. I'm hopeful that the Senate will act quickly to confirm Randall Tobias as our Global AIDS Coordinator, and that the United States Congress will fully fund my request for this lifesaving initiative. I'm also hopeful that other nations of the world will join us to combat the AIDS pandemic."

I couldn't have asked for a more effective endorsement of the program, or a clearer outline of my duties and authority. After the ceremony, I was eager to start—especially given the stakes. As I said in my own remarks that day, HIV/AIDS had already killed roughly 20 million people in sub-Saharan Africa, and if nothing was done, it would kill a fourth of the entire population within the next decade.

But there was one more step to complete before I could assume my role at PEPFAR. As the president mentioned, my appointment had to be confirmed by the United States Senate. I remember thinking, somewhat naively, that this wouldn't be a big deal. I also assumed, incorrectly, that my previous experience as CEO of a major pharmaceutical company might actually count in my favor. But as I quickly learned, nothing could have been further from the truth. My professional experience was viewed with suspicion in many quarters. And while the Senate hearing itself went fairly smoothly, prepping for it proved extremely onerous. This grueling exercise offered a foretaste of the many other bureaucratic challenges to come.

The August hearing would be overseen by Indiana Senator Richard Lugar, who served as chairman of the Senate Foreign Relations Committee. I'd known him for decades, and he and his staff were quite helpful as I prepared for my testimony. In addition to our long personal relationship, Senator Lugar had been singularly instrumental in gaining congressional approval for PEPFAR. Paige had even interned one summer in his Washington office and had had the opportunity to jog with him on more than one morning. But there was very little he could do to assist me with some of the most important requirements, such as gathering the mountain of personal documents and financial data the Senate confirmation process required.

Originally, when it was suggested by the White House Counsel's office, I responded that I thought I wouldn't need an attorney to shepherd me through this process. But I soon learned otherwise. In fact, I eventually paid more in confirmation-associated legal fees and other support services than I received in compensation during my first year on the government payroll and needed three Tobias Family Office employees to meet the deadline to fill out government forms and track down requested information. The more complex a nominee's life had been, and in some ways the more job-qualifying experiences he'd accrued, the more challenging the process. Among a great many other things, I had to submit the text of every speech I'd given in the past decade or so and provide details of every overseas trip I'd made, plus list anyone of note I'd spoken with during those trips. There were also extensive and intrusive financial disclosure requirements, plus rules that (to avoid possible conflicts of interest) forced me to resign from all of the boards on which I served and divest myself of certain investments that the government might, for whatever reason, consider problematic.

The requirements I've listed were only the tip of the iceberg, and over the years, they've grown even more detailed and stringent for the nominees who have followed. If you've ever wondered why more people with significant leadership roles in the private sector, and without the motivation of political ambition, don't go into high-level government service, this is certainly one of the biggest reasons. It's a circus. Honestly, if I were asked to do such a thing again, knowing what I know now, I would refuse. Even back then, if I'd fully understood what I was getting into, it would have given me even greater pause.

In the days before the hearing, I met privately with most members of the Senate Foreign Relations Committee, as is traditional with nominees for posts requiring Senate confirmation. This gives them a chance to get to know you (and you them) privately and for the nominee to make his case one-on-one. So, over the course of several days, I traipsed from office to office on Capitol Hill, spending time talking with individual senators about why I should run PEPFAR. Some visits were purely warm and social with the senator expressing gratitude that I was signing on. But one topic that came up with a few senators on the left of center as well as the right of center was condoms. Or more specifically, whether I was for or against encouraging their use as a way to curtail the spread of HIV/AIDS.

Believe it or not, this particular form of birth control, used also to prevent the transfer of potentially HIV/AIDS-infected bodily fluids, was extremely controversial in some quarters. Some on the right, especially those associated with evangelical Christians, believed that distributing them encouraged sexual promiscuity. They were very much against their use and felt the U.S. government shouldn't condone such efforts, even though the science clearly showed condoms were quite effective in preventing HIV/AIDS transmission. On the other hand, some on the left who cared about it took the view that people were already having sex anyway and that access to condoms could prevent them from getting sick.

I listened to both arguments, sometimes at great length. It certainly wouldn't be the last time.

The list of senators I spoke with included future president Joe Biden, who at the time was the committee's ranking Democrat, but viewed by many as more of an old-style backroom politician than a serious player in foreign policy matters. Our meeting took place in a nook of the Capitol Building, while he was between appointments. Unlike most other Senators on the committee, it did not appear that he had prepared for our meeting other than to read a short summary of my resume. He did however ask me biographical questions not specifically asked by anyone else, but that neatly summed up the reservations I'm sure many harbored about my suitability for the job.

"Are you a medical doctor?" he asked.

"No."

"Do you have a Master's Degree in Public Health?"

"No."

"Have you spent a lot of time in Africa?"

"No."

"Do you know a lot about HIV/AIDS?"

"No."

"Well, why in the world did the president nominate you for this position?"

In response, I told him what President Bush had told me. Namely, that the answer to all of those questions was no. The president already had a lot of people with those credentials. What he was looking for in a leader for the program was someone with a proven track record of running large, complex international organizations. The president's view, which I've come to see was prescient and absolutely correct, was that I could easily surround myself with qualified, capable people who could have answered some or all of Senator Biden's questions with a "yes." But my specific skills and experiences, in the President's view, were absolutely critical and in short supply.

After all the prehearing fact-gathering, studying, and glad-handing, the actual confirmation proceedings went smoothly and were somewhat anticlimactic. Both of my home state senators rose to speak about me. Indiana Senator Evan Bayh, a Democrat, my friend and a former member of the Lilly board, introduced me to the committee with a very gracious speech. Senator Lugar was equally gracious in his opening remarks. I got through the procedure in good shape and was unanimously voted out of the committee and recommended to the full senate, where the final confirmation vote would take place. However, several days passed with no action.

Years later, the public would be surprised and appalled by learning about Alabama Senator Tommy Tuberville's ability to single-handedly block, for months, the approval of all promotions of the most senior military officers requiring senate confirmation as leverage to try to get the Department of Defense to change a policy he didn't like. I soon learned that my confirmation was being delayed by that same procedural tradition, which allowed individual senators to put a hold on nominations, even for no obvious reason. Senator Jeff Sessions, I discovered, had done that with mine.

As is protocol, I dutifully requested an appointment with the senator to find out what I needed to do to satisfy his concerns. But he wasn't interested in a meeting. It turned out the hold had absolutely nothing to do with me. I was just a bargaining chip to get the White House to do something the senator wanted—something entirely unrelated to PEPFAR or me personally. I don't even recall what it was. The issue was quickly ironed out and shortly thereafter I was unanimously approved by the Senate, which sounds much more impressive than it was.

One might imagine that this confirmation would be done during a full session of that August body, with the nominee's name read out and then approved by a voice vote—perhaps with the nominee present. In fact, it happened while only three or four senators were on the Senate floor, plowing through a stack of routine boilerplate work. Someone introduced a resolution with several nominees (including myself) listed on it, the chair asked for unanimous consent, no one among the other three or so present said anything, and it was approved without objection. I only knew about it because I got a phone call telling me the approximate time to watch the proceedings on C-SPAN. The resolution including my name was passed with the perfunctory phrase, "Without objection, so ordered," and my confirmation was sealed. The record showed I had been unanimously confirmed by the Senate.

Not that I'd been entirely idle as I waited for this moment. According to protocol, a nominee isn't supposed to get involved in a Senate-confirmed job until they've actually been confirmed. It's viewed as presumptuous and disrespectful. But though you can't occupy the office you'll use in your official capacity, you can use temporary space set aside for that purpose and perhaps monitor meetings at the organization you'll oversee. But again, technically, you need to keep a low profile, sit at the back of the room, and not participate.

I tried to follow those rules. Mostly.

During the confirmation, there were lots of misconceptions floating around about my role with PEPFAR. The two biggest, in my view, were the ideas that I was probably just a significant donor to the president's campaign (I hadn't been) who was being rewarded with a high-profile ambassadorship and would be a do-nothing political appointee. Or that I would work for the benefit of the U.S. pharmaceutical industry. In addition, PEPFAR was seen by many who were already working on African development programs, or any development program for that matter, as a threat to their own funding. There was only a finite amount of money available for international development, which meant, in their eyes, that the $15 billion going to fight HIV/AIDS would come at the expense of already-existing programs or new initiatives they were pushing. So they did what they could to either derail PEPFAR entirely or to have some of its funding redirected to their own efforts.

Skepticism was rampant—even with the woman who would later become my chief of staff, Nazanin Ash. She, along with many others who'd been battling AIDS in the trenches for years, worried that I might be either a figurehead or, worse, a shill.

Nazanin, as I would soon learn, was an extraordinary young woman. Her name was Nazanin Samari Kermani when I met her. Raised in Los Angeles, her father had come to Kansas from Iran as a Ph.D. student and had stayed after the 1979 Islamic Revolution to eventually become a California bank executive. Her mother, who spoke no English at the time, followed him to the U.S. in an arranged but very loving marriage. She eventually became a teacher. Nazanin was a graduate of both Bryn Mawr College and the Kennedy School of Government at Harvard. She was later to receive the Kennedy School's Rising Star award. Following her Harvard graduation, she worked for a time in Kenya as a program officer for an HIV/AIDS initiative.

In 1993 she was appointed to one of the highly competitive positions as a White House Fellow. Each Fellow spends a year working directly with a cabinet secretary. Nazanin was assigned to spend hers as an aide to Secretary Powell. She asked Powell if instead she could work as an aide to me during the launch of PEPFAR, and he agreed. That was one of the luckiest days of my life. Nazanin became my closest advisor during my time in government—and a good friend. Later she, her husband Tim Ash, and her children all became treasured friends of my entire family. Justice Sandra Day O'Connor once told me that she always referred to the children of her law clerks as her grand-clerks. With that in mind, I refer to the children of my former chief of staff as my grand-chiefs.

Nazanin and those among the preexisting inter-agency AIDS staff soon understood that being the ceremonial head of PEPFAR wasn't what I had in mind. I got my first chance to explain this during an unexpected meeting at the State Department, just before I was confirmed. I happened, by chance, to hear about this gathering (to which I wasn't invited). I assume I wasn't included because I wasn't yet confirmed, although, to my mind, the subject under discussion was obviously something for the new AIDS Ambassador to decide. Nonetheless, people were clearly continuing to manage their various programs, mostly business as usual.

The gathering, chaired by Dr. Joe O'Neil, who headed the White House domestic AIDS office, included the current key inter-agency players in HIV/AIDS, and I'm certain I surprised them by showing up. I took a seat along the wall instead of at the conference table. Although I didn't know it at the time, Nazanin also found a seat among those in the back row.

"We were both backbenchers at a meeting where the interagency AIDS reps had gathered around the table to decide which contractor they would hire to write the PEPFAR strategy," she recalled. "Because Congress had unexpectedly inserted a requirement for a strategy document into the law, in the view of this group, it was just a paper requirement that had to be met—just a box to be checked." Unbeknownst to each other, Nazanin and I were both befuddled by the idea that we wouldn't develop and write the strategy ourselves because in our view it would be the most important first step—the essential road map for what we were going to achieve and how.

As I listened to the other attendees speak, I could tell that many still saw PEPFAR in exactly the wrong way—as a new amalgamation of independent interests with me as a figurehead. That wouldn't do. I put up my hand, rolled my chair up to the table, and used some very direct language to lay out the road map I had in mind.

Nazanin, who sat near me, said that before I spoke, she could feel herself slowly "losing faith in government" (her own words). She recalls me rising and telling the group something that made clear that that was not going to happen. "Why wouldn't we write the strategy ourselves?" she recalls me saying. "It's not just a ceremonial document that's going to sit on a shelf. It's going to be the road map for how we are going to achieve our goals. It's an alignment and communication tool, and it's something we should own and take very, very seriously."

These words greatly relieved her. It was the moment she realized that I would lead PEPFAR personally and not serve as some sort of figurehead. It had certainly been my desire to make sure everyone knew that I intended to take full responsibility for getting things done and that now it was time to put a detailed plan in place and execute it.

As the meeting concluded, Nazanin decided it was a good time to introduce herself and to break the news about her arrangement with Secretary Powell as to how she would spend her time as a White House Fellow.

"That was when I came up to you afterward, introduced myself, and said I was coming to work for you," she recently reminded me.

A NEW AGENCY WITH A NEW STRATEGY

Chapter Twenty-Five

The organization's goals were clear, but the strategy for accomplishing them wasn't.

It didn't take long for me to start wondering what I'd gotten myself into. I wasn't settling into a well-established government job at an already-functioning agency. My initial small team and I had to build everything from the ground up. And I do mean everything. When I arrived in Washington, D.C., to start work, I spent some of my time during my first days on such mundane tasks as finding a place to live, getting a security clearance, and obtaining office space for the organization.

In the meantime, we worked from temporary quarters to get PEPFAR up and running. The organization's goals were clear, but the strategy for accomplishing them wasn't. For instance, after I was finally confirmed, I was handed a single three-ring binder containing a PowerPoint presentation. I was told it comprised the concept for the program, all well-conceived but at a very high level. The rest I would obtain from the language in the enabling legislation and conversations with the people who had been instrumental in getting PEPFAR to that point. And when I asked for some idea of what the planners thought the organization chart and required job descriptions might look like, I received a bare-bones outline drawn on a single sheet of paper.

And by the way, at that point, the program was not yet referred to with an acronym. But if it had been, it would not have been PEPFAR but rather EPFAR. The working name was Emergency Plan for AIDS Relief. The "P" for "President's" was added in our early days because it seemed important to those of us working on the launch that President Bush get full credit for what he was creating.

It seemed like a less-than-auspicious launch pad for an effort with such an ambitious brief. But it was also an opportunity to mostly shape it rather than to reshape it. I saw it as a big positive that PEPFAR was to address three clear five-year goals, meaning the debate about what we were to accomplish would be short. First, we were to find ways to dramatically reduce new cases of HIV/AIDS by two million projected patients. This was to be achieved through innovative efforts such as a newly implemented prevention program for mother-to-child transmission.

Prevention initiatives would also focus on massively expanding testing and behavior change efforts based on "Abstinence, Be Faithful, and Condoms" or "ABC," which was in some ways mandated in the legislation. Second, we were to implement treatment efforts for seven million already-infected patients. This would be done largely through antiretroviral treatment programs and a massive increase in the behind-the-scenes capacity necessary to make that happen. This included the creation of facilities, infrastructure, and management systems. And third, we were to provide care and support to some ten million people living with HIV/AIDS, including palliative care, as well as care for those otherwise impacted, such as the hundreds of thousands of AIDS orphans left behind.

To say I already felt a sense of urgency about our mission would be an understatement. By this time, I had come to understand the worldwide AIDS epidemic as one of the biggest threats our planet faced. The scale of the humanitarian disaster, and its potential to worsen, was so great that it was difficult to grasp. Some 8,000 people were dying of the disease daily—the equivalent of 20 fully loaded Boeing 747 aircraft crashing every day, killing everyone aboard.

Each victim had a name and a family, and their deaths impacted both the global economy and the economies of the countries where they'd lived. Imagine trying to run a company when, each year, perhaps 30 percent of your workforce either dies or becomes too debilitated to continue. You'd have to constantly recruit and train newcomers, and absenteeism would soar because so many had to take care of sick relatives.

Increasingly, that was the economic situation in places like South Africa, Uganda, and Mozambique. But that was hardly the only issue. No matter where they erupt in the world, political unrest and terrorism always spring from the same soil—hopelessness. HIV/AIDS wreaked havoc in impoverished regions where hope was already in short supply. Perhaps not surprisingly, President Bush felt that heading off this sort of turmoil was one of PEPFAR's most important secondary goals. It didn't take a psychic to foresee the sorts of national security and economic problems that a continent cast into turmoil by AIDS might cause.

However, the president's reasons for creating and championing this program were in no way Machiavellian. Through my conversations with him over time, I know the humanitarian belief that we should do this was his primary motivation. He thought that the American people had the economic and technical wherewithal to help and that we had an obligation to do so.

The legislation that created PEPFAR and included the requirement that we put together a strategy document and submit it by a certain date didn't allow much time to think about it. However, as I'd learned during the meeting where I first met Nazanin, this sort of legislative mandate was apparently seen by many veterans of the bureaucracy as mostly a "check the box" exercise. Many seemed to feel that because Congress was requiring it to be done so quickly, it couldn't possibly be done thoughtfully and therefore might not bear much semblance to reality as the real plans developed. In fact, it was assumed it could even be outsourced to a "Beltway contractor" who likely wouldn't ultimately have any involvement in the implementation.

I took a different view. As I'd said in that first meeting, instead of creating something that merely satisfied a mandatory requirement, I wanted to build a real strategic plan from the beginning, and before anything else was done. So, I spent the better part of eight to ten hours a day leading and personally participating in writing PEPFAR's strategy, along with a core group of staffers, among them Nazanin Ash, Dr. Joe O'Neill, Dr. Mark Dybul, Dr. Bill Steiger, Ambassador John Lange, and several others.

Mark Dybul was a very effective scientist and administrator who had also been fighting AIDS since its early days in the U.S. He was a veteran of Dr. Tony Fauci's lab at the National Institutes of Health, was one of the principal conceptual and technical architects of PEPFAR, had important relationships across the government that were very helpful to me, and would not only become my friend and one of my most important partners in developing and leading the organization but would also one day succeed me as the United States Global AIDS coordinator. Initially, Mark was the program's medical director.

Dr. Joe O'Neill was a longtime practitioner in the AIDS world, with degrees in both medicine and public health from the University of California, Berkeley, and the University of California, San Francisco, plus experience fighting AIDS in northern California. He was at the time serving as the director of the White House Office of National AIDS Policy, a small office with an important but mostly domestic focus. He was on the team that drafted the early conceptual plans for what would become PEPFAR. His efforts, along with those of his colleagues Carol Thompson and Tracy Carson, were significant in those early stages of work prior to my arrival—from the initial concept to the approval of the enabling legislation. Joe was initially one of my two deputy coordinators.

Dr. Bill Steiger was Special Assistant to Secretary Tommy Thompson at the Department of Health and Human Services, with the portfolio of international affairs and global health. He was very important in building the critical relationships between PEPFAR and HHS and in the ongoing interagency success of our efforts.

Richard Armitage was at the time the Deputy Secretary of State and a longtime confidant of Secretary Colin Powell. While never directly involved in PEPFAR, he wisely suggested to me that, at least until I had the organization up and running and my own team in place, it would be a good idea to have an experienced senior foreign service officer on my staff who knew his way around the State Department. He then offered up Ambassador John Lange. John had great credentials. In addition to having a long interest in global health issues in Africa, he had risen through the ranks of the career foreign service to become the Chargé d'Affaires (number two) at the U.S. Embassy in Dar es Salaam, Tanzania. When terrorist attacks occurred there and simultaneously at the U.S. Embassy in Kenya in 1998, because of the absence of the U.S. Ambassador to Tanzania at the time, John found himself in charge of the embassy.

Eleven people were killed and 85 seriously injured, and John was subsequently decorated for his leadership and heroism. The attack was eventually attributed to an organization few had heard of at the time—Al-Qaeda. He later served as U.S. Ambassador to Botswana. For a time, John was the second of my two deputy coordinators.

My goal was to create something like the plans I was used to putting together at AT&T and Lilly and had seen in other corporate boardrooms, with specific goals and measurable objectives and with specific people assigned to achieve outputs and outcomes.

Very early on, we developed a rigorous data-gathering and analysis capability led by Dr. Kathy Marconi. I'm not sure who recruited her, but her Ph.D. in sociology and MS in Health Information Management made her a perfect fit and built an underappreciated capability that would be critical to our success. The efforts of Kathy and her team allowed us to track progress toward our numerous objectives and determine which of the many efforts PEPFAR oversaw actually delivered results, which didn't, and how they could be improved or defunded.

The team members, during those first early days of PEPFAR, were pioneers and change agents, doing something in a way and at a scale that the U.S. Government had never done before. Crucial too was the support of a number of people in more senior positions in the White House and elsewhere in the Administration. It required deep collaboration paired with rigorous accountability for results, overseen by a leader empowered with the singular authority to approve inter-agency strategies and funding allocations. Twenty years later, as I write this, I'm eager to recognize those founding and early members of the program's concept, design, and implementation teams in helping the president develop a conceptual plan, get it on paper and translated into legislation, and then—during their time working with me—launch PEPFAR and build the foundation for its success.

With the help of my own files and a few former PEPFAR colleagues, and without trying to parse the relative levels of their individual contributions, large or small, I've simply noted the names of many who played roles of one kind or another in Washington and around the world. Undoubtedly, there will be some that I missed. I apologize profusely for those whose names I haven't been able to pull out of my files or the recesses of my memory. Regardless, I am deeply grateful for the contributions of all those who are memorialized here, along with those who are not. The list includes:

Sylvia Alayon; Richard Armitage; Nazanin Samari Kermani Ash; Dr. Deborah Birx; Amy Black; Josh Bolton; Warren "Buck" Buckingham; Andy Card; Tracy Carson; Julie Chitty; William Dilday; Dr. Mark Dybul; Gary Edson; Dr. Tony Fauci; Adrienne Parrish Fuentes; Dr. Julie Gerberding; Michael Gerson; Sarah Gorrell; Reuben Granich; Michael Grillo; Alex Hammond; Peggy Hoyle; Ambassador Cameron Hume; Ambassador Jimmy Kolker; Heidi Kraft; Christine Kucera; Michelle Moloney-Kitts; Ambassador John Lange; Senator Richard Lugar; Nithya Mani; Dr. Kathy Marconi; Sara Pacqué-Margolis; Frances Marine; Lee McBrearty; Myron Meche; Kristie Mikus; Administrator Andrew Natsios; Dr. Joe O'Neil; Secretary Colin Powell; Elissa Pruett; Karina Rapposelli; Secretary Condoleezza Rice; Nadine Rogers; Carolyn Ryan; Ken Schofield; Ambassador Kristen Silverberg; RJ Simonds; Secretary Margaret Spellings; Dr. Bill Steiger; Karen Stewart; Ann Thomas; Carol Thompson; Secretary Tommy Thompson; Tom Walsh; Carrie Whitlock; and Mitch Wolfe.

In the beginning, perhaps not surprisingly, a lot of people thought PEPFAR would conduct itself like many other federal entities. The marching orders would come from the Washington,

D.C., headquarters, and the people in the various target countries (who might be locals or international NGOs) were expected to carry them out to the letter. Indeed, that was the concept in the minds of many of those involved in the planning prior to my arrival. But I had other ideas.

Once more, building on my corporate experience, I saw a big difference between determining "what" we would set out to achieve and deciding "how" we would go about achieving it. I was therefore focused on centralized strategic goal-setting with clear measurables, along with as much decentralized implementation as made sense. I believed that Washington should set overall targets and then work with agencies in various countries on how to best implement and achieve them, with an emphasis on identifying and engaging local partners and supporting their ideas and approaches. While their methods could vary depending on circumstances, it was very important that everyone stay focused on those three overarching goals and not be distracted by their own personal agendas. And at least in the long term, I was interested in bringing in as many local organizations as possible to accomplish this. I wanted the "boots on the ground" to have intimate knowledge of the situation, the trust of the people who would need their help, and skin in the game. I also wanted to build local capacity so the programs would be sustainable when the outsiders went home.

I didn't want us to micromanage from half a world away in Washington. But we also didn't want to stray too far in the other direction, particularly so in giving local governments and bureaucrats unfettered control over PEPFAR funds. It took a great deal of discipline, work, and leadership to develop the right approach because a lot of vested interests, international and domestic, governments and NGOs, and even members of Congress with interests in specific potential implementing organizations, wanted us to simply hand over the cash and leave them alone. For example, very early in my tenure, Ken Hackett, the highly respected head of Catholic Relief Services, came to see me both to get acquainted and to try to convince me that his organization should help implement PEPFAR's agenda—in exchange for significant funding from our $15 billion budget, of course. In an effort to sell the international charity's acumen, he mentioned the work it did in one African country.

"We've been there 26 years and have a very successful program," he said.

Over time, as they understood what was required to implement programs that focused on our goals, Catholic Relief Services became a helpful partner. But during that first meeting, I said, "Ken, stop right there. If your principal selling point is that you've been there 26 years, that's not what I'm looking for. I'm looking for people who want to do what needs to be done, train and support local people to do that work, and then back away as much as possible in favor of the local capacity they've built. Sure, we may need to be there a long time to help with technology, money, and capacity building, but a permanent lead presence as a point of pride isn't what I have in mind."

With our strategy in hand, I next enlisted the frontline leadership assistance I needed. I learned that there was a regularly scheduled meeting of the U.S. Ambassadors to the various sub-Saharan African countries planned for Johannesburg, which coincided quite fortuitously with my Senate confirmation. So I invited myself, and within days, maybe hours, of officially taking office I was on a plane to South Africa. At that meeting, I essentially told them, "I have a new job, and you do, too. If this is going to be successful, I need you as my partners."

Not surprisingly, they had lots of questions, and not surprisingly, I had only some of the answers. My recollection is that they were some combination of apprehensive, suspicious, grateful, and enthusiastic, but one way or another, they were on board. They quickly helped pull together in each of their countries an interagency team of people who were mostly already deployed, from the State Department, the Department of Health and Human Services, the Centers for Disease Control, the Department of Defense, the Peace Corps, the Department of Commerce, and others. I was amazed to learn how many people from how many places in the government were already on the ground working on HIV/AIDS, but with no coordinated strategy or leadership and totally inadequate resources. I asked them all to, in effect, leave their "organization-specific uniforms" at the door and think about their tasks going forward not as efforts for their specific agencies but as integrated United States government programs under the President's Emergency Plan. They were, for the most part, eager to sign on.

After a great deal of work, we released PEPFAR's strategy document in early 2004. I was proud of what we produced. It was a comprehensive guide that detailed our goals (prevention, treatment, and care) and then in some detail outlined how we planned to accomplish those goals. We then started coordinating with the teams in each country, determining how we could best work together in their cities and villages to implement our strategy and turn it into actual lives impacted and saved.

Given the gravity of the situation, we had no time to waste. We began by working with and expanding the programs of certain nongovernment agencies already operating in the target countries. The idea was to get a fast start by quickly reinforcing existing efforts already making a difference because those programs were up and running. But to some degree, this first phase was an approach I inherited, a result of the focus on more centralized control that existed in the minds of the planners before my arrival. It was also an opportunity for a fast start because designing more sophisticated follow-up efforts for the longer term that specifically targeted our objectives would require more time. By the end of February of 2004, roughly a month after Congress appropriated the first of PEPFAR's funds, we'd already moved approximately $365 million toward those preexisting organizations, which I considered an astonishing accomplishment—and still do.

Obviously, deciding (in the interest of speed) to allocate some top-down funding to those existing big international NGO programs somewhat undermined my assertions that this was going to be an effort largely implemented at the local level. But everyone, including the big NGOs themselves, soon learned I was totally serious about quickly pivoting to a more local focus.

By the middle of 2004, each of the 15 focus countries had completed five-year plans that, when taken together, comprised the heart of our overall implementation program. We had by then authorized a total of $865 million, the additional half billion dollars skewed heavily toward the country-identified programs. Periodically, we would meet with the leadership from each country to appraise results against objectives. Going forward, it was envisioned that each year each country team would present its operational plan for the next year, including specific programs they wanted to fund or continue to fund, the measurable objectives of those programs, who would carry them out, and how success would be measured.

Assembling PEPFAR's strategy required our core staff to put in plenty of long hours. But getting things organized and everyone pointed at least mostly in the same direction was the easy part. What came next was the hard, year-over-year work of making a difference with real people in a globe-spanning effort, making sure we truly saved the lives we set out to save. It required billions of dollars, the work of tens of thousands, and close attention to a million details.

Often, it was a case of two steps forward and one step back, and sometimes two back. But I was very pleased with the progress we made and extremely proud of the people in Washington and around the world who helped make it happen. As for myself, I had a great deal of traveling in front of me. Before my duty ended, I would visit every country on our intervention list (often multiple times) and receive more AIDS tests than, arguably, any other person on the planet.

GETTING (ALMOST) EVERYONE ON THE SAME PAGE

Chapter Twenty-Six

I just wanted to save lives, by whatever methods worked most efficiently. If that meant distributing condoms on a grand scale, I was all in.

Helping PEPFAR deliver on its many promises required monumental organizational and logistical efforts and the work of tens of thousands. But it also required tact and diplomacy. We had to address, acknowledge, sometimes humor, and occasionally simply ignore the various VIPs, private organizations, individual members of Congress, and various government departments that felt, for a variety of reasons, that they deserved a say in what we did.

One of the first issues I faced was a lingering distrust among AIDS organizations and activists of both PEPFAR in general and me in particular.

PEPFAR, it was intimated, was a program that would gut other AIDS projects, particularly the newly established Global Fund, a multinational effort that operated independently but was loosely under the UN umbrella and based in Geneva. As the former CEO of a major pharmaceutical company, I was seen in some circles as someone who would have a bias toward steering PEPFAR cash to U.S. drugmakers.

Hard to believe that when I was first approached about this job, I actually considered my professional background to be a plus.

I came to realize, as time passed, that too often the government's general view about political appointees from the private sector with experience and expertise is that you shouldn't have any job that you're actually qualified to have. Because, if you possess a background in one aspect or another of a particular industry, it's automatically viewed by many as a conflict of interest. Most AIDS advocacy groups initially saw me that way.

I'd actually anticipated the turmoil created by AIDS activists (however well-meaning they might have been) during my days at Lilly. Many, in my own experience, seemed to unintentionally obstruct the development of new drugs by stirring up controversy and advocating for ever-increasing government oversight. With my direct support (when the decision was made by the Lilly research organization), the company had exited what little AIDS work it was doing because, first and foremost, we simply lacked the in-house expertise to achieve any competitive advantage. But another concern, which ran a close second, was the feeling many of us had that the entire endeavor was rife with unhelpful advocacy politics. The thought that this was a big target of opportunity for the pharmaceutical industry didn't occur to me.

Unfortunately, some people in the governments of the various PEPFAR host countries (some as powerful as they were unscrupulous) seemed to see the program itself either as a huge opportunity to increase their power or line their pockets or as a potential threat to their own authority that they wanted to bring to heel.

PEPFAR's plan was to distribute money directly to frontline non-government organizations rather than through government health ministries and then to carefully monitor where the cash went and whether it achieved what had been agreed to before deciding whether to renew grant contracts. This amounted to a radically new way of distributing foreign aid. No wonder I had to spend so much time explaining the concept—sometimes quite firmly—to so many leaders, both foreign and domestic. For instance, I remember one particularly difficult conversation with Manto Tshabalala-Msimang. She was, at the time, the controversial Minister of Health in South Africa. For a long time, she had denied that AIDS even existed.

In our first meeting, when I was actually expecting to be thanked for what we were offering to do, she told me point-blank that PEPFAR wouldn't be allowed to sponsor programs in South Africa unless we gave our funding directly to her so that she could decide how it was spent. I told her we wouldn't do that, and after some prickly negotiations in the days and weeks ahead, we got our way. Our U.S. Ambassador to South Africa at the time, Cameron Hume, was an early and enthusiastic advocate for PEPFAR and enormously helpful in managing our relations with the government.

Some of the schemes we encountered were a bit more sophisticated. For instance, the president of Nigeria informed me that he'd decided his country should manufacture generic forms of AIDS-related medications and that he wanted to use PEPFAR funds to buy those drugs for use in his country. I politely declined. We found out later that one of his close relatives was slated to run the company that would make them.

The term "generic drugs" had become something of a holy grail to AIDS advocacy groups. They were seen as an obvious and more cost-effective way to treat the infected. In actual practice, a generic drug is a compound using the same chemical formula as a name-brand product and manufactured under the same highly controlled processes, overseen by the FDA, as are those made by research pharmaceutical companies. Legitimate generic drugs are substantially cheaper than the original name-brand compounds because the producer doesn't have to recoup the very large research and development costs associated with creating the original product. They simply have to competently create a no-name equivalent with the same formulation, quality, and intended use. From the very beginning, there was a lot of support for the term "generics" from well-meaning but naïve activist groups, who generally took the view that all generics were of the same quality as the originals, no matter who made them, under what circumstances, or even whether or not the patents involved were still in effect.

We wanted to protect the intellectual property of companies that originally developed specific drugs that had not yet passed the time when their patented formulation must be made available to other companies to be produced as generics. However, we were also totally in favor of using true off-patent generics, approved by the FDA and meeting the agency's standards, wherever possible. But, as illustrated by the dangers in the "plan" put forth in Nigeria, we wanted to make sure they were actually effective and not just some sort of scheme. So I worked out an agreement with Secretary Tommy Thompson at Health and Human Services, to whom the Food and Drug Administration reported and who was a strong advocate for PEPFAR. He supported an initiative at the FDA to institute a fast-track approval process for any generic AIDS drug candidate from anyplace in the world, not just the U.S., even if there was no intent to market that drug in the U.S.

This meant that any international generic could be examined for efficacy and safety by the FDA and, if it passed inspection, would become eligible for purchase as part of the PEPFAR program, in Africa or elsewhere. So, from that time on, when someone in one of the PEPFAR countries told me they wanted to acquire a so-called generic compound from their own nation, I could say, "Terrific, I will buy any generics that go through the generic drug approval process of the FDA, which means that it must demonstrate that it's equivalent to the drug that was originally invented."

Sometimes, when the possibility of FDA scrutiny was raised, the issue was simply dropped. However, a handful of generics, such as those from established companies in Israel and India, followed this road to approval and were acquired using PEPFAR funding.

Activists on both the political left and right also had issues with PEPFAR's congressionally mandated emphasis on abstinence. In other words, trying to convince people to stem AIDS transmission by just not having sex. Many very vocal groups accused us of either doing too much of this or too little.

Similar controversies arose on many different occasions over matters both great and small. For instance, another one of the questions that bedeviled me repeatedly was the issue of condoms and whether they were "good" or "bad." As I mentioned earlier, absolutely no one ever contested the fact that AIDS was a serious crisis in the nations PEPFAR served and that the groups of people it attacked varied from region to region. In the U.S. and Europe, for instance, the disease first gained a foothold and expanded among the gay male population. In Africa, however, it was just as common among women as men. Typically, females contracted it from males who had sex with an already-infected partner outside of marriage.

This was accepted by the members of Congress in a pretty bipartisan way. The idea of using condoms to combat it, however, most definitely wasn't. Democrats in general felt we should use this tactic more, while many Republicans, specifically social conservatives, thought easy access to prophylactics encouraged promiscuity.

I witnessed this divergence in action whenever I testified before Congress, which happened regularly during my government tenure.

On one of those occasions, I found myself before the House Committee on Foreign Affairs. As was protocol, the questions alternated between Republican and Democratic members in order of descending seniority. At one point, I was berated by a liberal Democrat for not purchasing and distributing condoms in what she considered sufficient numbers. Never mind that in my very first year as Global AIDS Coordinator I purchased more condoms on behalf of the government than had been purchased during the entire eight years of the Clinton Administration. It just wasn't good enough.

It was obvious that the congresswoman wasn't actually speaking to me, but rather trying to get a pleasing sound bite for her constituency (as often happened with politicians). I got through this as best I could. Then, when her turn was up, a Republican social conservative congressman promptly chastised me for buying too many condoms, saying the entire PEPFAR program should focus on abstinence and faithfulness to married partners. And yes, he too spoke not so much to me as to his constituency back home.

The "lifestyle modification" portion of the PEPFAR program was nicknamed ABC: abstinence, being faithful, and using condoms consistently and correctly. This wasn't an American invention. It was originally developed by Yoweri Museveni, the president of Uganda, when he recognized that AIDS was becoming an enormous problem in his country.

As I explained at the time to various and sometimes highly skeptical news outlets and organizations, abstinence focused heavily on teaching young people that the best way to avoid infection was to forego sexual activity until they were old enough for a committed relationship and then to be faithful within that committed relationship. Those two things together clearly helped lower Uganda's infection rates.

The final component of the ABC plan, the judicious use of condoms, recognized that there were individuals in high-risk situations who, either by choice or coercion, couldn't or didn't choose to follow steps A and B. Therefore, they needed access to condoms and lessons in their proper use.

This was controversial, but the ABC plan was baked into the legislation that created PEPFAR, so ignoring that approach was never an option. In reality, it never became the impediment to our work that its detractors thought it could be, in part because we never had a problem that I'm aware of with meeting the requirements. We simply did the things we were planning on doing anyway. In addition, even if adhering strictly to the legislative directive had become an issue, in my view, to paraphrase an old Chinese proverb, "Heaven is high, and the emperor is far away." Those who advocated for an abstinence approach seldom, if ever, found themselves in places like the hinterlands of the southern African country of Namibia, where the work of saving lives actually got done. Out in the field, and unknown to me, I'm sure the rules were occasionally bent or even ignored. The local people, who didn't have to deal with zealous members of the U.S. Congress, typically did whatever worked.

I found just such a situation in Windhoek, the capital of the nation of Namibia. There I met a very practical Belgian nun and physician, who had for some time run a highly successful HIV/AIDS program. When I arrived for a visit, she greeted me in her full nun's habit—the very symbol of Catholic conservatism and something that I hadn't seen in a while. And indeed, the clinic was funded by a Catholic missionary group. Yet, as I sat briefly with her in her office before the official tour started, I noticed a large bowl absolutely brimming with condoms. As head of PEPFAR,

I'd caused tens of millions of condoms to be purchased. But seeing them in a Catholic relief mission took me aback.

At first, I didn't say anything. But after spending the next few hours touring the facility, where I observed additional bowls of condoms, I felt like we'd developed a real rapport. So, when we found ourselves back in the privacy of her office at the end of the visit, I said, "Sister, I hope you don't mind my asking, but I can't help but notice the bowls of condoms. I'm surprised to see them here."

She told me that despite her Catholic convictions about not approving the use of condoms for birth control, I should understand that she distributed them in her clinic solely to prevent the transmission of AIDS. And besides, she told me, she knew she also had some cover. With a smile, she told me that her Cardinal, who had visited her clinic, was well aware of what she was doing and had assured her, "It's a long way from Rome to Windhoek!"

The nun knew that because she was saving lives—and that many of the rules cooked up half a world away simply weren't relevant on her corner of the planet—she had a more-or-less free hand to carry on. It was something similar to the way I saw my own brief. I certainly didn't go out of my way to violate the letter of the PEPFAR legislation. Indeed, quite the contrary. But I also didn't interfere unnecessarily with the best practices of local agencies. When it came to helping people, they usually knew what was best.

As for my own personal views, I just wanted to save lives, by whatever methods worked most efficiently. If that "whatever works" approach meant distributing condoms on a grand scale, I was all in. But if encouraging abstinence also worked to a degree, then that was also fine. I don't think that particular effort did any harm, but frankly, it was not an across-the-board approach in which I had much confidence. I strongly suspected it made much more sense to those in the hearing rooms of the U.S. Congress than in the bedrooms of the cities, towns, and villages of sub-Saharan Africa. Regardless, in my view, it was better to get on with the extremely urgent work at hand than to waste time complaining about the wording of our authorization documents. A lot of people spent a lot of energy worrying about and trying to change the law. If it came to it, I was prepared to put more effort into asking for forgiveness rather than seeking permission.

While it couldn't help with Congress, I nonetheless felt confident in taking this approach because of the support I received from the president and the shield it provided against agencies and groups, inside and outside the government, that sought to influence the program. To put it simply, one of the reasons PEPFAR succeeded was because I knew that when someone told me, "The White House says you need to do such and such," I didn't automatically assume this meant the directive had to be followed.

Let me explain.

Phrases like "The White House wants this," and "The White House wants that," are heard all the time in Washington. However, when I got such a request I typically asked, "Who actually said it? Was it the president himself? Or was it the pastry chef?" Because the president cared so deeply about this effort, I knew that if he truly desired something, he would let me know personally or through one of his closest aides. So in most cases, when these important-sounding instructions arrived, I felt secure in ignoring them. And in most cases, those requests would simply go away. No further action was required.

This might have irritated some White House staffers who weren't President Bush himself, but in truth, I didn't care. I suppose if I'd wanted to climb the ranks in Washington, I would have gone out of my way to please everybody. But that was far from the case. I hadn't volunteered for this particular assignment and wasn't interested in enhancing a political power base or angling for a new, bigger government job. I was there to manage PEPFAR and nothing else. It gave me freedom and flexibility to do what was right, or what I thought was right.

It proved extremely helpful in our plan to use already-existing local programs in rural villages, many of which happened to be faith-based, to jump-start PEPFAR. Indeed, if the president had told me I couldn't use faith-based organizations, as soon as I got the lay of the land, I would have said, "You can't do this without them." In all the countries where we set to work, no matter the spot on the map, faith-based organizations were already on the ground—large international groups, U.S. organizations, but most importantly local congregations. They formed the heart and soul of thousands of communities. In many ways, they were the backbone of our work. They served places where no one else wanted to go. In Ethiopia, the patriarch of the Ethiopian Orthodox Church told me, and it was very true, that you could go places in his country where there were no police, no roads, no water, and no sanitation, but the Ethiopian Orthodox Church was there.

I'd like to reiterate, however, that while I made no particular effort to censure people in the field who bent the rules slightly when it suited the local situation, I also felt the ABC approach could sometimes be productive. The ABC concept worked quite well in this environment, though, as previously noted, it had to be "customized" to reflect the reality on the ground, where even the seemingly cut-and-dried concept of being faithful was open to interpretation. For instance, there are some African cultures where it's very common for men to have two, three, or four wives. In those circumstances, it's important for the husband in such an arrangement to remain faithful within this group of wives.

The fact of the matter is that each letter in the ABC philosophy represented, sequentially, a fallback position if the letter before it didn't work. For obvious reasons, abstinence is close to 100 percent effective at stopping the sexual transmission of AIDS. If that strategy failed (and in my own view it often did), one could fall back to B, which was being faithful to a partner or partners. Because even if a man had four wives, it was vastly safer for all involved if he never went outside the individuals in his family. And if A and B didn't work or weren't practicable, there was C, which was condoms.

SEEING AIDS UP CLOSE

Chapter Twenty-Seven

I didn't expect to die while doing this job, but nevertheless it occasionally seemed entirely possible.

To say that PEPFAR changed my life would be an understatement. Before I took the job, I was essentially in full retirement mode. I showed up at the Tobias Family Office regularly but wore casual clothes instead of a business suit. I sat on several corporate boards, but I also divided my time throughout the year among Indiana, Montana, and Florida, and spent a great deal of time with family and friends.

It was pretty idyllic.

Exhausted after returning from a long trip, I found myself ruminating about that existence one Sunday night while I stood in the checkout line of the 24-hour Safeway grocery store in the Washington, D.C., neighborhood of Georgetown, buying eggs and some other essentials. I visited that store fairly regularly because it was the closest grocery to the small condo where I lived.

As I waited to pay for my purchases, I remember facetiously thinking to myself, "I have great help in the family office, someone who works for me at my Montana ranch, and people taking care of my properties in Florida and Indiana. So why am I standing here in line at 8 o'clock on a Sunday night, getting groceries? What's wrong with this picture?"

Of course, I wasn't serious. I knew that any inconveniences I endured were more than balanced by the good I helped PEPFAR accomplish. During those days, I made at least half a dozen trips to Africa. Each typically lasted ten days or so and included visits to multiple countries, where I spoke to everyone from government officials to frontline AIDS relief workers and the patients they served. It was vastly different from the numerous overseas trips I'd taken over the years for AT&T and Lilly and the other corporations on whose boards I served. They gave me a visceral, ground-level understanding of the human toll of AIDS.

My first such journey took place shortly after my congressional confirmation, when I accompanied Tommy Thompson, Secretary of the Department of Health and Human Services, on a tour to survey the situation. Thompson had lobbied intensely to have PEPFAR assigned to Health and Human Services until the president made it clear that he wanted an independent entity, nominally reporting to Secretary of State Colin Powell but without being integrated in any way into the existing State Department bureaucracy.

This made the long-planned trip somewhat problematic. Having the leader of PEPFAR shepherded around Africa by Thompson simply wouldn't do, and Tommy understood that. So instead, the journey was co-hosted by a triumvirate consisting of the secretary, myself, and Ambassador Richard Holbrook, a retired career foreign service officer and lifelong Democrat who, if Al Gore had won the 2000 presidential election, might well have become secretary of state. At the time, Richard lived in New York where he was an investment banker and also chaired the board of a not-for-profit AIDS advocacy effort on behalf of corporations doing business in Africa. We subsequently became good friends and eventually saw each other socially.

Holbrook was about my age and a great guy with a bigger-than-life personality. At the time, he was well-known (through his media presence) primarily for two things: serving as U.S. Ambassador to the United Nations and overseeing the peace process that created the Dayton Accords, which ended the war in the former Yugoslavia. I didn't know him personally until he called me out of the blue, shortly after my appointment.

"I just wanted to introduce myself and offer any help and support I can," he said. "You're a Republican, I'm a Democrat, so there are some things I can do to help you because I have relationships you're never going to have."

Before concluding the call, he offered me an unexpected bit of counsel.

"One thing that's going to come out of this miserable job you've taken on is that you're going to have the title of ambassador for the rest of your life," he told me. "Do not hesitate to use it. Because it will, without exception, get you the best reservations in restaurants for the rest of your life." We had a good laugh at the time, but the fact is, he was right!

And so, we found ourselves touring Africa together along with a number of others who were important to this effort, including Dr. Tony Fauci. It was a revelation. Of course, I was familiar with the statistics concerning the carnage of AIDS. But now, for the first time, I saw it up close.

During the trip, we divided our party into small groups to pursue different itineraries. I, along with Dr. Julie Gerberding, the head of the Centers for Disease Control (CDC) and someone who would become a big supporter of our efforts, visited the Ugandan countryside to watch healthcare workers delivering help to patients in a tiny village. While there, I spoke with a 12-year-old boy who sat in front of a mud hut that was his home. His father had died of AIDS and was buried out back, behind the family garden. His mother was HIV positive and part of a U.S.-funded treatment program. I learned that on that very day the boy had completed his last year of free public education. Going beyond grade school meant he had to pay fees, and there was absolutely no hope for him to do that. As I recall, the part of the country where he lived suffered from 60 percent unemployment. In summary, his father was dead from AIDS, his mother was dying from AIDS, at age 12 he'd completed all the formal education available to him, and he had little opportunity to get a job. That's hopelessness.

Over the years, I saw many different versions of this same, terrible scenario—parents either dead or dying of AIDS, leaving behind children to fend for themselves. In some cases, orphaned boys and girls no older than that unfortunate 12-year-old Ugandan became the heads of their families and assumed responsibility for their younger siblings. To this day, I find myself thinking about them. What I saw is so thoroughly burned into my mind that it never really went away.

That journey was the first of many on PEPFAR's behalf. Typically, my African excursions began not with a ride on a government plane but with a regular commercial flight. In those days, pretty much the only way to get to Africa from the U.S. was by flying into South Africa's capital city, Johannesburg. I and my small team would usually depart on a 747 either from New York or Dulles International Airport near Washington, D.C. The size of the group that accompanied me varied, but there was pretty much always a three-person nucleus composed of myself; my chief of staff, Nazanin, or a key member of the policy staff such as Amy Black; and finally, the person referred to as my "body man."

Amy was an accomplished and dedicated young woman who came to the State Department as part of a fellowship program for high-potential people. She was very committed to Africa and PEPFAR and was a very valued advisor and contributor to PEPFAR's success. The two body men during my time in this role were both energetic, recent college graduates who tackled all of the trip's logistical issues, such as handling luggage and arranging ground transportation and accommodations. The first was Alex Hammond, who signed on after holding the same job for the White House Drug Czar. Alex was a graduate of the University of Texas and quite coincidentally an Indianapolis native. He was eventually replaced by Lee McBrearty, an Auburn University graduate and a native of Fairhope, Alabama. Alex later went on to earn a law degree, and Lee his MBA. Both did an outstanding job of managing the complexities of our journeys and were great traveling companions as well. I'm very grateful to both for their dedication and friendship.

Though I might arrive from the U.S. on a 747, air travel within Africa could be more problematic. In fact, I believe it constituted one of the biggest potential dangers to my personal safety.

When it was necessary to travel to remote locations, I got around in twin-engine prop planes that sometimes sported a bit of duct tape here and there. We would take off from a major city airport and then land way out in the boonies where our programs were operating, often on a dirt road, because in some of the places we visited, actual airports were few and far between.

We had rules during both my AT&T and Lilly days that any flights that carried me or others had to meet well-established safety standards, including having two pilots. That, to put it mildly, was not the rule with many of these flights, where there was rarely more than one pilot. Sometimes, I would sit in the copilot's seat rather than in the cabin. On more than one bumpy trip, with an incoming storm looming and a perilous landing approach under way, I nervously scanned the control yolk and instrument panel, wondering if I could remember enough to land the plane if there was an in-flight pilot emergency.

I didn't expect to die while doing this job, but nevertheless it occasionally seemed entirely possible, given the number of dicey things I needed to do. I remember saying to Todd and Paige, "I just want you to know that if something ever happens to me, you need to know that I fully understood the risk. I've had a terrific life, and if something happens, I'm doing work that I think is important and worthwhile."

Again, I certainly didn't expect to die, but I meant every word of that. And during my time at PEPFAR, I never stopped traveling and taking calculated risks. But it was worth it. I met amazing people and had tremendous and mind-changing experiences. They were the sorts of things that I never would have encountered had I spent those years sitting on my front porch in Montana or gazing out at the Gulf of Mexico in Florida. I moved far out of my comfort zone, and the vivid memories of those travels—and the results they helped achieve—tell me that the hassle and the danger were well worth it.

While many of my trips involved meeting with government officials, just as many were spent in the field with grassroots organizations implementing our programs. Our intent was to work with people who achieved results in the AIDS battle, including those whose methods seemed somewhat unorthodox to Western eyes. That predilection was how I once found myself in the South African province of KwaZulu-Natal, discussing the fate of a chicken with a faith healer.

In this part of South Africa, that's what they called women in this profession who relied on traditional remedies mixed with a large dose of spirituality. We would probably say witch doctor. Some were born into this role, passing the craft from generation to generation. Some took it up because they or their elders felt it was their calling. They typically dressed in traditional garb, but with beaded headdresses with lots of feathers and other touches to signify the fact that their work was distinctly beyond the mundane.

If someone needed to get rid of evil spirits that were causing headaches, these people would burn the appropriate herbs and say the right words to cure the problem. Though the more modern faith healers could also set a broken limb. Midwifery skills were the stock and trade of many, and some had added to their abilities and credibility by taking emergency medical technician (EMT) training, thus learning to deal with injuries in a conventional way. But even then they would also burn the appropriate sacred herbs and wave the smoke over their patients to help them get well and to establish their credentials.

We'd developed an AIDS program with the cooperation of the chief KwaZulu-Natal traditional healer, and I visited to sign an agreement to finance her efforts to the tune of $2 million. The money was to, among other things, fund a program to put more of the area's faith healers through EMT training, plus purchase the necessary drugs and equipment for that work. Her objective (and ours) was to give them more modern medical capabilities without at the same time undermining their credibility as respected practitioners of the traditional ways of healing. In return, PEPFAR funding also allowed her to offer AIDS testing and provide treatment. The efficacy of having local, already-trusted people instead of foreign doctors perform these tests on villagers was pretty obvious. It was easier to get patients to go for treatment at places where they were used to going.

So, we had a signing ceremony. Afterward, as is traditional in that part of the world when a distinguished guest visits, they are typically gifted with some type of livestock. When I traveled to Africa on an economic development trip during Bush 41's presidency, I remember Vice President Dan Quayle was presented with a horse by the leader of a village we visited. Secretary Tommy Thompson was given a cow during our earlier trip, which he adroitly donated to a healthcare facility in the village he visited. The conventional wisdom on such matters soon became my standing policy: "Never leave the village with the cow."

In this particular case, however, it wasn't a cow I had to deal with. Instead, immediately after the document signing, one of the chief traditional healer's assistants handed her a chicken to present to me. It would have been insulting to reject it, so I thanked her profusely to make clear it was now my chicken. Then I said, "Now that I know about all the good work you're doing here, and that there are patients in need of nourishment to get well, I would like to donate my chicken to you to be used as food for those patients who would benefit from it."

When this was translated into Swahili for the traditional healer, she instantly got a twinkle in her eye and replied via the translator, who told me, "She wants to know how you would trust her to not just eat the chicken herself."

Thinking fast, I said, "Well, we've just signed an agreement for a great deal of money, and I'm prepared to trust that you're going to use it in the ways we've agreed. If I can trust you to carry out this agreement, I can certainly trust you to do the right thing with my chicken."

The traditional healer laughed in response, took the bird, and handed it off to an assistant. We continued with our meeting, and about 20 minutes later I happened to notice somebody passing by with the freshly plucked, dead chicken, taking it away to be cooked.

During my trips to Africa, I believe I might have also established a very unusual personal record. Though there's no way to prove it, I think it's likely that I've taken more AIDS tests than anyone else in sub-Saharan Africa, if not the world.

I became a living pincushion because it helped encourage average people in the places we visited to also get tested. Knowing your status was a key to AIDS prevention, and getting tested was the way to learn if you were infected. Just as in the U.S. at the time, there was a stigma attached to the procedure because getting the test seemed to imply that you were doing highly suspect things. So I tried to help change the narrative. Instead of telling people, in effect, "You need to get AIDS tested," we started using the phrase, "We need to get AIDS tested."

To drive this home, I took advantage of every opportunity to get an AIDS test in public—in front of local newspaper reporters and photographers, and on television. I'd also try to get the mayor or some other well-known person, perhaps even a movie star or celebrity, to take the test with me. The very first time I did this was with the mayor of Addis Ababa, the capital of Ethiopia.

Soon this became part of my shtick. I don't know how many times I did this during my government service, but I'm sure the number was at least in the teens. I once got tested in China with a man I was told was one of the country's biggest movie stars.

There was only one thing that worried me about this process—the skills and emotional state of the person doing the blood draw. This task often fell to a local tech who might be deeply rattled by the prospect of taking blood from a foreign bigwig and perhaps a local luminary while sometimes on live TV. So it wasn't unusual for their hands to shake as they stuck the needle in my arm—sometimes repeatedly.

Though the majority of my PEPFAR trips carried me to Africa, that wasn't the only place I visited. Two of the nations the program targeted—Guyana and Haiti—are in South America and the Caribbean, respectively. I remember, in Haiti, visiting a program that illustrated in a nutshell the sorts of attitudes and socioeconomic issues that could make AIDS prevention so very difficult.

It was an effort to help young women get out of sex work (one of the main AIDS transmission vectors) by training them to become hairdressers. The idea was to get them off the street and into a profession where they could earn a living. I asked one of the students, who couldn't have been much over 18, what she planned to do when she finished her training. Her response drove home just how different the world looks to someone struggling to survive than it does to some high-minded Washington, D.C., politician.

"I'm going to work in a salon during the week, but I'm going to continue being a sex worker on the weekends," she told me. "The money is just too good. I can't make that kind of money doing anything else."

Things like that cleared up any delusions one might have about just how difficult changing behavior could be.

I also went to various international gatherings, including the 2004 Global AIDS Conference in Thailand, where I was a featured speaker. Thousands attended this particular event, including many, many AIDS activists. And, as with activists in general, many of them were very angry about various things and wanted their voices heard. A couple of years earlier, Tommy Thompson had addressed this event, and the activists caused such a ruckus when he was trying to speak that he got angry and stalked off the stage—which was, of course, exactly what they wanted.

When it was time for me to speak, I got pretty much the same treatment. Protesters came to the front of the room and started shouting and waving signs that said things like, "He lies." It went on and on, and I couldn't get a word in edgewise. But instead of abandoning the stage to them, I just stood at the podium. For almost an hour. I figured if they had something to say, fine. But I wasn't going anywhere, and when they got tired of yelling, I'd make my remarks. I kept my place while the event's organizers negotiated with the protesters, who finally agreed that they would stand in front of me with their signs, but remain silent.

And so, I finally gave my speech. It was bizarre. Definitely the toughest crowd I've ever addressed.

I met fascinating people and enjoyed some unique experiences during my travels. But the things that made the greatest impressions and formed the longest-lasting memories were the somber encounters with the men, women, and children whose lives were wrecked by AIDS.

On one occasion, I visited the nation of Mozambique to see a home care volunteer program we funded. I went to a woman's home, which was a small, mud brick building with no windows and a dirt floor. We had to use a flashlight just to find our way. Lying on a mattress on the ground was an AIDS-infected woman who probably couldn't have weighed more than 70 pounds and who was in the last hours of her life. And seated on a corner of the mattress where she lay was her five-year-old daughter.

The little girl was already essentially alone, other than when volunteers stopped by. I asked what was going to happen when her mother passed and learned that no one knew for sure. Her father had already died of AIDS and there were no other known relatives. The sad fact is she was probably destined for the street.

Experiences like this were heartbreakingly common, and as I mentioned earlier, they changed the way I viewed the AIDS crisis. Believe me, seeing just one dying mother and soon-to-be homeless child very quickly turns what might be perceived as a somewhat esoteric issue into something very, very real. I think if more people had had such experiences, we as a nation would have probably felt a much greater urgency about AIDS. As I've said before, this issue wasn't front-and-center for me before the president asked me to serve. But after what I've seen, it will be for the rest of my life.

NAVIGATING WASHINGTON AND TACKLING AN EVEN BIGGER JOB

Chapter Twenty-Eight

I believed I'd done what I'd been asked to do and that it was time for me to head back to Indianapolis.

Though I traveled quite a bit during my roughly four years of government service, I spent most of my days in Washington, D.C., navigating the city's tangled bureaucracy. I began by running PEPFAR, but after two years, I would find myself leading the United States' entire foreign aid program.

During the interim between my PEPFAR nomination by President Bush and my Senate confirmation, I worked from a temporary space in the State Department, which keeps a very small number of vacant offices for use by high-level nominees. Since I nominally reported to Colin Powell, this made perfect sense.

But I worried about becoming ensnared in the organization's cloying bureaucracy. It was a tricky issue, and one of the reasons I wanted to move PEPFAR's offices to a separate building as quickly as possible. The other main reason was pure practicality. There was simply no appropriate space for us in the Harry S Truman Building (the State Department's headquarters). So we leased offices on Pennsylvania Avenue, just a few blocks from the White House.

I would have been much less concerned about potential bureaucratic interference if Powell was the only person with whom we interacted. I first met him in 1997 when he visited Indianapolis at my invitation to speak at a Lilly function. He'd recently retired from his position as Chairman of the Joint Chiefs of Staff, where he helped oversee the Desert Storm invasion of Iraq and the liberation of Kuwait. He was on the speaking circuit and, for the first time in his life, was making some money. At the time, he was probably one of the most famous people in the country.

His speech was on a Tuesday, which happened to be the day after the Monday night championship for the NCAA Division I men's basketball tournament, which that year took place in Indianapolis. It occurred to me that rather than flying in on Tuesday morning he might like to come early for the game, so I invited him and he accepted. There wasn't a hotel room available in the entire city, so he stayed at my home.

A Lilly plane picked him up, and we attended the game that evening at the city's downtown (and now long gone) RCA Dome. Not surprisingly, lots of people asked to have a picture with him, and he kindly obliged. This was in the days before ubiquitous smart phones, so usually the people who wanted pictures whipped out small, disposable Kodak cameras. I remember Powell saying that those cameras were the bane of his existence whenever he visited Iraq. Every U.S. soldier had one, and they all wanted shots with him, meaning that it would often take him half an hour to complete what should have been a five-minute walk from one building to another.

After the game, he headed home with me. I recall a couple of very telling moments from his stay: he very politely asked permission before using the house phone to make a long-distance call to his wife, and in the morning, he made his own bed.

That personal connection would make a difference a few years later when he helped convince me to run PEPFAR. He was an excellent leader and the sort of person you would follow anywhere. He knew the president wanted PEPFAR to act quickly and independently, and he never attempted to encroach on us. Typically, I scheduled meetings in his office from time to time to update him, and he would ask informed questions, offer advice, and very graciously provide help whenever I asked for it—mostly by appearing at PEPFAR events to impart more gravitas to the proceedings and boost media coverage.

For example, to this day I keep in my office a photo of myself and Tommy Thompson standing in the background while Powell holds up the very first copy of the official PEPFAR strategy at the State Department podium when we announced we were submitting it to congress and providing it to the media. He had nothing to do with developing that strategy of course, but he was interested in what was in it directionally, and at my request, he showed up for its unveiling. His mere presence earned it a great deal more attention than if I'd presented it alone.

As I said, if Powell and a few others had been the only State Department officials I dealt with, there would have been no issues whatsoever. It was the department's innate bureaucracy, and the mischief it might cause, that worried me. It was neither worse nor better than the tangles of red tape I'd encountered in other organizations, including both AT&T and Lilly, but it could have posed a major hurdle. No matter where you work, there are always entrenched managers who think things should be done a certain way, want certain protocols honored, or believe you desperately need their guidance and advice. This sort of mentality is the sworn enemy of any organization that wants to do things in a hurry. And PEPFAR, in order to save lives, needed to hurry.

Having Powell as my titular boss gave some of these middle management types the idea that PEPFAR was just another entity of the State Department and was therefore also under their bureaucratic authority. For instance, someone told me, "You've got 32 people in your headquarters, but we won't let you hire any more because of State Department headcount constraints." I was also informed that we were leasing too many square feet per person according to State Department protocol (even though the space had been acquired to accommodate the growth that was anticipated as we were creating a new organization and adding staff), so "they" were going to carve off some of it and use it for people who didn't have offices at the main State Department building. I told these folks to get lost—using suitably diplomatic language, of course. It was all incredibly petty and time-consuming, but that's par for the course because bureaucracies are typically petty.

In the end, the State Department bureaucracy wound up having roughly the same relationship to PEPFAR that in my experience the state of Indiana has to the University of Notre Dame. Which is to say, while Notre Dame is in Indiana, it's not of Indiana.

Once PEPFAR moved into its new quarters, I settled into a regular 7 a.m. to 7 p.m. work schedule. Shortly after I arrived at the office, my body man (in violation of government regulations against using employees for "personal services") would go to a nearby carryout place and bring back a yogurt with granola in it, plus a couple of boiled eggs. I'd eat at my desk and then kick off a round of meetings that could sometimes last all day and into the evening. They included meetings with PEPFAR staffers; talks to various Washington organizations and interest groups; media appearances; and interagency gatherings such as the PEPFAR steering committee that included representatives from USAID, the Department of Health and Human Services, the State Department, the military, and others. At the time, the United States Army was represented by the then Colonel Deborah Birx, who would become quite well-known when she played a lead role during the COVID-19 outbreak of 2020-22. From 2014 to 2020, Dr. Birx would serve as the United States Global AIDS Coordinator.

I've attended a lot of meetings over the years, but the sheer number of government gatherings and demands on time for speaking appearances around Washington put the corporate world to shame. I often saw them as "less than total value added." At Lilly, which when I arrived was also very meeting- and committee-oriented, it was an easier issue to address. Although I wasn't totally successful, I issued a directive that from then on, I didn't want to be told that something had been approved by a committee. I didn't want groups making compromise decisions based on what everyone could live with. I wanted leaders to make the best decisions, sometimes with so-called winners and losers, and take responsibility and be accountable, after listening and getting the best possible input and available advice.

There were also efforts to reduce the number of big-but-unnecessary meetings in crowded conference rooms. Mitch Daniels, during his time with the company, did something that I thought was very creative. He put up signs outside the Lilly conference rooms in his part of the organization that read something to the effect of, "No parking after 9:30 a.m. or before 4:30 p.m." It meant that you could certainly have big morning meetings to start the day, smaller meetings during the day with only people who needed to be there and could add value, or meetings at the end of the day. But at other times, big meetings were discouraged.

Powell, who was likewise not a huge fan of long, high head-count, open-ended gatherings, held short, 20-minute meetings with his senior staff every morning—an arrangement that harked back to his days in the army. He told me privately that he called them his "I'm OK and you're OK meetings." Such brief, regular gatherings kept people from imagining that their boss was irritated at them or was heading off in some direction that wasn't in sync with what they were doing. It was a way to form a daily human connection.

Unfortunately, in Washington, I couldn't simply cancel other people's meetings wholesale—particularly ones that included, say, a senator or an important constituent of the administration. So they continued to eat a larger portion of my schedule than I would have preferred. When I wasn't attending such gatherings, I handled numerous administrative tasks, made a lot of speeches in places of strategic importance (to get out the word about our work), and spent time on Capitol Hill courting individual members of Congress. It wasn't all fun, but it was vital. They provided our funding and could easily throw a wrench in the works if they felt like it (though many were incredibly supportive). So I needed to stay on good terms with all of them.

Meeting with these folks privately was sometimes a revelation. The same people who harangued me for, say, buying too many or too few condoms were often vastly more cordial with no cameras present. They still held the same political views, but they presented them in a more collegial way. This is not to say that these meetings always went smoothly. I faced constant requests for PEPFAR to spend money in politicians' home states or congressional districts. They might plug a not-for-profit located in their domain or tout some in-state manufacturer making a product that (in their view) we totally, absolutely needed. For example, the staff of a very prominent senator made arrangements for me to meet with the owner of a company that distributed audio versions of the Bible in Africa. They wanted us to use the same company to distribute audio information about AIDS. On another occasion, the staff of a prominent southern senator made clear to my staff privately that the senator wanted to be sure the condoms we bought were from a company in his state that was a major manufacturing employer—even though he was publicly opposed to the role of condoms in the ABC strategy.

This was part and parcel of the political experience.

I soon realized there was a huge, vexing difference between running a federal governmental organization and a private company. In the latter case, pretty much everybody, from the shareholders to the customers to the employees and management, generally wants the same thing—the success of the company and its products or services. Any disagreements arise over the proper approaches to achieve that goal, with the interests of each of the company's constituencies taken into account.

That's simply not the case in government, where you typically have several different factions with diametrically opposing goals. For instance, the government maintains various food security programs to supply vulnerable populations worldwide with wheat and other staples. The agencies working directly on these efforts want to get food to starving people as quickly and efficiently as possible, and they rightly see this as their overriding purpose. But agricultural interests see such efforts primarily as a support for U.S. agricultural output, while the transportation industry sees them as domestic U.S. jobs programs.

This is why, in my day, around 70 percent of the money appropriated by Congress to purchase grain for food-insecure populations overseas had, by law, to come from U.S. farmers. Furthermore, you couldn't ship grain from the U.S. to, say, Africa, unless it was aboard a U.S.-flagged ship, which was vastly more expensive. Often, the more efficient approach was to buy the food sources in parts of the world closer to the need. But that's simply the way it was—and, to my knowledge, largely remains. Once, I asked about getting this law changed, only to have the chairman of a House Agriculture Subcommittee flatly tell me, "That's never going to happen under my watch."

This sad state of affairs could (and still can) be laid at the feet of our elected officials. Too often their number one job, at least in their own minds, isn't to efficiently serve the public interest broadly. It's to get reelected. Though there were certainly some exceptions to this mindset, especially in the first four years of a senator's six-year term, too often the votes members of Congress cast and the policy positions they took were determined not by what was objectively the best course of action, but on whether it helped them keep their seats. That was twenty years ago, and the pressures on those officials are even greater today.

If you're a member of the House of Representatives, for instance, and you get elected in November, by December you're out raising money for your reelection. Today we have too many members of Congress touting the fact that they sleep on rollaway beds in their offices. They usually leave town on Thursdays to make personal appearances and campaign and come back Monday night, when they are in session.

This issue has only gotten worse since my years in government service. At that time, there was still a lot more cordiality and cooperation in Congress than seems to be the case today, though probably less than twenty years earlier. I wonder if people worked together better because their families lived in the same neighborhoods in and around Washington and their kids played on the same Little League teams. Did it help that Republicans and Democrats knew each other more personally as human beings? Did that make it much more difficult to demonize the opposition?

In Indiana, as I write this, we're very fortunate to be represented in the U.S. Senate by Todd Young, someone who would be successful at anything he chose to do in life, but who has chosen to serve in public office. He represents almost a throwback to a type of elected official that's too rare in today's politically charged world. Other examples would be former senators like Indiana's Dick Lugar, Howard Baker of Tennessee, David Boren of Oklahoma, or Congressman Lee Hamilton of Indiana. These were all people I have been privileged to know, and all cared more about policy than politics.

Another concern I have from my Washington days is the disappearance from Congress of regular Main Street citizens—people who aren't in politics for a career or to advance some narrow-minded or vitriolic point of view. This sort of person isn't independently wealthy and typically can't manage the cost of both getting elected and then living in two places at once. Yet they have the talent and desire to serve.

Unfortunately, these days, such folks, should they win a spot in Congress, can barely afford to pay their bills. In 2024, U.S. Senators and House members were paid $174,000 a year, an amount that hasn't changed in nearly 15 years. That may sound like a lot of money, but it goes quickly when the job requires maintaining a residence in your home state plus a place to live in Washington, D.C. I'm sure many who have been elected would love to move their families to Washington and have a proper residence in two locations, but unless they are independently wealthy, they simply can't afford it. So their family stays home, and the representative or senator must find very modest accommodations at (or near) the Capitol—or, at the worst, sleep in their offices.

Beyond our elected officials, those who serve as staff for our senators and representatives, and in government agencies, are also too often inappropriately maligned. Almost without exception, I found the staff in all branches of the government to be hardworking and intelligent, and again underpaid. The amount of decision-making that's delegated to these folks is enormous, and a great deal rides on their overworked, underpaid, and mostly very young shoulders.

By early 2006, I was satisfied that PEPFAR's foundation was in place and that our new strategy was bearing fruit. I was so confident, in fact, that I felt I could, in good conscience, declare victory and tender my resignation. I broached this topic with Condoleezza Rice, who had succeeded Colin Powell as Secretary of State in January of 2005. I believed I'd done what I'd been asked to do and that it was time for me to head back to Indianapolis.

But that's not how things worked out.

"The president and I would like you to consider taking the lessons learned from PEPFAR and seeing if we can apply that model more broadly to the way in which all United States foreign assistance is delivered," Rice told me.

She and President Bush believed PEPFAR's strategy and implementation—fast, nimble, efficient, and focused on measurable metrics of success—could transform America's entire approach to foreign aid. And they wanted me to lead a transformative effort to make it happen. I would become the first Director of United States Foreign Assistance, with the rank of deputy secretary of state, and concurrently administrator of USAID, also with the rank of deputy secretary. I would preside over the entirety of the nation's foreign aid efforts.

It was a huge vote of confidence in my leadership and in the strategy I'd put in place for PEPFAR, but the thought of remaining in D.C. didn't excite me. I felt that the project was worthwhile, but the timing was terrible. We were well into the Bush administration's second term, and it's widely understood that in most cases a president's biggest accomplishments happen during their first term—more exactly, during the *first two years* of the first term, when momentum, enthusiasm, and political capital are at their peak. PEPFAR was founded in that environment.

Now, however, I was supposed to tackle an even bigger task during the Bush administration's second-term doldrums. Political people were already focused on the next election cycle, and anyone who wanted to resist my initiatives could simply dig in their heels and wait me out. And I anticipated facing a *lot* of resistance. Trying novel strategies at a brand-new agency such as PEPFAR was tough. Attempting the same thing with established organizations filled with vested interests would be tougher.

But though the timing wasn't ideal, the fact remained that the president of the United States and the Secretary of State had asked me to take on the task. And so, in early 2006, I duly became the first United States Director of Foreign Assistance and was also nominated, confirmed, and sworn in as Administrator of USAID. With this promotion, my days of trying to physically avoid the State Department building were over. I was given an incredibly historic place from which to work—the recently restored office once occupied by Secretary of State George Marshall, the creator of the Marshall Plan, the wildly successful economic assistance program that helped rebuild Western Europe after World War II. I also kept the separate USAID office, located in the Ronald Reagan Building, that had long been occupied by USAID administrators, and split my time between both locations.

I can't resist offering another footnote about the federal bureaucracy. The Marshall office was of course incredibly historically significant. It was, after all, where the Marshall Plan had been launched, the most important development initiative in our country's history. It was made available to me by Secretary Rice. This was an incredible gesture because the space hadn't been occupied for decades. It had recently been restored as part of a general rehabilitation of the portion of the State Department headquarters known as "Old State" (its headquarters prior to the construction of its current Truman Building offices).

Some but not all of the furnishings that had been provided, however, were up to the standards the space deserved. I decided to have a decorator select and obtain, at my personal expense, among other things, appropriate Oriental rugs for the office, similar to what was visible in a historic photograph I had from Marshall's time. I then wanted to make a permanent gift of the rugs to the State Department with the understanding they would stay in that space when I returned to civilian life.

It sounds simple, but as with many seemingly trivial matters, the Washington bureaucracy turned it into a problem. Apparently, there were rules prohibiting using personal furnishings of this nature in an office, and there was no easy procedure for accepting the rugs as a donation to the State Department, with those strings attached. By the time those involved in building management got over believing it was a bad idea for me to have Oriental rugs in the office, even though I had purchased them myself, and then figured out how to handle the gift, I was almost sorry I ever thought of it.

But the rug issue, irritating though it was, proved only a minor inconvenience compared to the numerous other roadblocks I faced.

My brief was to lead a concerted effort to bring rigor to the nation's roughly $28 billion annual foreign assistance budget. If you ran an overseas U.S. government aid program, your objective was no longer to perhaps engage in empire-building by asking for a bigger staff and more funds or to use the money primarily as a carrot to get local governments to toe the line on U.S. political objectives. Now the goal was to help the host nation develop the expertise and skills to manage their problems themselves. We'd stick around as a safety net, and in some places handing over the work to the locals might take many years, even decades. But the ultimate goal was to put U.S. managers out of business by enabling locals to be self-sufficient.

We started by placing every country that received foreign aid on a matrix that listed, among other things, what they needed and the condition of the local government—everything from democracies with only a few needs to failed states lacking basic education, healthcare, court systems, and even the rule of law. Then we directed funds to those nations based on where they stood on the matrix, while also establishing clear objectives and metrics for success and standing up local groups to handle as much of the work as possible. It was like PEPFAR but on a much larger scale.

As one can imagine, this wasn't greeted in all quarters with extreme enthusiasm. Not when the strategy boils down to, "use development dollars strictly for targeted development, teach the locals to do what you do, and make your job redundant." Even the objective of no longer allowing local heads of state to use development cash as they pleased (as an enticement to toe the line on U.S. policy points) was not popular with those outside development circles. Once, when I briefed President Bush and Vice President Cheney on what we were changing in this regard, the vice president, who over the years in his various roles had made use of development funds to enlist support from friendly foreign leaders for one effort or another asked, "Why would you want to do that?"

Matrix-guided funding adjustments also proved quite vexing because many of the folks involved in international aid saw the distribution of government money as a zero-sum game. In other words, there were only so many slices of the aid pie, and if someone got a bigger slice, that inevitably meant someone else got less. This is why people interested in a particular cause wouldn't hesitate to throw rocks at other organizations, even if their work was also worthy. If you were promoting, say, education, you were very aggressive in using any tool you could find to make sure "your" funds were not redirected toward healthcare, without regard to the relative merits.

Elected officials could also take a proprietary (in the worst possible sense of the word) interest in foreign aid programs. For instance, a powerful senator or representative with a lot of immigrants from a particular country in his or her district might exert pressure to fund some organization doing relief work in that country. Members of Congress tended to view foreign aid dollars in the same way one might view a charitable foundation. They wanted to get as much money as possible for the causes that interested them, with no thought to any overarching strategic framework.

All of the agencies distributing foreign aid had their own patrons in Congress. This was back in the days when individual senators and representatives could add an "earmark" to a piece of legislation, requiring that a certain amount of funding go to a particular program or organization. One literally couldn't vote for the bill without voting in favor of the earmark (or, more often, earmarks). Needless to say, strategically and efficiently distributing money was impossible if the way to use those funds was mandated in the appropriations legislation.

However, I can say with a great deal of pride that during my watch there wasn't a single earmark placed on funds associated with PEPFAR. I could accomplish this because, as I stated earlier, I had no political agenda. I just wanted to do the work, implement our strategy, and go home.

Nevertheless, plenty of groups and individuals tried to sway my thinking. Occasionally, I was even approached by world-famous celebrities who wanted to influence our foreign aid work in some way. For instance, I once met with Brad Pitt, and separately also had lunch with his then-wife Angelina Jolie, who at the time was a United Nations Goodwill Ambassador. But going back to my PEPFAR role, I probably had the most contact with Bono, the front man for the rock band U2. He'd met President Bush in 2002 to enlist his help in the fight against HIV/AIDS, and the two struck up what must surely be one of the most unlikely friendships in recent memory.

Bono became one of PEPFAR's biggest celebrity supporters, and we met several times over the years. Once, while I was at the World Economic Forum in Davos, Switzerland (which I attended several times), I got a message in my hotel room asking if I could meet him for a drink. And so, after that day's official events, I found myself in the bar at Bono's hotel, drinking a pint of Harp Irish beer (from Bono's home country) and talking with him friend-to-friend late into the night. Pretty heady stuff for the boy from Remington. And then, to top it off, the actor Richard Gere, who was at a table across the bar and was also interested in AIDS, stopped by our table to say hello.

Bono also visited my Washington, D.C., office a couple of times. Once, when he was doing a concert in the city, he sent tickets to several of us he knew in and around the White House. We had incredible seats, plus backstage passes.

I remember him warmly because he possessed a characteristic that set him apart from some of the other celebrities who professed an interest in our work. Bono actually did care, and he did whatever he could to help, whether there was a camera pointed at him or not. He would quietly visit some of the nondescript places where the work was done, talk to people on the ground and people in government, work aggressively to raise money and awareness, and urge politicians to make the decisions they needed to make in order to help their citizens.

Bono did a lot of this, and he did it quietly and very much under the radar. As such, he exemplified one particular group of "political" celebrities: those deeply involved in the battle against HIV/AIDS, but not necessarily interested in letting the world know about it—unless that might somehow help the cause. The other group of celebrities was best typified (at least in my view) by former talk show host Oprah Winfrey. At this time, she was at the very pinnacle of her fame. Yet her reputation among development people on the ground (totally deserved or not) was different. While I'm sure she too did care, unlike Bono, she never went anywhere without a big camera crew. They documented her every move, as well as the cause she was championing at that particular moment.

In Bono's case, it was all about the battle against AIDS. In Oprah's, it seemed to be all about Oprah. I would call it an early form of "virtue signaling," though the term hadn't been invented yet.

Celebrity encounters constituted a very small part of my work, of course. My new title gave me many new responsibilities and placed me in regular, much closer contact with Secretary of State Rice as part of her senior staff. We shared a common view about what we were trying to accomplish, and I was more involved in her day-to-day operations. I enjoyed the same respectful relationship with her that I had with Powell. I found her to be very smart, very experienced, and more of a political creature than her predecessor. This made her very adept at avoiding the landmines of government that in the end had thwarted Powell's interest in continuing to serve as Secretary of State in Bush's second term.

We occasionally met socially. For instance, I attended a concert of the National Symphony at the Kennedy Center as her guest. Condi was a skilled pianist and, at one point in her life, had aspired to a career as a concert pianist. The Center maintains a Presidential box, which the president himself almost never uses. However, senior White House and cabinet secretaries, in descending order of rank, can reserve it. The box accommodates about a dozen people and has its own sitting area, bar, and bathroom, similar to a suite at a major sports stadium. I also attended a few small meetings with either her or her senior staff at her condominium in the fabled Watergate complex. I hold her in great respect.

With my new titles and responsibilities, the number of meetings I attended increased, along with their gravitas. I became a member of what's known as the Deputies Committee, composed of the deputy secretaries of state, deputy secretaries of defense, deputy secretaries of the treasury, and so on. That group met to prepare issues for presentation to the National Security Council, which is made up of certain cabinet members and the vice president and president.

I attended gatherings where the weightiest governmental decisions were discussed. As Director of United States Foreign Assistance, I was responsible for funds that could help make certain foreign policy objectives happen, such as assisting counterinsurgency programs in Afghanistan or Iraq, so I was occasionally asked to nod my head yes or no (or offer an opinion) about readily available development funds when important and relevant decisions were being made. As I write this, I'm sure the person currently with my same responsibilities is sitting in the Situation Room doing the same thing with respect to aid for Ukraine or the people in Gaza.

The Deputies Committee always met in a "sensitive compartmented information facility," or SCIF. These were the rooms where the most classified matters could be discussed because they were shielded from electronic and other forms of eavesdropping. Many major government office buildings had them, including the Pentagon and the State Department (where the section housing the secretary's office and those of other high-ranking officials was basically one giant SCIF). They could also be set up temporarily, pretty much anywhere. For instance, President Bush had one at his Crawford, Texas ranch. But the most famous SCIF was and remains the Situation Room in the White House. Twenty years later, I still can't share much specifically of what went on during these gatherings because they were, and remain, highly classified. We couldn't take any notes or talk to anyone who wasn't in the room with us about what went on.

I also continued my international travels, but the itinerary differed substantially from my PEPFAR days. As, on occasion, did the tone of my reception. Sometimes it was warm. And sometimes it was very warm.

For instance, I was deeply involved with reconstruction activities in Iraq and Afghanistan. In Afghanistan we were, perhaps naively, putting gazillions of dollars into getting the local farmers to stop growing poppies (the feedstock for both morphine and heroin) and instead plant conventional field crops. At the same time, we also tried to eradicate the country's poppy crop by spraying herbicides on thousands of acres of farmland.

As one would imagine, this approach angered both the farmers, who made less money growing conventional crops, and also the Afghan drug lords, who were very unhappy with our efforts and frequently fired on our people. Equally unhappy were the drug cartels in Peru, where I actually came under fire. We helicoptered into the countryside on one occasion to see a demonstration of a modified spade that could pull up entire coca plants (from which cocaine is made), roots and all. People who were armed with these (and paid with U.S. funds) would fan out into the Peruvian coca fields and, while protected by soldiers, take out entire plantings in a fairly short time.

Just as in Afghanistan, this angered the local cartels, and they registered that displeasure in the same way as their Afghani counterparts. They left us alone while we were on the ground, puttering around with the special spades and talking to the locals. But as soon as we got back in the helicopter and took off, we realized someone was taking potshots at us. Fortunately, hitting us with small arms from a quarter mile away was beyond our attackers' skills. It's a good thing they didn't have some sort of portable anti-aircraft missile that day, or I might not be telling this story.

But the encounter that brought the difficulties of our drug control efforts into sharpest relief didn't involve gunplay. It was a cordial but breathtakingly unproductive meeting I had with Bolivian President Evo Morales. He was the first indigenous person (the Bolivian equivalent to someone who we would call a Native American) to win Bolivia's highest office. He'd started out as a farm worker raising coca plants and rose to lead a union representing coca workers. You read that right. Bolivia had a union for coca plant workers. And its sitting president once led it.

Not surprisingly, Morales had a rocky relationship with the U.S. government. It was so bad that he'd never even met any high-ranking American officials. But then, out of the blue, I was invited to meet him in the Bolivian capital of La Paz, which I planned to visit in my capacity as the chief of USAID. This made me the highest-ranking American official to ever sit down with him.

But breakthroughs were not forthcoming—quite the opposite, in fact. The programs I oversaw in Bolivia strove to get rid of the drugs flowing into the U.S. from there and to help local coca growers find other livelihoods. But Morales would have none of that. Instead, he spent our time together trying to convince me that putting coca growers out of work was a bad thing and that we needed to shut down our programs and get out of his country. Not long after our meeting, he decided to kick out the U.S. Ambassador to Bolivia.

So, I think one could ultimately conclude that my "boots on the ground" inspections of our anti-drug efforts were sometimes not well-received by the locals.

Or rather, a certain well-armed subset of the locals.

While the Bush administration remained in office until 2009, circumstances resulted in my early departure. On April 27, 2007, I resigned as both Director of U.S. Foreign Assistance and Administrator of USAID. This unexpected turn happened because I got drawn into what became a big Washington scandal involving a woman who was arrested for allegedly running an escort service. One day my USAID media officer was contacted by Brian Ross, at the time an investigative reporter for the ABC News program 20/20. He said he wanted to talk to me. It wasn't unusual for a reporter who didn't really need to talk with me personally to call my office to obtain the information they were seeking, so I asked the staff to handle it—only to be informed a couple of days later that Ross was persistent. "He says it's a personal matter and he needs to talk to you."

I got back to him at the conclusion of a downtown meeting, as I stood on the sidewalk next to busy Pennsylvania Avenue waiting for a car to pick me up and take me back to the office. When I reached him, he said he wanted to talk about something that had apparently been in the local news—the beginnings of an investigation into the activities of a Washington woman accused of running an escort service. According to Ross, she had shared with him her telephone company billing records. He then told me the reason he was calling me was that my telephone number was in her outgoing call records. "Do you have any idea why your telephone number would be in her records?" Ross asked. Of course I didn't and should have just said so and terminated the conversation. I don't know if, in the end, it would have made a difference, but blindsided as I was, I made (in retrospect) a very naïve decision to think out loud and try to figure it out.

"Well, I have occasionally had massages for back pain at my Ritz Carlton condo," I said. "They are arranged by the concierge staff there. I suppose if this is all a mistake and she's actually running a spa that does business with the Ritz Carlton, then she could have my number," or words to that effect.

That was all it took. It wasn't long before Ross reported that I'd hired an escort service to come to my condo. I returned to my office and immediately consulted with Condi's chief of staff, Brian Gunderson, an experienced leader in Washington with impeccable judgment and a friend for whom I had and have great respect. I wanted to get his perspective on how this might play out. This couldn't have come at a worse time for what I was trying to accomplish in the refocusing of foreign assistance resources. We had just released a new budget that shifted $4.5 billion among countries receiving U.S. foreign aid, prioritizing funds where they were most needed to accomplish the strategic goals we had established. A number of countries received increases in funds, but 80 countries received cuts. Compared to the way foreign aid had been administered in the past, this was unheard of. The vested interests advocating for the various countries that would get less funding, including members of Congress, were already screaming. I'd recently been severely lectured in a Congressional hearing by chairman Tom Lantos of the House Committee on Foreign Affairs, a highly respected Democrat from California with his own opinion about where our development dollars should go. He accused me of "acting like you are still a CEO who thinks he can make whatever decisions he wants to make without Congressional oversight." I quickly recognized that whatever I did about the Brian Ross matter would be a no-win situation. It would be impossible to lead the Administration through this budget battle with this distraction. It would quickly be about me and not about the merits of what we were trying to accomplish.

I decided that the fastest way for the Administration to get back to the business at hand was for me to not prolong this situation. So, with reluctance, I turned in my resignation to the president, said my good-byes, and went home. I hoped that by exiting the spotlight and with no facts to back up the Brian Ross story, ongoing interest would quickly fade. But I couldn't have been more wrong. From that point on, the facts didn't matter. I was in the vortex of a massive scandal, and there seemed to be little I could do about it. ABC News almost immediately dropped further reporting on the broader story. And while there was never any additional reporting at all regarding me, the media echo chamber continually repeated Ross's assertions.

Finally, I hired a well-known Washington attorney and told him, "I don't know where this is going, but I'd like to at least try to clear my name, so help me figure out how to deal with it." He then asked the U.S. Attorney's Office in Washington if they would be willing to meet so we could confirm they had no interest in me. Because of the news story and my somewhat high profile, they were willing to spend an hour in a conference room in Washington asking me about what I might know—which was nothing. They quickly reached the same conclusion I had already asserted: as it pertained to me, there was simply no "there" there. From that meeting, I was astonished to learn that the phone company's records included exactly one outgoing call initiated to my number. If I had it to do over again, I clearly would have addressed it more aggressively. But

I didn't. It is right at the top of the decisions in life I deeply regret and wish I could have a do-over.

Though I'm not at all happy about the way my time in Washington ended, I nevertheless feel great pride in what was accomplished. We called it "transformational diplomacy." It meant that we used foreign assistance funds strategically to try to transform circumstances on the ground. You could describe that in a lot of ways, but at the end of the day, we needed to have in mind and be able to clearly articulate what we wanted to accomplish in each situation. And then, we needed to measure in some fashion whether the money we put in place actually did what we wanted it to do.

I'm happy to say that transformational diplomacy has continued, more or less, ever since we first initiated it. The concept has been repackaged by subsequent administrations to look like a new idea, but the principles we put in place years ago are, in most cases, those that still drive U.S. foreign aid.

Beyond this transformation or our broader development work, I'm particularly proud of PEPFAR's achievements. I have in my office a photograph that was taken in Uganda in early 2004. It's a picture of me standing with a smiling and reasonably healthy-looking man. Some weeks before, infected with AIDS and days from death, he'd become the very first patient to receive antiretroviral drugs (ARVs) through PEPFAR.

That very special pioneer is a Ugandan citizen named John Robert Engole. I recently had a chance to commiserate about him with my friend Jimmy Kolker, who served as the U.S. Ambassador to Uganda when PEPFAR launched and later worked on my staff in Washington.

Jimmy recalled that John's story was, at that time, both horrifically tragic and depressingly, discouragingly typical. He'd taught history at a rural high school until he was diagnosed with AIDS. His wife and extended family abandoned him, and he was shunned by his community. Soon he was on his last legs, languishing in a clinic in the Ugandan capital of Kampala. The facility was affiliated with a faith-based NGO called Reach Out Mbuya and run by an intensely committed Danish woman named Margrethe Juncker (a physician and Reach Out's co-founder). Her clinic, with very limited resources, took care of hundreds of patients in a city where the disease killed so many that coffins were sold on street corners.

When the first ARVs were airlifted into Uganda in March of 2004, Juncker decided that John should get the initial dose. There was certainly no time to waste. His deeply compromised, almost nonexistent immune system left him wide open to infections and other medical issues. He also had an itching rash, which was a common visual sign of late-stage AIDS.

"I asked her months later why she picked him," Jimmy recalled. "Was it because he was at the clinic the longest or because he met some specific medical criteria? But she said it was for none of those reasons. Instead, she replied disarmingly, 'He wanted to live.'"

And live he did. At the time of this writing, Engole is well into his 50s and feeling good, with his HIV so thoroughly suppressed it's not even detectable in his system. He stayed at the clinic until his health returned (though he still has some residual medical issues), then went back to school, resumed teaching, and remarried.

"He turned up well-dressed and chatty when I was in Uganda in 2012 and asked to see him," Jimmy said. "He missed a ceremony I attended in 2019 at Reach Out for the 15th anniversary of the initiation of treatment, but a half dozen others from the original cohort of patients were there, and their stories were both miraculous and perfectly ordinary. Many were now grandparents, and their professions ranged from security guards to health assistants. All beamed with appreciation and gave moving testimonials about what it meant to them to have the chance to simply enjoy being alive."

Fast forward to the mid-2020s. Beginning with that first patient in Uganda, PEPFAR is now credited with saving more than 25 million lives over the past 20 years. The rate of AIDS-related deaths in Africa has declined by 68 percent since its peak in 2004. New HIV infections are down 42 percent. And PEPFAR investments ensured that 5.5 million babies were born HIV-free.

Because of its success, up until now, PEPFAR has enjoyed bipartisan support within Congress and among a diverse array of stakeholders. In addition to the $15 billion appropriated for the initial five-year program, another $100 billion has been invested so far. In fact, uniquely in this time of so much partisan acrimony, President Joe Biden recognized the program's 20th anniversary in his State of the Union address and President Bush's role in creating it. Unfortunately, as I write this, reauthorization is being held up by misguided members of the House who want to be certain that no PEPFAR funds are provided to any organizations that also encourage or perform abortions—a reminder of the same groups' obsession with ABC. Former President Bush has strayed from his post-presidency practice of not commenting on political matters to use his best efforts to break this logjam.

I believe that the empowerment given to me by President Bush and the very clear goals that he personally endorsed were a big reason why, two decades later, PEPFAR is generally viewed as the most successful international development program in U.S. history.

Despite my initial reluctance to do so, leading PEPFAR proved to be the greatest privilege of my life and gave me the opportunity to do what I believe was the most important work of my professional career. I learned so much about the desperate needs of the people of sub-Saharan Africa and the rest of the developing world, and I met extraordinary women and men who dedicated their lives to alleviating human suffering.

After my departure from government, I retained relationships with many of those I worked with. I was invited to attend the unveiling of Condoleezza Rice's official secretary of state portrait. I had lunch at that event with my friend from those days—Michael Gerson, President Bush's chief speechwriter, one of the conceptual architects of PEPFAR, and an incredible human. Unfortunately, that was the last time I saw Michael, who died of cancer at a much too young age.

The Powell family invited me to attend Colin Powell's funeral in 2021 at the Washington National Cathedral, which was an incredible honor.

Over the years, I've also received a number of very generous compliments, directly and indirectly, from President Bush himself. For instance, a while back, Steve Goldsmith, the former mayor of Indianapolis, told me a story reported to his wife Kate by a friend who was an advisor to Bono in his efforts to fight AIDS. The friend told Kate about a photo shoot for the July 2007 cover of *Vanity Fair* magazine that she attended. President Bush and Bono were both featured for their work in Africa, but during the shoot, the president said in front of her that the person who should be on the cover was Randy Tobias. More than anything, that's an indication of the president's very generous and admirable qualities.

I had a private lunch with President Bush in his suite at the Conrad Hotel when he visited Indianapolis some years after he left office. He was in a very happy mood, talking about how great it was to be retired and how proud he was of what we had achieved with PEPFAR.

And most recently, in the spring of 2023, Mitch Daniels, who was retiring as president of Purdue University, made one last appearance in his decade-long "Conversations with the President" program, in which he conducted one-on-one fireside chats with noteworthy individuals from all walks of life. I was in the audience for that final session, which featured President Bush. It took place in Purdue's Elliott Hall of Music, which that night hosted a capacity crowd of 6,000. During the gathering, Mitch asked Bush what presidential accomplishment he was most proud of, and the first thing he mentioned was PEPFAR. He hailed its 20th anniversary and the 20 million lives it saved. Then he said that Randy Tobias was in the audience and that his leadership was instrumental in making it all possible. I can't imagine a better validation of my efforts and those of the thousands of others involved, then and since.

PUBLIC SERVICE AND PHILANTHROPIC CAUSES

Chapter Twenty-Nine

This wasn't the first time in my professional life I'd been placed in such circumstances.

I returned to private life with very few firm ideas about what to do next. I couldn't just automatically resume where I'd left off because government regulations had forced me to resign from every position I held before PEPFAR.

After some consideration, I decided to decline invitations to return to corporate boards. I'd been away from my CEO role long enough that I was out of touch with the current corporate issues they addressed every day. And besides, it just didn't seem like it would be enjoyable anymore. After the Enron scandal of 2001, in which accounting irregularities by the company's management led to the largest (at the time) bankruptcy in U.S. history, the federal government adopted stringent new regulations pertaining to corporate boards and the ways in which they were to operate. Some of these requirements were well-founded, and some were overkill. But regardless, the time demands on directors significantly increased. I'd had enough of all of that. I was ready to do something else.

I was asked to rejoin the National Collegiate Athletic Association's corporate advisory committee, and I also returned to the board of the Indiana University Foundation, which I'd sat on previously from 1986 to 1995. Indeed, since my 1964 graduation from IU, I've maintained a longstanding relationship with my alma mater. Over the decades, I helped with numerous projects, beginning in 1983 with my service as a member and ultimately the chair of the Dean's Advisory Council at the Kelley School of Business.

Over the years, I have financially supported IU in a number of ways, including a chair in leadership at the Kelley School of Business and a scholarship for the Wells Scholars Program in my parents' names.

But the centerpiece of my efforts was (and remains) the Tobias Center for Leadership Excellence. Housed at the Kelley School of Business on IU's Indianapolis campus, it develops top-notch leadership talent in the corporate, public service, education, and nonprofit communities.

It was launched in 2004, shortly after I went to work at PEPFAR. But the project was years in the making. It came about after lengthy discussions with Gerald "Jerry" Bepko, a well-respected friend and the then-chancellor of Indiana University-Purdue University Indianapolis, a collaboration between Indiana's two major state universities that was usually referred to as IUPUI.

Jerry wanted to know if I was interested in supporting some sort of project on IU's Indianapolis campus. I was intrigued, and during our conversations, its mission slowly took shape. I told him about my long-standing interest in leadership development that emphasized practical, hands-on training. I wanted to create something that would help Indiana's businesses and institutions by delivering quantifiable results in the form of effective leaders. For that reason, I approved of the idea of placing it in Indianapolis, the state's center for both governance and business. I told Jerry that if we built something around that outline, I'd commit.

It took some doing to get the project's other stakeholders on the same page. Many envisioned a think tank that would put out academic papers, not educate young leaders—which, to put it mildly, wasn't what I wanted. I viewed this not as philanthropy but as an investment. In return for a $5 million donation, I wanted an outcome that benefitted the state. If the timing had been different, I'm sure I would have applied the lessons I learned at PEPFAR to the arrangement.

We eventually came to a meeting of minds. I told Jerry that I would fund the new center with $1 million per year for five years. However, if Jerry (who was preparing to retire from IUPUI) became the center's first director and worked to build the sort of hands-on institution we'd discussed, I would give him the check for the entire $5 million up front. It would serve as an endowment, with the center living off the interest from that lump sum, to the tune of about 4 percent per year. I'm not sure if this is what swayed Jerry to take the job, but he did. I surprised him by increasing the donation amount to $5,250,000, which was presented to him by Paige and Todd, in their roles as directors of the Randall L. Tobias Foundation. The added amount was the equivalent of the annual earnings payout on the endowment, thus enabling the Center to get up and running immediately.

I'm pleased to say that another $2,500,000 has just been added to the Center's endowment. Some years ago, I made a gift of real estate to the university with the provision that if they ever decided to sell it the proceeds would go to this endowment. As I write this, it's recently been sold.

For obvious reasons, I had nothing to do with the center's activities during my time in government. However, I think Jerry did an extraordinary job getting it off the ground. Some of his ideas and initiatives exist to this day. But when he retired, the job was handed off to a Kelley professor with an interest in leadership, but who I think we can generously say lacked the leadership skill set for the position. The leadership center carried on, thanks to others on its staff and a certain amount of momentum left over from Jerry's tenure, but there was little in the way of innovation. It was very much adrift.

At some point, I took stock of the situation and decided that the leadership center could use new leadership. I talked to IU President Michael McRobbie about this and also sought out Idie Kesner, the then-dean of the IU Kelley School of Business. She agreed with my concerns and replaced the director with Kelley professor Julie Manning Magid, who at the time of this writing still serves as the center's executive and academic director. In addition, Julie has also become vice dean of the Kelley School and head of Kelley at IU Indianapolis.

I really can't say enough positive things about Julie and what she did to revitalize the Tobias Leadership Center. Today it offers a unique array of programs using practical techniques to develop young leaders. As mentioned earlier, candidates are drawn from the business world, but also from the public service, education, and nonprofit communities. Some 15 to 20 of these Tobias Fellows, most of whom could be called mid-career executives, pass through the program annually—everyone from Lilly executives to high-ranking staffers at the Indianapolis Fire Department. They spend one weekend a month together for about nine months, receiving presentations from visiting faculty while also participating in some very interesting, and novel, fieldwork. On any given weekend, they might, for instance, go to an army base for a military leadership exercise; visit the IU Athletic Department to learn how coaches build teams; get hands-on lessons about teamwork by training to be part of an Indianapolis 500 pit crew; or visit a southern Indiana monastery to learn how the monks who live there govern themselves. It's an eclectic syllabus, to say the least. I think it's turned into a wonderful program. At the time of this writing, it is two decades old and still going strong.

But this was only one of my post-PEPFAR projects. Another effort took me well out of my comfort zone—serving as chairman of the Indianapolis Airport Authority.

This opportunity came to me, appropriately, from out of the blue. Shortly after I returned to Indianapolis, I was offered the job by the recently elected Indianapolis mayor Greg Ballard. Though at one time, I was a licensed pilot and had flown (as a passenger) thousands of miles all over the world on all kinds of aircraft, I certainly had absolutely no experience with helping to run an airport—particularly one as large as Indianapolis International Airport, which currently hosts around 9 million passengers annually and is also home to the second-largest FedEx air cargo hub in the world. At the time, the facility was also in the midst of a massive upgrade. The centerpiece was the Colonel H. Weir Cook Terminal, the first post-9/11 "greenfield" terminal to be built in the U.S. It was to cover 1,275,000 square feet and include two concourses, 40 gates, and a vast main lobby filled with restaurants and shops.

In addition to the terminal, a new air traffic control tower and administration building were being constructed between two active runways. All of this had to be accomplished while the airport continued to function. The work was already well under way when I signed on, but there was still plenty to do.

Clearly, this would not be a "ceremonial" position. I told the mayor that I would only accept it if I could lead the airport as a business, not a political entity. The task was big enough without worrying about getting calls from people in the mayor's office telling me that I had to give a contract to a particular company, or other such shenanigans. Mayor Ballard was happy to do that because it was consistent with his own view. So I took the job.

To make the airport board more business-oriented, I immediately made one small, almost cosmetic-seeming change. But while it might seem trivial on the surface, its symbolism proved powerful.

Traditionally, during meetings, the board sat in a row on a raised platform, just as a congressional committee might sit, with other attendees and the public facing them. I immediately retired that format and had everybody sit around a big conference table, as one would at a corporate board meeting. And I reduced the sheer number of gatherings from once every two weeks to (typically) once a month. This came as a great relief to airport staffers, some of whom had spent an enormous amount of their time simply preparing for the next board meeting. I also encouraged the appointment of board members who possessed business skills that would be useful for the task at hand.

Furthermore, I wanted to give lots of attention to making the new terminal a great customer-friendly experience for travelers. This wasn't an uphill battle, because the airport staff and the construction companies already felt the same way.

Though I'd never had anything to do with overseeing an airport, I felt confident. After all, this wasn't the first time in my professional life I'd been placed in such circumstances. As I've already stated on several occasions, it's axiomatic that while the specifics of running different sorts of enterprises vary, about 80 percent of the skills a leader needs are the same. As for the other 20 percent that are relevant only to a particular endeavor, one simply needs to study and seek help from the experts around them.

I greatly enjoyed my up-close look at how such a facility operates, and I quickly came to appreciate the extraordinary capabilities of its staff. John Kish, who at the time was the airport's executive director responsible for both its operation and the massive construction project, was doing a very effective job leading that staff. Marsha Stone, one of the senior members of the airport's executive staff then and now is, I'm proud to say, a graduate Tobias Fellow. The entire complex is basically a small city, with some 40,000 airport and airline employees serving the tens of thousands of passengers surging through the place every day. The airport also has its own police department, fire department, and healthcare facilities, and the staff takes great pride in the fact that, no matter how bad the weather, the runways never close. It's a major operation that goes well beyond plane landings and takeoffs.

My work with the airport wasn't a full-time job, but it came fairly close. It was pretty common for me to spend a portion of, say, four out of five days of each workweek dealing with airport issues. It might have been a couple of phone calls, answering a question or approving something, or going out to the airport for meetings.

Unlike at Lilly or PEPFAR, however, I wasn't brought in to "fix" anything. The construction projects and day-to-day operations were already well-handled by very competent people. I, instead, spent my time looking at the "big picture" and making sure everything stayed on track and came together on time and under budget. And of course, we focused on making Indianapolis International Airport the most customer-friendly airport in America.

This was no small feat, and it required attention to myriad details. For instance, I remember saying repeatedly that, when the new terminal opened, I hoped to never see anybody sitting on the floor next to an electrical outlet intended for vacuum cleaners because it was the only place where they could charge their laptop. Today, of course, there are sometimes chargers under every airport waiting area seat. But back then, what we were trying to achieve was much more novel. I think that the new terminal may have been one of the first such facilities in the country to offer dedicated charging ports.

That terminal and the other associated projects also constituted the first major U.S. airport construction since 9/11. So, all the security changes and difficult work-arounds that had been made in other facilities since that time could be incorporated into our basic design. Many other airports are far more inconvenient because they weren't physically created with this in mind. So you may have to go through security once and then go through it again in another area. Not in Indianapolis. Also, a lot of thought was given to efficient baggage handling to make sure it went smoothly both from a customer and a security point of view.

These were examples of the kinds of things that the board and the staff worked hard to make happen, and I'm very proud of everyone who was involved in the work. The airport is a real gem for the city and the state. And it's not just me who thinks that. At the time of this writing, the Airports Council International-North America has named it the Best Airport in North America for the 11th year in a row.

I stayed with the board until the fall of 2010, when geography, of all things, forced my departure. We moved to a new home just outside of Marion County, meaning I was no longer eligible to serve as an Indianapolis mayor-appointed board member. But by that time, I and the myriad others who worked on the airport's reconstruction had already made our mark. Recently, I flew into and out of the main terminal for a European trip, and I'm just as proud of that airport today as I was when it reopened.

Soon after leaving the board, I found other things to keep me busy. I continued my longstanding membership (at a much scaled-back level) on the Indiana University Foundation board, which solicits charitable contributions on behalf of the school. I first joined in 1986 and became an inactive member from 1993 to 1999, when I was CEO of Lilly. It wasn't a conflict-of-interest issue. I just didn't think, given my workload at the company, that I had enough spare bandwidth to offer to the foundation. After I retired from Lilly, I became active again, serving until 2003, when I had to resign from pretty much everything for PEPFAR. As mentioned earlier, I was reinstated when I left public service and stayed with the foundation as an active member of the board until 2018 when I became an emeritus director.

In 2013, Indiana Governor Mike Pence appointed me to the Indiana University Board of Trustees. I served a three-year term, the last two years as chairman. As I approached the end of my third year of service, which concluded in July of 2016, I asked the governor not to reappoint me for a second term.

I'm a great believer that one should know when to leave. As I've often said, when it's time to go, it's time to go. And my view was that age 75 (a landmark I reached in 2017, during what would have been my fourth year on the IU board), was a good time for me (and, in my view, for people in general) to stop sitting on boards and other positions of similar responsibility. To put it bluntly, it was time to bow out gracefully and hand things over to the next generation. I did not want to become the Senator Diane Feinstein of board members.

I also wanted more time to myself. I wanted to get up every morning and enjoy a long-neglected morning ritual—reading the *London Times*, the *New York Times*, the *Washington Post*, *Politico*, what remained of the *Indianapolis Star*, bulletins from the *Indianapolis Business Journal*, the *San Francisco Chronicle*, the *Los Angeles Times*, the *Athletic*, and more. And to be frank, I wanted to make sure that I never missed anything my grandchildren did.

Also, on the personal front, in 2009 Marianne and I divorced. I was 67 at the time and could not imagine we could happily spend the rest of our lives together. Rather, I had concluded that it would be best for us to go our separate ways. When I told her my intentions, I don't think she was shocked. She accepted my decision, and we respectfully and amicably moved on. With the benefit of hindsight, it's safe to say that what drew us together in the mid-1990s was the fact that we'd both lost our spouses. While we had a number of other common interests, we were united by our sense of loss, which clearly wasn't the best foundation upon which to build a marriage.

Over the years, we'd grown apart and our interests diverged. However, we by no means had an acrimonious relationship. Far from it. We'd worked together on several community projects and had mostly enjoyed a comfortable rapport.

In the years after our divorce, we would occasionally run into each other at events around Indianapolis and always stayed friendly. Marianne passed away on July 12, 2023, at the age of 82. Her memorial service provided an opportunity for me to reconnect with her children, Jim and Katie, and catch up on their lives for the first time since our divorce. I have the greatest respect for Marianne, the life she lived, and her resiliency when faced with tragedy and loss.

My work with the Tobias Leadership Center and a handful of other projects at IU and elsewhere continued to some degree, but mostly informally. During IU President Emeritus Michael McRobbie's long tenure, I served him occasionally as a sounding board. Since I no longer occupied any formal positions with the university, I was free to offer the unvarnished opinions and observations he sought—but only when asked. I've played a similar role for others in the university—when asked. And I also helped the leadership center in every way I could.

Also, beginning in 2014, at the request of Julie Manning Magid, we started hosting an annual December gathering of all the current and past Tobias Fellows at our home. Usually, about a hundred people attend, and it serves as a bonding event for former fellows and a recruiting vehicle to attract new ones. I also help recruit subjects for the center's Oral History Project, in which well-known leaders share their professional and life experiences via comprehensive interviews that are available online in both transcript and audio formats. I myself was interviewed by the project's director, Dr. Philip Scarpino, which required numerous multi-hour sessions spanning several months. The oral histories so far available include those of Father Ted Hesburgh, the longtime president of Notre Dame; former U.S. Senator Richard Lugar; former Indiana Governor Otis Bowen; several former IU presidents; the extraordinary, multifaceted leader and my friend of more than 60 years, Jim Morris; and many others.

A few years ago, I also endowed the Tobias Chair in Leadership at the Kelley School of Business. It is currently occupied by Associate Professor Erik Gonzalez-Mulé, chair of the Department of Management and Entrepreneurship. While currently it has no connection to the Tobias Leadership Center, part of our vision going forward is to develop ways to link the activities of the professor who occupies that chair with the center and also provide center-related programming at the Kelley School in Bloomington. A lot will depend on financing. However, I'm already quite happy with how the program is growing and flourishing.

I count the Tobias Leadership Center among my three most important professional legacies. Another is my work at Lilly. I don't take any specific credit for the enormous success the company enjoys today, but I do take credit for helping to put it on a strong financial and strategic footing beginning nearly 30 years ago.

However, I think my most impactful achievement was helping to launch and guide PEPFAR. The achievements of that organization and the millions of lives it helped save have already been well-documented in these pages. I'm proud of what was accomplished, but I'm even prouder of the fact that the template we produced—favoring local groups over distant bureaucracies; helping countries help themselves; and focusing on measurable metrics of success—not only continues to be used but has even become something of a "default" approach to international aid programs.

Helping to develop that results-oriented mindset is perhaps the most important legacy of all.

ANOTHER TERRIBLE LOSS

Chapter Thirty

I've always felt that Todd, in spite of the issues he faced, didn't have to die.

On June 26, 2012, the entire Tobias family faced another enormous personal tragedy—the untimely passing of my son, Todd.

The death of someone so young—he was only 41—always comes as a shock. However, those of us closest to him knew for some time that, barring a miracle, it was likely inevitable. Todd, just as his mother had, faced numerous emotional and psychological challenges during his life. And as with his mother, eventually, they got the better of him.

I won't belabor his struggles in these pages because I don't want anything to detract from the life and accomplishments of the vibrant young man whose company I cherished. Rather, I think it's important to remember that he struggled valiantly throughout adulthood with formidable personal demons. And that, for most of those years, in spite of resounding emotional shocks, he held them at bay. It was only at the end, at the very end, that he succumbed.

I believe, however, that something useful can be gained by once more traversing this painful emotional territory. Perhaps, as was the case with his mother, talking about what happened will benefit others facing similar situations and spotlight the way mental health issues are handled, or rather, mishandled, by the American medical system. Because I've always felt that Todd, in spite of the issues he faced, didn't have to die. Intervention and long-term treatment might have saved him. But in his case, as with his mother's, our medical structure seemed utterly incapable of doing what needed to be done.

In retrospect, the very first issues likely surfaced when Todd was a teenager. As mentioned earlier in this narrative, he spent those years in Bernardsville, New Jersey, while I worked at AT&T's headquarters. He made friends easily and his peer group included local kids whose families had lived in the area for generations, along with the sons and daughters of corporate executives whose employers kept their headquarters in the area.

One of Todd's best high school friends was the son of one of the senior officers in the Bernardsville Police Department. This was a good thing because on one or two occasions the doorbell at my house would ring at around midnight and there would be the police officer with Todd and a couple of his buddies. They'd been out partying someplace and got caught.

I must admit that while I wasn't happy about this behavior, I didn't see it as a huge issue. To put it simply, Todd and his friends weren't the first teenagers to discover beer and to want to run off and have fun together. Only much later did I wonder if this might have been the very beginning of the alcohol abuse that would steadily grow as the years passed.

Todd graduated from Bernards High School in Bernardsville in May of 1989. During those days, our biggest concern about him wasn't his extracurricular partying with his friends but his academic performance. He lacked direction and motivation, and schoolwork didn't come easily to him. He wasn't particularly interested in high school, and he also struggled through his first two years at West Virginia University. However, during his junior and senior years, his classwork vastly improved mostly because he found an academic subject—English and writing—that he enjoyed.

He graduated from WVU in December of 1993 with a Bachelor's Degree in English and immediately moved to Indianapolis, where he worked for a while at a bookstore while waiting to start graduate school. Following his mother's death in May of 1994, he moved to Bloomington in the fall and subsequently earned a Master's in Comparative Literature at IU with a concentration in film studies, graduating in May of 1997.

Yet even with another diploma in hand, he still didn't seem particularly well prepared, either academically or psychologically, for a conventional career. This was of course troubling, but once again not particularly unusual. Like a lot of people his age, Todd wasn't sure about what he wanted to do. He did, however, possess a strong desire to write.

Todd was always very close with his mother, and her death was devastating. As I mentioned earlier, it was made immeasurably more traumatic by the fact that he was the one who discovered her, unconscious from carbon monoxide poisoning in our garage. She lingered at the hospital for two days before passing. Todd felt extraordinary guilt. If he'd found her sooner, he believed, he could have saved her. And if he'd found her a bit later, she would have died then and there, sparing her further suffering. Discovering her when he did was, at least to him, the worst of all possible worlds.

That idea seemed to lodge in his mind, and I don't think he ever escaped it.

Todd married Amy Rae Brim on May 31, 1997. They moved to Denver, where he worked at Westview Press in Boulder and also freelanced. They had two children, the first of whom, Ella, was born on September 29, 1999. Todd kept up his pursuit of writing and proved extremely good at it. After moving back to Indianapolis in February of 2000, he did an internship with Indianapolis Monthly magazine (where he quickly found himself writing major feature stories) and also freelanced for national publications. His and Amy's second child, Sam, was born on April 1, 2003.

During this time, he also developed the idea for *Indy Men's Magazine*. As discussed earlier, it was founded in 2002 and published its last issue in May of 2007. During its heyday, Todd seemed simply overjoyed. I think those five years were the very best of his life. They were also great for me because during that time we worked together writing *Put the Moose on the Table*. Unfortunately, even though *Indy Men's Magazine* won national writing awards and proved very popular with its audience, it was never able to sustain itself financially. After Todd closed it, I don't think he ever really found himself professionally again.

Things headed downhill after that. Todd had struggled for years with depression and low-level alcohol abuse, but now those issues reasserted themselves with a vengeance. Paige and I realized that his drinking was growing much, much worse.

I want it understood, however, that he didn't simply withdraw from the world after the magazine folded. During that time, he kept writing and saw his work published in various high-profile venues. He was even looking for new projects. At one point, he worked with Jerald Harkness, the son of former NBA star and ex-Indiana Pacer Jerry Harkness, to develop a sort of video version of *Indy Men's Magazine*, among other things. I've been proud to watch Jerald take his career on to great success.

However, through it all, Todd's mental state grew more brittle, and his alcohol consumption increased. Paige and I tried to intercede in pretty much every way we could imagine. And again and again, we were thwarted by the same sorts of roadblocks that prevented Marilyn from getting help. Todd also resisted, and we got little support from those who were then in his support system, who felt conflicted and were not prepared to support the recommendations of the experts against Todd's wishes.

The mental health system in this country is profoundly broken. People who are suffering from a disease such as cancer typically want to seek medical care. But in the case of mental illness, many sufferers not only don't seek help, but resist it. This fact of life often goes unacknowledged. In many cases, the law actually prevents people with severe psychological issues from being forced to seek treatment, even to save their lives. That's what we faced with Todd.

Nevertheless, we tried everything we could think of. Paige would speak with him. I would speak with him. We'd speak with him together. To no avail. We even hired a "professional interventionist" who helped us develop a plan of action. Under this person's guidance, we drove to Todd's home early one morning, knocked on the door, got him out of bed, and told him that we were going to help him. Our objective was to get him to agree to ride with the interventionist to an Indianapolis inpatient substance abuse clinic, where he would be admitted into their program.

We actually got him to do that, but again without unified insistence and tough love from the rest of his support system, and with no commitment himself, he only stayed a week. And that wasn't nearly enough. Truth be told, he was in such dire straits that the professionals felt he likely needed a year of inpatient treatment.

Todd's drinking began to consume him, and the physical damage it did became obvious. We realized that the only way to save his life was to force him to get the help he refused to seek on his own. Paige and I hired an attorney, took Todd to court, and got a judge to commit him to a mental health facility for treatment. This was incredibly emotionally exhausting and no doubt one of the most painful decisions I've ever made, and in the end, it was all for nothing. The judge indeed issued an order compelling Todd to receive treatment for up to 90 days. But within a week he convinced his doctors to put him out on the street again. That, I feel, was truly the beginning of the end.

In late June of 2012, he was rushed to St. Vincent Hospital, suffering from organ failure. A couple of days later, while surrounded by his family, he was taken off life support. He died shortly thereafter.

He's been gone for more than a decade, yet I still think about him every day. And I wonder what else I could have done to save his life. So many different factors conspired to make his existence difficult. The world, in a sense, ganged up on him. But even though Todd's life was tragically short, it was by no means a failure. He did extraordinary things, and he succeeded in becoming the polished, professional writer he longed to be.

MEANT TO BE

Chapter Thirty-One

We did pretty much everything a couple might do for a 200-guest wedding. Except we only invited 40.

The years after I returned to Indianapolis from Washington, D.C., held more than their share of heartbreak and upheavals. The passing of Todd hit like a thunderbolt, and even today it still weighs on me. But in spite of everything, life—as it always does—went on.

And it continued to offer surprises. The years between the conclusion of my government service and now have also brought new adventures, a new grandchild, and most surprising and welcome of all, new love.

These days, I spend the balance of my time enjoying the company of my wife and best friend, Deborah Flanagan Tobias. Having her enter my life was a surprise, but a very, very welcome one. She plays a vitally important role in our extended family and has made a profound impact on my happiness and personal morale.

We met for the first time in June of 2009 thanks to the benevolent machinations of some mutual friends.

After Marianne and I agreed to divorce in 2008, I found myself in possession of our Lake Wawasee home—a place where I hadn't actually spent much time during the previous decade. I was just too busy. Because of this, the only people I knew in the area were people from other parts of my life, such as Indianapolis residents or people who were associated with IU. But Sandy Buhrt (the wife of Mike Buhrt, owner of the contracting company that built my house in 1999), wasn't satisfied with my borderline hermit-like existence while at the lake. She advised me that, now that I was on my own and would be spending more time at Wawasee because Paige and her family also owned a cottage there, I should get to know my neighbors.

"How would you like me to introduce you to some people around the lake—maybe from Chicago or Fort Wayne or wherever—that you might like to know?" she asked me.

It seemed like a good idea. I agreed, and she and Mike, both of whom are amateur chefs and wine aficionados, volunteered to cook dinner, select the wines, and compile the guest list. One of the people on that list was a neighbor from just down the road whose name I didn't recognize—Deborah Flanagan.

An Indiana native, she'd visited Wawasee literally every summer of her life. She graduated in 1973 from the University of Dayton with a degree in secondary education. But instead of pursuing teaching, she built a spectacularly successful career with the technology firms Infotron, StrataCom, Cisco Systems, and Juniper Networks. She'd been divorced for more than 20 years and, at the time, kept her main residence in San Mateo, California, just outside of San Francisco, near where she had been based before retiring.

Deborah and Sandy had been friends ever since the Buhrts had also built her Wawasee home. It sat just down the road from me. We were practically neighbors but had never met. Because during my infrequent weekend visits over the past few years, I pretty much just closed the front gates and kept to myself. I wasn't trying to be antisocial. I just viewed the lake as a place to get away.

When I looked over the Buhrts' guest list, Deborah's name was the only one that didn't ring a bell. So, I decided to give her a call. I told her that since we hadn't met, it would be nice to get acquainted before the gathering. I asked if she'd like to stop by over the weekend for a drink, and she said that though she'd love to, there was a scheduling conflict. She was going to visit her sister's family in Chicago to watch her great nephews play in a Little League game and wouldn't return until that Sunday afternoon.

I offered that if she'd like to come down to my house the evening she came back, I'd be happy to put something on the grill. She loved that idea because she wouldn't have any food in her kitchen when she returned, and this would solve her dinner conundrum. I think it's safe to say that neither of us saw this as anything other than an opportunity to get acquainted with a neighbor.

And yet, we hit it off immediately.

This development took us both by surprise—to put it mildly—because neither of us was in any sense "looking around"—quite the opposite, in fact. After becoming single, I remember jokingly telling the staff at the Tobias Family Office that if it ever seemed like I was becoming even remotely interested in anybody, their job was to talk me out of it. Well, needless to say, they didn't. Indeed, after they met Deborah, they started to encourage our budding relationship.

The same went for Todd's two children, as well as Paige, her husband, and their three kids. At the time, my Button grandchildren were 10, 9, and 6, with the fourth, Ava, not yet born. According to

Paige, shortly after her crew met Deborah for the first time, Emily, on behalf of herself and her siblings, asked her mother, "How would you feel if Boo Boo (the grandchildren's nickname for me, which I will explain in a bit) married Deborah?" Which is quite a thing to say at age 10 after meeting someone for the first time.

In the early part of 2010, as she and I became more excited about our chemistry and comfortable with our growing closeness, it gradually became clear to both of us that we were going to get married. It was such a foregone conclusion that I don't remember us even talking about it that much as a specific decision. Neither of us would have been comfortable remaining in some sort of permanent committed relationship without getting married, as people our age sometimes do. Yet, there also wasn't some specific moment when we made that decision. It just sort of … happened.

At some point during the progression of our relationship, we visited with Gary Thrapp, a longtime friend of mine and a preeminent Indianapolis jeweler. We were actually there to talk about a watch, but the conversation gradually turned to possible eventual engagement ring designs. It was all fairly low-key and theoretical, but it gave me a good idea of what Deborah wanted. Shortly thereafter, in secret, Gary and I collaborated with his designer to make that "theoretical" ring real.

Everything came together on March 27, 2010. I needed to go to my house in Captiva to check the status of a kitchen renovation project that I'd undertaken to get the property ready to sell, which was then my plan. Deborah, after she took care of some things in the San Francisco area, intended to fly to Florida so we could spend a few days together. But I had some surprises in store. Surprise number one was the fact that I'd given the boat I kept at Captiva, a 48-foot Grand Banks trawler, a new name. It would now be called

Meant to Be—the phrase the two of us had begun to use to describe our relationship.

Then came an even bigger surprise. Though Deborah obviously knew that an engagement was in the works, she had no idea I had the completed ring with me when she arrived that weekend. However, she became quite suspicious when, while sitting on our lanai, I popped the cork on a very expensive bottle of chilled Dom Perignon champagne.

I also formally popped the question shortly thereafter, and Deborah responded with an enthusiastic yes. Afterward, we emailed our families with a picture of her on the *Meant to Be*, wearing the ring. We told everyone that the Easter Bunny had delivered some "carats" early that year.

To say that the Button kids, Emily, Connor, and Jack, and Todd's two children, Ella and Sam, supported this development would be an understatement. They were thrilled. But though both Deborah and I were likewise excited, neither of us saw the need to make our wedding into a big production. Originally, we planned to go someplace like Hawaii or the Caribbean to tie the knot, with just a handful of guests or more likely none at all. But when this strategy was floated, Emily made it very clear that was not going to happen! She believed all of her siblings and cousins not only wanted to attend the ceremony but also participate. Furthermore, she wanted to help with the arrangements.

This was par for the course for her. She has always been the "family planner," and right now, at the age of 26, she serves as Director of Operations for Indiana Senator Todd Young in Washington, D.C. But even at a very young age, she was in charge of making dinner reservations for us during family vacations. She displayed an almost supernatural ability to get tables at particularly difficult eateries—even places that allegedly didn't take reservations.

And so, not wanting to disappoint her, her siblings, and her cousins, we scheduled a more formal wedding for June 19, 2010.

The grandchildren and their parents visited us in Captiva in early April, shortly after our engagement. Deborah told Emily she could be as involved in the wedding preparations as she wanted. Well, it didn't take long to learn just how deeply involved she intended to be. We were all sitting around one day, toward the end of their stay, when I noticed Emily having an animated conversation with someone on her mom's phone. Then, still in the midst of the call, she turned to Deborah and said, in a very businesslike manner, "Deborah, could you pick me up after school next Wednesday at 3:30?"

This was a fairly surprising thing for an 11-year-old to say to someone who was still quite new in her life.

Deborah, though a bit taken aback, nevertheless agreed. Emily then told the lady she was talking to that the two of them would see her next Wednesday at 3:45 p.m.

"I arranged a cake tasting," she said after she hung up.

What?!

The following week Deborah indeed collected Emily from school and took her to the tasting. They picked out our wedding cake, and on June 19th we got married at our current home in Carmel. At the time, it wasn't quite finished, so about 48 hours before the nuptials, the builder and all of his subcontractors loaded everything construction-related, from tools to lumber, onto an 18-wheeler and parked it out of sight in a nearby cul-de-sac. Then a cleaning crew tidied up inside and out, and my longtime event planner, David Jackson, disguised everything that still looked incomplete with a sea of flowers, potted plants, and rugs.

We wound up doing pretty much everything a couple might do for a 200-guest wedding. Except we only invited 40. We were joined by most of our extended family including Deborah's siblings Diane and Donald, with their spouses Bob and Maryanne, her dear cousin Rick Pfleger and his wife Claire, and her nephew Robert Okon and his wife Julie, the parents of the three grandnephews. Among the friends with us were Bill and Janet Biddle and John and Lynn Smart, Deborah's close friends from her Saint Louis days, Teenah and John Foster, and Nazanin Ash, my Washington, D.C., chief of staff. The ceremony was officiated by Mitch Daniels, who at that time was Indiana's governor. We took our vows on the rear terrace of the house and then held the reception in what would soon become our great room. A string trio performed before and during the wedding, and a small band played at the reception. Well, the grandchildren wanted a formal wedding, and they certainly got one!

If you look at our pictures of the wedding party you see Deborah and me, Deborah's best friend, Cathy Conners, and my brother, Roger. There were also our five Tobias and Button grandchildren, our three Tobias grandnieces, and Deborah's three grandnephews, Michael, Matthew, and Andrew Okon—eleven in all. The girls all wore matching dresses, and the boys were decked out in khakis and Brooks Brothers blue blazers with matching ties. And when it was time to cut the famous cake, we invited Emily to help us.

At the time, Paige was pregnant with her fourth child, Ava. So today, when Ava looks at the wedding photos, she points to Paige's bump and says she was there too.

Ava was scheduled to be born in 2010 by caesarian section. Paige had been given the choice of either August 19th, Emily's birthday, or August 20th. Emily let Paige know in no uncertain terms that she did not want to share her birthday. Thus, Paige chose the 20th for Ava's debut to avoid having two daughters sharing such a big landmark.

There was, unfortunately, one honored guest whom we dearly wanted to attend, but whom fate wouldn't allow—Deborah's younger brother, David. As a child, he'd been deprived of oxygen during a botched surgery, which left him with a collection of cognitive deficits. He was a delightful conversationalist with a vivid imagination, but he struggled with several limiting issues, including an inability to read and write, and difficulty remembering names. It was as if his mind was a brightly lit house with a few broken light fixtures. Certainly, only a few of them were broken. But enough to make a difference in the way he coped with the world.

After David and Deborah's parents died, and to some degree while her father was still living, Deborah, along with her cousin Rick Pfleger, became her brother's primary financial backstop, necessitating her spending more time in Indiana, where he lived. Because of this, it's fair to say that David was at least partially responsible for Deborah and me meeting. Her presence in the state at her Lake Wawasee home only grew after David contracted leukemia. It went into remission for quite a while but came back with a vengeance shortly after Deborah and I met.

When we initially planned our wedding, we did so with the hope that David could participate in some way. But it soon became pretty clear to anyone who was realistic about the matter that David was going to die. And when it came to his own mortality, David was the most realistic of us all. One day, when I had known him for perhaps a year, he asked me to come alone to visit him at the apartment he shared with his wife, Kaye. He said he wanted to speak with me very privately about something. Such a thing had never happened before.

"I know I'm going to die," he told me. "I would like to know what it's going to be like."

I think he always assumed, because of my time at Lilly, that I was a doctor. At the very least, he seemed to hold me in high regard. But in truth, I didn't have a great deal of insight into the dying process. So, I told him I would look into the matter, which I did by reading a book on the subject and seeking advice from the dean of the IU School of Medicine, who was a longtime friend. Afterward, armed with the best information I could find, I sat down with David and tried to give him an unvarnished view of what a person in the final stages of a long illness might expect.

I told him, among other things, that he'd find himself gradually losing interest in normal, day-to-day activities. Particularly food. He might also start to lose energy, sleep more, and want to spend less time talking with visitors and more time reflecting on his life. Then, toward the end, he might enjoy a brief resurgence of energy and clarity for a few hours, followed shortly thereafter by death. Scientifically, this is known as terminal lucidity, though it's sometimes referred to colloquially as a "last hurrah" or "burning your reserves."

As it turned out, David's final days unfolded in almost exactly this way. He died on April 29, 2010, at a hospice. Two days before his passing he roused from a coma and was sitting up in bed cracking jokes with his family and friends. Then he slipped back into unconsciousness and a few hours later passed away peacefully. I have to say that having him confide in me in such an intimate way was a great honor and a very profound experience. It was amazing that someone facing such circumstances could muster such a courageous, intellectual interest in what awaited him. And it was humbling that, of all the people in his life, he chose to speak with me about it. It's an experience I'll always treasure.

Interestingly, in a roundabout way, David helped decide the nickname by which the grandchildren would refer to Deborah. Bear with me, because I must first share a fairly long tale about how I came to be known among the family's younger set as Boo Boo. The groundwork was laid shortly before I departed Lilly, when I went to Pasadena, California, where Paige and Tim then lived. I wanted to spend time with them because they would shortly have their first child (Emily). On the night before Paige was scheduled for a cesarean section, she, Tim and I went out to dinner. In the course of the meal, they presented me with a book about being a grandfather, which included a couple of pages listing the word for "grandfather" in 100 different languages. At the time, I wasn't too keen on being called "grandpa," (although sometime later that's what Ella and Sam called me and I came to like it just fine). Anyway, we looked through the list for an alternative and, after some deliberation, settled on Babu, from the Swahili.

But as Deborah likes to say, grandparents don't get to decide what their grandchildren call them; grandchildren themselves do that, regardless of your plans. That turned out to be the case with Emily, who simply couldn't get her tongue around Babu. So instead, she called me Boo Boo, which I wasn't crazy about. I occasionally corrected her, but by the time she started (sporadically) calling me Babu, Paige and Tim's second child, Connor, had arrived, and suddenly I was Boo Boo again.

Eventually, I bowed to the inevitable and accepted the title I'd been given. Indeed, I leaned into it so hard that to this day friends of our grandchildren, with whom Deborah and I are privileged to have wonderful relationships, also refer to me as Boo Boo.

The name Deborah selected for herself stuck far better than mine. And it was first coined by her brother David. During his younger days, he called his grandmother Woo-Hoo because that was how she announced herself whenever she walked in the backdoor of Deborah's parents' house. Deborah adopted a companion to that name that mirrored my own, so now I'm Boo Boo and she's Hoo Hoo.

I think they all knew, from an early age, that Marilyn was Paige's mother. In fact, when Ava was about four, she said, "Deborah, I know who Marilyn is. Marilyn is Mommy's mother, and you are my grandmother." I think that was pretty profound for someone so young, but it certainly captured the sentiments of her siblings and cousins.

As the grandchildren have gotten older, some took to calling Deborah by her given name. However, I don't think any of the grandchildren or their friends would ever be comfortable calling me Randy. So Boo Boo I am, and Boo Boo I shall remain.

It's amazing to contemplate how quickly Deborah, a.k.a. Hoo Hoo, became an integral, cherished part of the grandkids' lives. The earliest and most intense example of this occurred during the arrival of Ava, the last of the six. On the day of her caesarian, the doctor was delayed by an emergency. So Paige and Tim, cooling their heels in their hospital room, asked if we wanted to stop by and keep them company. Deborah, who still felt new to the family, wasn't comfortable about (in her view) intruding on such a private moment, but I told her if she didn't go, I wouldn't go either.

She reluctantly assented, and shortly thereafter we joined Paige and Tim in their room. Deborah, who's always very observant, noticed a faint "tick, tick, tick" sound and asked what it was. Paige said she was hooked up to a monitor, and that we were hearing the baby's heartbeat. Well, tears immediately streamed down Deborah's face. It suddenly hit her that this child, her grandchild, was already in the room with us, waiting to be born.

Finally, a nurse came in and wheeled Paige out, with Tim following. Within half an hour, Tim came back with Ava, and Deborah and I got to hold her for the first time.

A lot has been written about the bond that develops between infants and their parents. Well, I think Deborah experienced something similar with Ava. In the blink of an eye, she went from being single for a long, long time to being both married and a grandmother. It was a massive transition, but (as Deborah will tell you herself) a joyous one.

Not surprisingly, she and Ava formed their own strong connection —one that deepened during her first years thanks to our service as her "go-to" babysitters. If Paige had something to do, or if she needed to focus on her other kids, she would send a message saying, typically, "If you've got other commitments I can make other arrangements, but it would be really helpful if you could take Ava."

It's safe to say that we never ever had other commitments. Or at least, none that took precedence over Ava. Deborah's strategy has always been to say yes first, then consult her calendar to see what needed to be canceled or rearranged to make it happen.

Actually, we did (and do) the same for all of the grandkids, both Todd's and Paige's. Because they and their various interests, from writing to sports to music, always come first.

Ella (Todd and Amy's firstborn) had come into the world on September 29, 1999. As a youngster, she was very interested in dancing and also very good at it. Deborah and I often attended her recitals. Like her father, she's a writer. During college, she even interned at *Indianapolis Monthly* magazine, just as Todd did years earlier. She graduated from DePauw University in 2022 with a focus on English and a concentration in writing. She recently completed a Master's Degree in Public Relations and Advertising at DePaul University and accepted a job as an account executive in a Chicago PR agency.

Her great-grandfather (my father, Roy) would have been very proud of this because he graduated from DePauw 93 years earlier. I think he always hoped that either Roger or I would attend his alma mater. But nearly a century later, it was his great-granddaughter who accomplished this. Ella was also the first of the grandkids to attend graduate school. I've teased her that if she wanted to save a few bucks, I could easily modify her DePauw t-shirts with a Sharpie for DePaul use.

There's something else that I'd like to say about Ella. She was only 12 years old when her father, Todd, passed away. That was a lot to handle at such a young age, but she did it magnificently. She's a very mature young woman who has faced more than her share of trauma. Both I and her grandmother admire her greatly.

Connor, Paige's second and my first male grandchild, was born on January 31, 2000. When his brother Jack came along on November 8, 2002, it set off a childhood rivalry that went on for years, until I put my grandfatherly foot down.

Let's just say the two boys developed a classic older/younger brother relationship—lots of pushing and shoving. And it was never clear (at least to us adults) who started it. Though to Deborah and me, it always looked like Connor started things and Jack would get mad and retaliate. It's probable that some of the time we had not seen the initial provocation!

Of course, none of us adults enjoyed this particular brand of brotherly interaction. It all came to a head during one Christmas at Captiva. They were pushing and shoving, knocking each other down, and crying and blaming each other. Finally, I'd had enough, and I did something I pretty much never do because I pride myself on being calm and "under control."

I got angry.

In the middle of one of their spats, I took them both aside and said, "You do this one more time and I am personally taking you to the airport and putting you on a plane and sending you home. Because I'm going to have no more of this."

Paige says the two boys remember that warning to this day because it was so out of character. But it really straightened out the situation. From that moment on, brotherly rivalry (at least in my presence) ceased to be an issue. What makes this really interesting is that if you saw them today, you'd never think for a minute that sibling strife was ever an issue. They couldn't be nicer, gentler souls, or more loving to each other or to their grandparents.

They certainly have a lot in common. Connor and Jack were both serious cross-country runners in school. The first time I introduced Jack to Deborah, back in the summer of 2009 when he was just six years old, he looked up at her and said, "I'm going to run around the house 100 times," and took off. Every two or three minutes he'd go blazing past us, and at some point, he reported completing 100 laps. I think it was actually more like eleven.

For a very long time, until the birth of Ava, Jack was also the youngest of the grandkids. But when his little sister arrived, he was, at the age of nine, no longer the baby. Which didn't sit well with him. The spring after Ava's birth, both Emily and Connor headed off to summer camp, and it seemed to Jack that there was nothing of similar interest going on with his life. So, I asked him, "Would you like to go someplace with Deborah and me, just the three of us?"

I told him he could pick the destination, and after some consideration, he selected Mount Rushmore. We signed off on his choice, but I gave Jack the responsibility of arranging our travel plans, lodgings, and itinerary.

"Dory will help you, but you need to figure out where we're going to stay," I said. "And she will help you figure out airplane reservations. This will be a good opportunity for you to learn how to plan a trip."

The Dory in question was Dory Cook, one of the Tobias Family Offices' longtime employees. Our new Carmel home included space to house the offices' work area, so all Jack had to do was go through a door in our kitchen to reach her. Together they figured out how to fly to Rapid City, South Dakota, which required a plane change in Minneapolis. When Jack presented all of this to Deborah and me, he proudly announced that we were staying at the La Quinta Inn & Suites located just off a highway cloverleaf in the Rapid City suburb of Wyndham.

Next to the hotel, he told us, sat the WaTiki Indoor Waterpark Resort, which he excitedly reported was "the largest indoor waterpark in all of the Dakotas."

And so, when the appointed day arrived, Jack, Deborah, and I arrived at the La Quinta. We'd barely dropped off our luggage in the room before Deborah had all three of us in swimsuits and over at the waterpark, where she and Jack climbed the highest ladders and raced down waterslides with abandon. The next day, we visited Mount Rushmore, took a steam locomotive up a mountain in the Black Hills, and visited a drive-through nature park called Bear Country U.S.A. Then we drove back to the airport and came home.

Originally, we considered doing this sort of one-on-one experience with all of the grandchildren, but for one reason or another, it's mostly only worked out with Jack. Pretty much every summer since Mount Rushmore, we've gone somewhere. He's a huge sports fan (and currently a senior at the University of Oregon with an interest in sports management), so our trips generally revolve around a baseball game, plus whatever else is of interest in that city. Deborah, Jack, and I have been to Chicago for a Cubs game and the musical *Hamilton*; to St. Louis to see the Cardinals along with the City Museum and a play at the Muni; to Milwaukee for a Brewers game and a tour of the Harley-Davidson Museum; and to Cleveland for baseball and a visit to the Rock & Roll Hall of Fame. Fortunately, Sam, the family rock and roll expert, was able to join us on the Cleveland excursion.

Connor also loves sports and played lacrosse both in high school and at Vanderbilt University. Tim and Paige were always kind enough to include Deborah and me on the annual Vanderbilt Family Weekends, which often included a lacrosse match, giving us a chance to see him in action. He graduated in 2021 with a degree in history and economics.

Afterward, he spent about a year as a management consultant for NTT Data but quickly realized the work didn't provide much in the way of joy or fulfillment. What he really wanted, he decided, was to teach and perhaps eventually become a school administrator. He landed a one-year fellowship (which turned into two years) teaching English at a school in the Canary Islands. This is an opportunity to both gain teaching experience as well as advance his fluency in Spanish. Afterward, he'll likely come back to a teaching position in the United States and perhaps to graduate school.

In the fall of 2024, Connor was still teaching in the Canary Islands and loving every minute of it. I'm incredibly proud of him for figuring out what he really wants to do and pursuing it, rather than just trying to make the maximum amount of money doing something he doesn't like. As evidenced by the joy he has displayed during his multi-summer employment as a camp counselor, I believe it's highly likely that a teaching career will suit Connor very well.

Todd and Amy's second child, Sam, was born on April 1, 2003. I was incredibly honored that they chose to name him Randall Samuel, though, for most of his life, he's gone by Sam. Of course, his birthdate made him the target of more than a few April Fools' Day jokes, such as the standard, "Is *today* your birthday? I completely forgot!"

Sam was only nine years old when his father died, and I think it may naturally have been even harder for him to bear at his age than it was for his older sister, Ella. Not surprisingly, he faced more than his share of struggles during his teens, which he's managed to overcome with flying colors. He's now completed two years at Mesa College in San Diego, making straight A's, and in the fall of 2024, he began classes at UCLA where he was accepted into a program to advance his own writing aspirations. And he's written some beautiful things, including an essay about his dad that brought tears to my eyes.

Recently, he returned briefly to Indiana and had dinner with Deborah and me. It was a lovely evening, and we're so proud of the man he's become. I don't think we'll see him living back here in the Midwest, but who can predict with any certainty? Sam has said that he sees himself as a California person now, and it sure seems to be a good fit.

"I kind of anticipate that I'm going to stay there," he told us. "I'm guessing I'll get a degree and then put down roots there. I love California and I love what I'm doing."

When it comes to talents, he's definitely his father's child. Just like Todd, he's deeply interested in writing. He also took up the guitar at a very young age (again, just like his father) and is very serious about it. But unlike Todd, he's also become a surfer. Which makes Christmas shopping for him pretty easy. So far, we've given him a surfboard and, in 2023, a guitar.

After Todd's passing, I grew closer to my nephew, Eric. When Eric lost his father (and my brother and best friend, Roger) we became even closer. Nothing could make up for the loss of Roger and Todd, but I found a surrogate son with Eric and he found a surrogate father in me. We've spent a lot of time together, hunting pheasants in South Dakota, hunting quail in South Georgia, and enjoying our extended family times at Lake Wawasee. One of our most significant shared passions is IU athletics. We often attend football and basketball games together, and if we can't manage to attend in person, we share our enthusiasm and frustration via text during the games. Exactly as Roger and I used to do.

Deborah and I feel very fortunate that all six of our grandchildren are very close to each other and love being together. It's been that way pretty much forever. Even Ava, who's considerably younger than her siblings and cousins, has never been pushed aside or ignored by the others. When she was five years old and the extended family was gathered one summer at the Wawasee house, she composed, produced, and directed her own musical. We were all given parts, most of which were birds. I think I probably had a "minah" role! And even after all this time, we can still sing from memory the show's signature tune, "Seeds in the Air and We Don't Even Care."

Deborah and I love to have the kids and grandkids around, but we also enjoy being alone together. I'm reminded of a deceased friend whose own marriage summed up what I think makes Deborah and my relationship so special. Recently, we attended her funeral, shortly after she had celebrated her 70th wedding anniversary. In the course of the service at Second Presbyterian Church in Indianapolis, it was mentioned by each of her three sons, and by the minister, that she and her husband had been proud of the fact that during seven decades of marriage they had never run out of things to say to each other. They had never grown bored with each other's company.

Though Deborah and I haven't been together for nearly as long, the same holds true for us. At this time in our lives, we spend more time together than most younger married couples. And we never run out of things to talk about. So much so that one of our primary shared activities is conversation.

We also pay a lot of attention to sports. On weekends, during the fall, we watch college football on Saturdays and the NFL on Sundays. We also take in a lot of college basketball, either on TV or in person—most often IU and Deborah's alma mater, the University of Dayton. We're also very interested in Duke because of my role there and the fact that Paige and Emily are graduates. In fact, we've gotten interested in all the schools our grandchildren have attended.

Among other things, Deborah and I also have experienced great joy in supporting the IU Athletics Women's Excellence Initiative, an effort launched in 2021 by my close friend, IU Vice President and Director of Athletics Scott Dolson. It exclusively supports IU's 13 women's sports programs and enhances the student-athlete experience for the university's more than 300 varsity female athletes.

The university wanted to acknowledge our gift, and I suggested naming something for Deborah within women's athletics. And so, in late October of 2022, we visited the Bloomington campus for the dedication of Deborah Tobias Field, the women's field hockey facility. The women's field hockey team refers to it as "The Deb," and their motto is "Protect the Deb." They've installed a plaque with those words beside the door of their dressing room and now have a tradition of touching it as they go out to take the field. We've begun a custom each fall of furnishing the team with quarter-zips that say "Indiana Field Hockey, Deborah Tobias Field" on the front and "Protect the Deb" (and the year) on one of the sleeves. We've enjoyed the personal friendship that has developed with Coach Kayla Bashore and her colleagues. We've often observed that if we had a daughter playing college field hockey, we'd for sure want her to have the opportunity to grow and develop as a person under Kayla's nurturing influence.

Though Deborah and I are both quite enamored with sports, our philanthropic interests have reached far beyond them. During my time leading and helping to launch PEPFAR and my subsequent leadership of all United States foreign assistance, I saw so much accomplished. But I also witnessed a development culture that too often measured success based on how much money was raised and appropriated and not on tangible achievements.

Often this wasteful behavior was done with the best of intentions by organizations that didn't grasp already well-understood lessons about what development practices work and what don't. I saw a lack of focus on clear goals and metrics and an absence of innovation and local ownership.

An opportunity to address this issue came about on my 75th birthday. Among the many bold initiatives undertaken by IU President Emeritus Michael McRobbie during his 14-year tenure at the helm of the university was the creation of the Hamilton Lugar School of Global and International Studies. IU has long had an important role in international matters across a wide spectrum, for example, offering courses in more foreign languages than any other U.S. university. But those extraordinary resources were scattered across many parts of IU, existing without the benefit of the many available synergies. In 2015 McRobbie brought those assets together to form the Hamilton Lugar School, now a true leader within higher education in the study and teaching of international affairs. Deborah wanted to do something special with her own money to mark the occasion of my special birthday, so we began conversations with Dean (and former U.S. Ambassador to Poland) Lee Feinstein and his colleagues at the Hamilton Lugar School, which led to the launch of the Randall L. and Deborah F. Tobias Center for Innovation in International Development. Deborah wrote a significant check and I matched her funding with an equal deferred gift. The goals that we agreed upon for the center were very clear and driven largely by my own experiences.

In a nutshell, we wanted it to identify and share best practices in the delivery of development assistance; create reliable metrics to assess the effectiveness of aid, including through the identification of clear and measurable outcomes, with particular emphasis on developing self-sufficiency where possible; stimulate research into innovative approaches in the field, including effective partnerships with the growing roster of international donors; and train and engage the next generation of leaders in the field of development assistance. I'm pleased to note how proud Deborah and I are to be associated with this venture and what has already been accomplished under the very capable leadership of the Center's Director, Sarah Bauerle Danzman, Associate Professor of International Studies at the Hamilton Lugar School. And we are incredibly energized by their plans for the future. It's certainly been money well invested.

Deborah and I have also done quite a bit of traveling together. This is somewhat of an unusual development, given our professional lives. Because both of us jetted around the world on innumerable business trips, we for the most part looked forward to spending our retirements not walking through airports. Yet, in spite of that, during our marriage, we've made several epic journeys together, from France to Cuba. We even spent a month on a chartered 757 with about 50 other people, traveling around Oceania. We started in Hawaii and then went to New Zealand, Australia, and other points of interest. There was an onboard chef and two university professors who offered lectures about our various destinations before we arrived. It was quite an adventure.

We also spent two very memorable weeks in Africa, where I had a chance to show Deborah some of the things I was involved with during my PEPFAR days. We went as part of an official IU excursion that checked in on AMPATH Kenya, a partnership between Moi University, Moi Teaching and Referral Hospital, the Kenyan government, and a worldwide consortium of universities led by IU. The object was to develop holistic, sustainable healthcare in Kenya and also globally. Back in the day, I put some PEPFAR money into the effort—not because of its IU affiliation, but because it offered (and continues to offer) what's truly the best AIDS program in sub-Saharan Africa.

During the trip, we got a chance to visit a woman in a remote part of the countryside who was a participant in one of AMPATH Kenya's AIDS programs. We tagged along with the person who provided her with medications, giving Deborah a feel for what PEPFAR was really like at "ground level." It was an emotional moment—the sort that, many years ago, transformed my own perspective on AIDS from an academic issue to a viscerally human one.

But that wasn't the trip's most compelling moment. That occurred when we visited the program's facilities in the Kenyan city of Eldoret, during which a young female doctor came up to me and asked, "Are you Ambassador Tobias?"

I told her I used to be, and she started crying.

"I met you before, when you visited Kenya eight or nine years ago," she said. "I have a photograph of you and me standing together, hanging on the wall in the living room of my apartment. You just have no idea the impact you had on my life. You came to my country when I was a young doctor, just beginning to practice, with so few resources and so much hopelessness. You demonstrated that you personally cared. You gave us significant resources from the American people. But just as importantly, you personally gave us hope. I can't thank you enough."

Deborah and I both shared a tear with her.

I was proud to see her again. Proud of what she'd accomplished. And extremely humbled to have been a part of such a vast effort that saved and changed so many lives. In retrospect, I should have told her, "You have no idea the impact all of this has had on my life as well."

FULL CIRCLE *Chapter Thirty-Two*

Change is inevitable.
But family is eternal.

It's said you can't go home again, but I've got something that gets me pretty close.

Deborah and I commissioned two paintings of the places that shaped our character and that still matter deeply to us today. Deborah's canvas is a picture of Our Lady of Lourdes, the school and church she attended while growing up in the Irvington neighborhood on the Indianapolis east side, the focal point of her family's existence. Mine, perhaps not surprisingly, is a rendering of downtown Remington as it was in the 1940s and '50s when I grew up. Both were done by the acclaimed Midwestern artist John Michael Carter, who worked from period photos and also made personal visits. He did an extraordinary job with each.

For me, he conjured a time and a milieu that exist now only in my memory. My painting shows Remington's main street business district, circa 1950, looking north. Railroad tracks, which in 1860 became the town's reason to exist, run from east to west. On the northeast corner of the block, in the lower right of the canvas, one can see a limestone building with a reddish awning. That's the State Bank of Remington, my father's bank. The bigger brick building next to the bank is Peck's grocery, where I worked on Saturdays as a teen. There's a green pickup truck parked on the street in front that represents the one owned by my dad's close friend Chester Biddle, the father of my friend Bill. Chester frequently drove into town from his farm to share a morning cup of coffee with my dad and other locals at Woody's Snak Shop (barely visible in the canvas's lower right corner). Likely among those locals was Ronnie Gillam, the principal attorney in town and the father of my friend Ronnie Q. His office is visible across the street from Woody's in the lower left corner. They were often joined by other good friends of my dad, maybe Ward Lewis, owner of a local auto parts business and the grandfather of my friend Mike Merkel, or Hollis May, owner of the local Ford dealership and the father of my friend Jeffrey.

When I gaze at this painting, I fondly recall that long-gone era. Over the years, the town has grown, but only slightly, from 869 residents in 1940 to 1,356 in 2020. The businesses in Remington are now more spread out, with many located several blocks north along the main highway and the nearby interstate interchange. The railroad in the center of town, the town's original reason for existence, is no longer the focal point. So the mix of downtown businesses has changed. No more State Bank of Remington, no more Peck's, and no more Woody's Snak Shop. But along with a lot of other remnants of my youth, my parents' home on Brown Street still stands. Back in the 1950s, if you stepped out our front door and turned right, within a block the street led you to the Bellows's family home and immediately behind it to orderly rows of corn and soybeans. It's the same now. Almost exactly the same.

I know all this because today, in my 83rd year, I spend more time in Remington than I have since I left it for college. And recently, for the first time in more than six decades, I visited my childhood home.

I got this priceless opportunity thanks to a chance encounter at a Remington High School Alumni Association Annual Dinner. Remington High School's last class graduated in 1971, after which it was merged with the school systems in several adjacent communities to create the Tri-County School Corporation. About 250 people annually attend these dinners, which is a pretty good turnout for an organization that hasn't added a single new member in more than half a century.

While there, I learned from Lanny Sigo, the brother of a childhood classmate, that his niece, Darcy Allegrini, and her husband Tommy, had recently acquired my old family home and were in the midst of renovating it. My parents sold it in 1962 to Carl and Deloris Pampel, and when Carl died in 2018 the property was acquired by their granddaughter Darcy. I mused idly that it would be great to tour the place someday, and—Remington being Remington—my words almost immediately got back to the Allegrinis. In short order, I received an email from Darcy with a very warm standing invitation for a tour when they finished their renovation. Eventually, I found myself, with Deborah at my side, paying a visit for the first time in 62 years.

We knocked on the back door (visitors, just as in my day, typically use it instead of the front door) and were welcomed onto the home's enclosed porch. The first thing I noticed was a familiar-looking exquisitely refinished upright piano. Upon closer examination, I realized from the wood detailing that it had been my mother's. I even have a photo of myself as a young boy standing next to it, playing a duet with her on my cornet.

That was the most meaningful of the family artifacts I saw that day, but by no means the only one. The home's basic layout hadn't changed much, but some of the details had. The kitchen was still in the same place, but the bar where the Tobias family ate breakfast together (and took their Lilly vitamins) was long gone. And my brother's bedroom and the guest bedroom had been combined to create a spacious master suite. However, surprising traces of our tenure remained. My own bedroom looked the same. In the basement (where, just as we did, the Allegrinis keep shelves of home-canned produce), we found the ping-pong table my father built back in the 1940s. And upstairs sat a carved wooden sideboard that matched my parents' dining room table, which I still have. When they moved, they took the table but left the sideboard.

The yard, which formed the backdrop of so many of my childhood adventures, was also a mix of the new and the familiar. The spot where I spent the better part of a summer building an elaborate foxhole, complete with a camouflaged trap door, bore no trace of my efforts. But the creek that I canoed as a child still traced its way along the edge of the property. And a line of pine trees near the creek, which I watched my grandfather plant as a windbreak when I was five or six years old, now towered in their mature majesty after seventy-five years of growth. So did a massive, sprawling cottonwood tree that I remembered from childhood. It's said that everything seems bigger to a kid than it does to an adult. Well, this particular tree looked just as imposing to me as a grownup as it had when I was young.

Seeing the place after more than half a century affected me deeply. But I didn't realize how deeply until the next morning, when I woke up feeling utterly depleted. I told Deborah I wasn't feeling myself, and she, in her wisdom, told me the likely cause.

"I think you had a bigger emotional experience yesterday than you realize," she said.

I believe she nailed it. I was struggling to process some very different feelings: elation over visiting my parents' house after such a long absence, nostalgia from all those formative memories, and distress pondering what it must have been like for my mother to part with (among other things) her much-loved piano.

The reason my parents moved almost immediately after I left for college was likely rooted in my father's Depression-era pragmatism. With both of his boys gone, he probably saw no need for a four-bedroom, two-story home that would become increasingly difficult for him and my mom to navigate as they aged. So, they instead moved to a two-bedroom, one-story house where they spent most of the rest of their lives. There was less room, so this meant leaving things behind—including the piano. It wasn't (at least in my mind) ideal, but I can understand their thinking, or at least his. Why linger in a larger, pricier house than they needed?

As did my parents until the end of their lives, I too now own a small home in the Remington area.

It sits on the working, 320-acre corn and soybean farm that I purchased in 1998. Located only a few miles from the land where my father grew up, it's still overseen by Bill Biddle and his son, Bryce. I bought it to maintain a connection to the community at a time when my last remaining relative there was my aunt (my dad's youngest sibling), Helen Butcher.

In 2017 I built a small shed on that property to store the necessary equipment for launching clay birds. I've enjoyed shotgun sports much of my life and have mostly focused on hunting upland birds like pheasants and quail. I've introduced Deborah to the sport, and we shoot clay pigeons at the Remington farm for fun and to keep up our skills. But as the years passed, the farm became far more than just a place to indulge my hobby. I added a more extensive shooting layout, as well as a cozy, two-bedroom farmhouse with a stone fireplace in the living room, plus a large garage and storage facility. Whenever we can, Deborah and I spend time there. It's hard to explain how relaxing it is to unwind in a place where the dominant sounds are birdsong, the buzz of insects, and the wind rustling the corn.

When making my rounds in town, I can still greet a few of Remington's current and former residents by name. The list includes Mike Scott, who owns the Remington IGA grocery—successor to Peck's, the grocery store where I once worked that is featured in my painting. He also knew my dad. But time has taken its toll. For example, in the spring of 2023, I attended the funeral of my lifelong friend, Alice Medley. As I mentioned in an earlier chapter, when I was 14 years old, I worked with her at Peck's. I sang at her wedding, and she and her husband, Bill, named their first son after me. Over the years we stayed in touch, and I'm still in contact with Bill and two of their children, Sandy and Jeff. Alice was 87 at the time of her passing.

Alice lies in Remington Cemetery, a quiet patch of monument-filled turf that sits on the town's northeastern periphery, overlooking a flat, horizon-spanning swath of farmland to its north and east. The cemetery is the final resting place of my great-grandparents, Theopolis and Elizabeth Tobias; my grandparents, Harry and Leva Tobias; my parents, Roy and Fern; my brother Roger and his twin, Gordon, who died shortly after birth; and many other family members and friends. Calling it peaceful would be an understatement. It seems like a fine, restful place to spend eternity. When I walk among the stones and read the names they bear, it actually feels like I'm walking down Remington's 1950s streets, looking at long-familiar names on mailboxes.

Remington's changed over the years, but while there are some scars, for the most part, time has treaded lightly. Not like much of the rest of the country, which during my lifetime passed through one cultural, economic, and political upheaval after another. For instance, my adventures as an Indiana University student during the early 1960s sound almost anachronistic today. They took place during the last, tranquil moments of the post-World War II era, before concerns about things like fall formal college dances were supplanted by protests, the sexual revolution, and worries over the draft. And I served in the military just as the Vietnam War turned into a lightning rod of controversy that pitted generation against generation.

Similar seismic changes also roiled my career. I spent decades working for a company that was so vast, respected, and ubiquitous that it was assumed to be a permanent part of the U.S. landscape—until it literally vanished overnight. As for my personal life, I've endured the loss of family members who were centerpieces of my existence and whom I never imagined being without.

But that, as I've learned from hard experience, is the way of things. Jobs, homes, friends, and loved ones all come and go, no matter how much we might wish otherwise. Change is inevitable. Our task, as I've alluded to throughout this volume, is to learn whatever lessons these disruptions might offer and then soldier on—older, wiser, and never daunted.

If you're an IU alumnus, that last phrase, "never daunted," may strike a chord. It's from the university's famous fight song, "Indiana, Our Indiana," which has been performed at every football and basketball game and other university functions since 1912.

Here are the full lyrics:
> Indiana, Our Indiana
> Indiana, we're all for you
> We will fight for
> the Cream and Crimson,
> For the glory of Old IU
> Never daunted, we cannot falter
> In the battle, we're tried and true
> Indiana, Our Indiana
> Indiana, we're all for you!

I've sung it myself many times over the years in many places, including while in the stands at Assembly Hall and Memorial Stadium. But only recently did I realize how perfectly "never daunted" sums up the Tobias family's multi-century, multi-generational American saga. And how my own journey through the tumultuous last half of the 20th century and the early 21st shaped my hard-won beliefs about how best to cope with—and benefit from—change.

I think about the generations of my family a lot these days because in recent years I've spent a great deal of time researching its past. It's populated with figures who coped with disruptions far more drastic than anything I've personally faced. For instance, I can't help wondering what inspired Tobias Tobias, sometime in the 1820s, to forsake his ancestral home of Wales, take a ship across the vast Atlantic, and then travel deep into the North American continent to try his luck in a half-settled wilderness called Indiana.

I'll likely never learn for certain what circumstances drove him or even whether he was going *away* from something or *toward* something. But I think I understand why he chose the path he did. He decided that the best solution was change—radical change.

He wasn't alone in making such a drastic decision. Consider the millions of people who, facing danger or poverty in their home countries, chose, like Deborah's Irish ancestors and like my progenitor, to pack up their meager belongings and go to a mysterious, faraway land called America. It was a leap of faith and an act of courage so breathtaking that it beggars the imagination. Those were the folks who built this country.

Now, consider for a moment what was likely a far larger group—the ones who could have left but didn't. They too faced danger and poverty in their homelands. Perhaps the potato famine in Ireland, or the pogroms in imperial Russia, or political chaos and war in China. But instead of taking advantage of a lifetime opportunity for the price of a steerage ticket to the New World, they shied away, perhaps paralyzed by uncertainty or fear of change. To their minds, simply staying where they were and vanishing from history seemed less traumatic than plunging into the Great Unknown.

For some, this probably worked. But in hindsight it's easy to see the heartbreaking price many of these timid souls paid for their decision (or rather, indecision). They failed to grasp a fact that Tobias Tobias seems to have instinctively understood and that still applies to this day: those who embrace change earn at least a fighting chance at a better life. Those who resist it or avoid it often have no chance at all.

The America my family arrived in fairly writhed with change. Economic booms and busts came and went. Cities rose seemingly overnight. Even the nation's leader was replaced every four or eight years. Beginning 200 years ago, the Tobiases rode such changes like surfers catching waves. They started out as farmers and frontiersmen. Then they spent two generations running a family mill. And when that business died, they returned to farming.

Then my father got the chance of a lifetime—a scholarship to DePauw University. But he graduated just as the Great Depression struck. His first job was behind a desk in the accounting department of the Northern Indiana Public Service Company, but as the ravages of the Great Depression deepened, he found himself serving as a lineman for the company until he too was laid off and returned to Remington to work as a farm laborer.

This, as some might recognize, is the moment when a great many people would simply accept their fate and put away their ambitions. But then, out of the blue, he was offered a job at the State Bank of Remington. He had no experience in banking. A different sort of person might have decided to stay with what they knew. But Dad didn't see it that way. Even though the times brought an understandable aversion to unnecessary risk, he was eager for a better opportunity, in spite of the enormous change it represented. When a chance came along, he grabbed it.

And just like that, the trajectory of an innocuous milling and farming clan changed beyond all recognition. Dad married my mom, who had herself earned a college degree in a time when nothing of the sort was expected, or sometimes even condoned, for women. Then they had two sons, who like their parents attended college. One became an executive with one of the 20th century's most successful retailers, while the other achieved a high position with the nation's largest company, followed by leadership at one of America's preeminent pharmaceutical manufacturers. Not bad for a family that started the 1900s as custodians of a gristmill on the banks of the Muscatatuck River. And it all began with Tobias Tobias's decision to leave the Old World for the New.

Driven in part by a desire to learn what moved him, in the fall of 2024 (just a few months after I toured my childhood home in Remington), Deborah and I visited Wales.

Our trip started with a few days in London, followed by the "bucket list" opportunity to take part in an English driven pheasant shoot at the invitation of the Anglo American Shooting Society.

If you've ever watched a movie about the English gentry, there's almost inevitably a scene where everyone goes on a "driven shoot," dressed in tweed jackets with ties, plus fours, long colorful socks, and wellies, equipped with elegantly made double barrel shotguns, with the nine or ten "guns" lined up in a field at assigned "pegs" as a line of "drivers" flushes birds toward them. After five days of this very challenging but incredibly enjoyable pursuit, Deborah and I moved on to Wales (one of the four countries, along with England, Scotland, and Northern Ireland, that make up the United Kingdom).

On Saturday, November 9, 2024, for the first time in two centuries, a member of my branch of the Tobias family trod the roads and lanes of the village of Llanfihangel Aberbythych Carmarthenshire, and the ancient settlements nearby, where Tobias Tobias lived his early years, as did others in the Tobias clan.

With the help of a wonderful local genealogist, Elinor Gilbey, we toured the countryside and visited landmarks in the places where my ancestors lived, including St. David's Church in Abergwili where Thomas and Catherine were married and are buried; St. Michael's Church in Llanfihangel Alberbythych where Tobias Tobias was baptized; St. Tybie's Church in Llandybie where David T. was baptized; and a tiny nearby village named, of all things, Carmel.

We know that in addition to their son David, Thomas and Catherine, my fifth great-grandparents, had seven other children, all of whom remained in Wales. And we know that David and Elizabeth Tobias, my fourth great-grandparents, besides their son Tobias Tobias, had six other children. Their sons John and Enos also emigrated to the United States to the same southern Indiana community as Tobias, but the four other siblings remained in Wales. Tobias is not a common name in Wales, so the odds are high that I may be related to any we can locate who are still in the area and may be descendants of these earlier generations.

We visited a cemetery in the nearby village of Llanarthney, Carmarthenshire where Elinor has discovered a significant number of Tobias graves. Elinor is continuing to investigate who these people were, on my behalf, so the search continues.

During these excursions, as we tramped through verdant fields and gazed at old stone buildings, it dawned on me that perhaps I was looking at the question of why Tobias Tobias left for America incorrectly.

Knowing the particular challenge he faced didn't matter. Knowing the particular opportunity he sought didn't matter. What *really* mattered, and what really changed his descendants' lives, were his bold actions. He was, as the crowds at Assembly Hall like to sing, Never Daunted.

Rising from a small Welsh village to where our family is now does seem, at the very least, improbable. But the truth is, it would have been *impossible* if, during perhaps a dozen key moments of the Tobiases' American adventure, just one of my ancestors decided to make a "safe" choice about his or her future. To stay put. To refuse an unusual opportunity. To stick with a dying trade because it was all they knew.

In other words, to refuse the call to change.

In achieving what I have in life, I recognize I stand on their shoulders. But I like to think that I've honored my lineage by also never (or rarely) being daunted by change. And I hope that by my words, but more importantly my actions, I've demonstrated the principles and values that can help motivate and educate future generations going forward.

I want to emulate some of the leaders I've known and observed during my life—the sorts of people who've left behind what I call "footprints." The ideas and the policies they championed not only survived them but continue to inform the practices and values of the people, businesses, and organizations with which they were involved.

For instance, I'm quite proud of my efforts at Lilly, which I believe helped enhance the foundation for what's so far been a very prosperous 21st century. And today, I'm so incredibly proud of the leaders who followed me as CEOs: Sidney Taurel, John Lechleiter, and Dave Ricks. As one measure, when I became CEO in 1993, the company was in significant difficulty and a hostile takeover target, with the price of a Lilly share down to $12.50. When I retired at the end of 1998, the share price was $96 and the company was again on a sound footing with a new, focused strategy and a refreshed and maybe even reinvented culture. And now, 25 years later, through the work of the leaders who followed me and thousands of extraordinary Lilly people around the world, as I write this, a share of the company's stock is valued at well over $800, nearly nine times the price when I retired. And Lilly is currently the twelfth most valuable company in the entire world.

Of course there are also the millions of lives saved and improved by PEPFAR. I take a great deal of pride in my involvement in that effort and in the results achieved by the thousands of goodhearted people across the planet who formed the organization's bones and sinew. I was able to take the lessons I'd learned in business and apply them to this massive governmental effort—strategies that are still taught by my IU philanthropic programs and which have become part of the DNA of PEPFAR and other federal organizations.

Speaking of our philanthropy, I've been very blessed to have accumulated the unexpected resources that enabled me to "pay it forward" in ways I could never have imagined when I graduated from Indiana University and began my career. I feel very good about a number of those efforts, large and small, beginning with the Tobias Leadership Center. From its launch in 2004 and with its extraordinary accomplishments over nearly 20 years, I fully expect that 20 years from now, and beyond, it will continue to produce young leaders and publish useful, actionable research. As I write this, 324 Tobias Fellows have graduated from the Center's year-long keystone program.

And there's also the Tobias Center for Innovation in International Development. With individual commitments from both Deborah and me and a mission to build on what I learned during my time as an ambassador, running the nation's International Development Program, it too is already meeting and exceeding our expectations.

And most recently, with a significant commitment from Deborah and me, an equivalent commitment from our good friends John and Sarah Lechleiter, and additional matching funds from IU Health and the IU School of Medicine, we're excited about the vision and aspirations for what will be known as the Tobias-Lechleiter Institute for Clinical Trial Excellence. The vision for this institute is to create a world-class capability that further develops the underutilized potential synergies that were envisioned when Methodist and IU hospitals initially came together to form what is now IU Health and were then joined in a partnership with the IU School of Medicine. Our expectation is that this institute will take a leading role in the development and deployment of life-changing medicines, therapies, and procedures—something of great interest to both the Lechleiters and Deborah and me.

During my life, I've traveled to virtually every corner of the world and owned homes in Indiana, New Jersey, Pennsylvania, Tennessee, Florida, Illinois, Colorado, and Montana. But recently, I've been drawn ever more strongly to my Hoosier roots. Our Carmel house on the outskirts of Indianapolis serves as both our primary residence and the location of the Tobias Family Office. During summer, Deborah and I (and, as often as possible, many other family members) regularly decamp to Lake Wawasee, where I enjoy lake life—including my collection of vintage wooden boats. In the winter, we spend close to three months at our home on Longboat Key, Florida—again joined from time to time by children, grandchildren, nieces, and nephews. Indeed, my most important priority is to devote time and attention to the next generations of my family.

Deborah and I want to leave a lasting, positive impact on the lives of our six grandchildren, who are the eighth generation of our Indiana family: Emily, Ella, Connor, Jack, Sam, and Ava. Also, my nephew Eric, his wife Laura, and their three daughters, Anna, Abbie Grace, and Elizabeth; and my beloved daughter Paige and her husband Tim. Along with Deborah, these are the people I care most about and for whom I want to leave "footprints" when I'm gone. And with planning well underway for the July 26, 2025, Wawasee lakeside wedding when Emily and Jack Morris celebrate their vows, it's not unreasonable for me to think that I might someday meet the ninth generation of the Indiana Tobiases.

I want to make sure that my grandchildren are all well-educated and have the opportunity to live comfortable and productive lives consistent with their own abilities and their chosen professional pursuits. I want to be sure they are fully prepared and equipped to accept responsibility for their own wellbeing—and that they do so. I harbor no aspirations for them to follow in my footsteps. It would be fine if they do, but I wouldn't think of trying to mold them into a Randall Tobias 2.0. Instead, I want them to be "Themselves 1.0." To be successful at whatever they choose to pursue, to the maximum of their own capacities. And I want, most of all, for them to be happy.

That legacy was bequeathed to them not just by Paige or Todd or by me as their grandfather, but by all the Tobiases who came before me. Step by step, decade by decade, generation by generation, they faced change fearlessly and, in many cases, found a way to benefit and advance.

I believe it's not impossible, given the fact that both my parents lived to be 90 and the ever-increasing quality of healthcare, that I could be around for another 20 years. Yet, I also think that at this stage in my life, it's perfectly reasonable to understand my time might be shorter and to contemplate what I will leave behind. I hope that legacy goes well beyond the academic centers and physical facilities that bear my name or the boxes I've occupied on various organization charts. I hope my legacy also resides in the realm of values, ideas, and lessons learned. And perhaps the most important lesson learned is this: Change is part of life. Don't fear it. Instead, embrace it and learn to recognize the opportunities it inevitably brings. This is the throughline of this book and the most important "footprint" I hope to leave in both the professional and academic worlds and with my family.

I intend to add to my personal legacy for as long as I can, in part by spending time with my grandchildren. I want to continue to help and encourage them to develop their own values while they also build happy, and perhaps instructive, memories of their Boo Boo and Hoo Hoo. Because eventually, inevitably, those memories will form our truest, most lasting legacy.

People come and go. Careers rise and ebb. Change is inevitable. But family is eternal.

So too is faith in a brighter future.

May it ever be so.

ACKNOWLEDGMENTS

As I believe this narrative repeatedly shows, little in life that is truly worthwhile gets accomplished alone. For me, nowhere has that been more true than in the creation of this book. I want to take a moment to recognize and thank some of those who were essential in bringing *Never Daunted* to fruition.

The only logical place to begin expressing my gratitude is with my beloved "office family," each of whom has shared nearly every aspect of my life, professional and personal, for well over four decades. Without them, my life, and the story in this book, would have been very different. Maureen Radigan, my longtime AT&T executive assistant, was by my side professionally and personally from the early 1980s until I departed for Lilly in 1993, and we've continued to stay connected. Following my retirement from Lilly, Dory Cook joined the Tobias Family Office in September 1999. Even though she retired in 2016, she still returns twice each year to fill in for vacations. Eleven months after Dory's arrival, Laura Lashmet signed on in August 2000. Meg Linden came aboard in May 2004. Each of these four people has played such an incredibly important part in my life, as well as in the lives of Deborah, Paige, Todd, and others in the family. From the critical to the mundane;

ACKNOWLEDGMENTS

the transition from AT&T to Lilly and from Lilly to retirement; the management of a ranch in Montana and a farm in Indiana to overseeing a number of other properties and construction projects; to helping to analyze, buy, and sell various business investments; to other matters of financial, tax, and estate planning; to travel planning; to event planning and hosting in our homes; to managing calendars; to buying and selling boats and vehicles; to helping run a thoroughbred racing and breeding operation; to running the family foundation; to listening to political candidates and development professionals and others hoping for an opportunity to tell their story; to providing support during illnesses and surgeries; to sharing both joy and tears when celebrating the births of grandchildren or helping with the planning for both weddings and funerals; they have each been there through all the victories and setbacks, looking out for my best interests, every moment of every day. To Maureen, Dory, Laura, and Meg, I love each of them unconditionally, and will until my last breath.

For many reasons, I'm very grateful to my good friend and spiritual advisor, Chris Henry, senior pastor of Second Presbyterian Church in Indianapolis. This is the church where I have been a member since returning to Indianapolis in 1993 and where I currently serve as an Elder. After my marriage to Deborah, we spent some time "shopping around" to find a church home where both of us, given our different faith histories, would together feel comfortable and welcome. Ultimately, even though Deborah will always remain a cultural Catholic, Chris made Deborah feel so incredibly welcome in joining the Presbyterian Church during his first meeting with us to discuss the possibility. There were tears of joy all around. Chris, his wife Sara Hayden, and their sons, Sam and Ben, have all become treasured extensions of our family.

ACKNOWLEDGMENTS

I'm indebted to my first cousin once removed, Vicki Tobias, whose long-time passion for genealogy and tenacity in searching far and wide to document the details of the Tobias family contributed greatly to the backstory of this book. She has generously shared her findings with me over the years, helped answer my questions, and in some cases kvetched with me when together we could not find answers to the unanswerable. I'm hopeful that my work here will be a partial payback for all she has given me over the years. I'm also grateful for the work of two talented genealogists in Wales, Susan Rainey and Elinor Gilbey.

More specifically to the book, guiding this work from manuscript to finished volume required the services of an entire team of experts, beginning with project manager Alyssa Chase, who brought in seasoned professionals that included graphic designer Carla Blackwell; copy editor and proofreader Corina Lebegioara; and indexer Kelly Talbot. Their work shepherded *Never Daunted* from a rough draft to a polished book.

One of the flagship programs of the Tobias Leadership Center is its oral history project. I'm grateful to Julie Manning Magid, the Center's executive and academic director, as well as vice dean of IU's Kelley School of Business, for encouraging me to participate in the program, and to Dr. Philip Scarpino, an expert in oral histories who directs the program and has conducted several hours of interviews with me on three separate occasions. The resulting oral history proved an invaluable resource for this book.

During my years at AT&T headquarters, one of my colleagues and close friends was Al Partoll. Al was initially an AT&T attorney who handled federal appellate litigation. He later focused on strategic planning and other matters and retired as an AT&T executive vice president. Of equal relevance, he was simply one of the company's best minds. This placed him in the middle of many of the most

ACKNOWLEDGMENTS

important decisions of the times. I asked Al to read a draft of the section of this book pertaining to AT&T, and his suggestions were extremely helpful. I'm very grateful for his contributions.

One of the most important responsibilities of any CEO, indeed any leader, is identifying and developing talent. During my early days at Lilly, when I asked to see the files of people who were thought to have the potential to someday rise to the top ranks of the company, John Lechleiter's was one of the first I read. As I interacted with John, it became clear that he would someday be a candidate to lead the company—something I told the board at the time of my retirement. Following the successful tenure of my immediate successor, Sidney Taurel, and to no one's surprise, John indeed became one of the most effective and significant CEOs in the company's nearly 150-year history. Deborah and I have also come to treasure our personal friendship with John and his wife, Sarah. John read the parts of this book pertaining to Lilly and generously offered his insights. Those suggestions—some from his perspective as my colleague and as a former Lilly CEO and some, by his own admission, inspired by his days as the undergraduate editor of the Xavier University student newspaper—were all extremely helpful.

In the body of this book, I've already written a good deal about Nazanin Ash. Let me simply say here that anything I may have accomplished during my time in the government bears her fingerprints as well. In spite of the time pressures from her current role as the CEO of Welcome.US, Nazanin read everything in the first draft pertaining to my time in Washington, D.C., reminded me of some important facts, and made invaluable suggestions for which I am incredibly grateful.

I'm indebted to my daughter, Paige Tobias Button, in more ways than I can possibly express here. The title of this book,

ACKNOWLEDGMENTS

Never Daunted, perhaps best describes her own journey—and ours together. Paige read the first draft in its entirety. Her suggestions were very helpful, and her belief that the book would be, in her words, "an incredible gift to the grandchildren" made my heart sing.

My wife, Deborah Tobias, has been a rock of support during this undertaking. She too read the near-final manuscript and offered great observations and encouragement. She took the view that when I was in the mood to work on the book—occasionally late into the night like a college kid cramming for finals—that's what I should be encouraged to do, whether the timing was convenient for her or not. Beyond that, she has come to play many roles in our family, including those of wife, grandmother, aunt, ever-present cheerleader, and all-around generator of family joy. The day I fell in love with Deborah was a great day for the extended Tobias clan.

Sometime after my retirement from Lilly, my son, Todd Tobias, made the audacious proposal that I might actually have it in me to write a book. The result was our 2003 collaboration, *Put the Moose on the Table: Lessons in Leadership from a CEO's Journey Through Business and Life*. The process of writing that book, and the father-son bonding that resulted, was one of the highlights of our relationship. I am forever grateful to Todd for talking me into that project. Without it, I would never have had that experience, nor would I have had the confidence or motivation to write this volume. I miss him every single day.

This takes me to my partner in this endeavor, Sam Stall.

Sam is a 1984 Ball State University journalism graduate who has authored or co-authored more than two dozen nonfiction books, three novels, and innumerable magazine and newspaper stories. For sixteen years, he occupied almost every masthead position at *Indianapolis Monthly* magazine from intern to editor-in-chief. It was Todd who first connected us.

ACKNOWLEDGMENTS

Todd worked for Sam when he was an intern at the *Monthly*, and later Sam served as a freelance contributor to *Indy Men's Magazine* from its first edition to its last. For a while, Todd convinced me to write a monthly business column for the magazine. But the time and mental commitment required to write them to the high standard that I expected of myself, and that Todd expected of me, in the midst of an already full calendar of other commitments, became more than I could handle. Enter Sam. Each month I would sit down with him and discuss my thoughts on some business- or leadership-related subject. Sometimes the topics themselves were generated during those conversations. Sam would then take those thoughts, turn them into a well-crafted draft column, and return it to me. I would edit it, occasionally tweak it, and sometimes rephrase parts of it to sound, at least to me, more like my own voice. And just like that, we had a finished column.

Sometime in 2018, remembering the questions I wish I'd asked my grandmother about her days teaching Richard Nixon's mother, I decided that I wanted to write a memoir whose "target audience" would be my grandchildren and their grandchildren. I immediately thought of Sam, my admiration for his work, and the ease with which we collaborated. It was a process I totally understood not only from that experience but from years of working with very talented corporate speech writers in the same way—channeling thoughts from my brain to their brains and keyboards and on to a finished document. In December 2018, Sam and I shook hands and began the journey that produced this book. And I will admit that I think both of us are rather proud of ourselves.

Reviewing my calendar from that time, I can identify 36 scheduled telephone conversations that probably averaged two hours each. And I know there were more than that. I'm sure the emails we exchanged count in the hundreds. As with those *Indy Men's Magazine*

ACKNOWLEDGMENTS

columns, Sam asked questions to stimulate my thinking about topics and times contained in our outline for the book. He would ask, I would talk, and he would take notes and record. Occasionally, I would sit down before a blank computer screen and write something myself. Eventually, sometimes after Sam had also done additional research to provide richer context, draft material would appear in the shared online software we used. I would then add, subtract, and edit. And sometimes I would just wish I could have expressed myself as well as Sam expressed me! It took nearly six years of such work to reach the finish. Bottom line: The story is mine, but the book is ours.

Sam Stall will forever be linked to the Tobias family and its history. Words cannot convey my gratitude to him, not just for the result, but for the joy of the journey.

RLT.

INDEX

Numbers

12 Springs Ranch, 207–211

A

ABC (abstinence, be faithful, condoms), 254, 270–271, 274–275, 295, 313

activists (AIDS), 265–266, 286–287

addiction (alcohol/substance abuse)
    Tobias, Marilyn, 172–173, 176–177
    Tobias, Todd, 330–334

Afghanistan, 305–307

AIDS. *See also* PEPFAR
    AIDS ambassador. *See* Global AIDS Coordinator/AIDS ambassador
    AIDS Conference, 224, 286
    antiretroviral (ARV) drugs, 241, 254, 311–312
    Engole, John Robert, 311–313
    Global AIDS Coordinator/AIDS ambassador. *See also* PEPFAR
        ABC (abstinence, be faithful, condoms), 254, 270–271, 274–275, 295, 313
        achievements, 311–315, 328, 371
        AIDS activists, 265–266, 286–287
        airplane flights to remote locations, 281–282
        AMPATH Kenya, 355–357
        body men, 281, 292
        building central team, 256–259
        bureaucracy, 289–297, 299–300
        celebrities, 303–304
        condoms, 245, 254, 269–272, 275, 294–295
        coordinating local teams, 260–264
        creation of role, 232–238
        faith-based organizations, 274
        five-year goals, 254–255, 262–264
        generic drugs, 267–269
        getting AIDS tested, 285–286
        Global Fund, 265
        host country officials, 266–269
        long hours, 263, 277–278
        meetings, 292–295
        nomination announcement, 238–243

INDEX

orphans, 280, 287–288

prevention, treatment, and care, 254–255, 262

resignation, 298

Senate confirmation, 243–251

sex workers, 286

South African faith healer, 282–285

strategy development, 253–262

strategy document, 249–251, 256, 262

visiting frontline locations, 278–288

AIDS ambassador. *See* Global AIDS Coordinator/AIDS ambassador

AIDS Conference, 224, 286

Air Force (IU Air Force ROTC), 49

airplanes

flights to remote locations, 281–282

pilot's license, 53–55

Alayon, Sylvia, 259

Alcatel, 126

alcohol/substance abuse

Tobias, Marilyn, 172–173, 176–177

Tobias, Todd, 330–334

Allegrini, Darcy, 361–362

Allegrini, Tommy, 361–362

Allen, Bob, 43, 65–66, 93–94, 120–123, 125–126, 131–133, 137

Al-Qaeda, 258

Amazon, 112

ambassador (AIDS). *See* Global AIDS Coordinator/AIDS ambassador

AMPATH Kenya, 355–357

Anglo American Shooting Society, 368–369

antibiotics (Lilly), 142

antidepressants (Prozac), 174–175, 188, 193, 200

antiretroviral (ARV) drugs, 241, 254, 311–312

antitrust suit (AT&T), 104–105, 128–130

Arbuckle, John "Jack," 89

Armitage, Deputy Secretary of State Richard, 257, 259, 261

army, 37, 39, 47

artillery school, 48–52

Fort Sill, 48–52

pilot's license, 53–55

artillery school, 48–52

arts (Business Committee for the Arts), 85–87

ARV (antiretroviral) drugs, 241, 254, 311–312

Ash, Nazanin (neé Samari Kermani), 248–251, 256, 259, 281, 341, 380

Ash, Tim, 249

asthma (Tobias Button, Paige), 71–75

AT&T

AT&T Phone Centers stores, 108–109

ATMs, 125

Baby Bells, 106, 116–117, 119, 126

Bell Laboratories, 100, 104, 107, 117, 120, 124, 126

cell phones, 111–113

chairman and CEO of AT&T Communications, 121, 151–152

Chinese Ministry of Telecommunications proposal, 151–152

386

INDEX

corporate reorganization, 120–123, 131–135
divestiture
   creating plan, 104–107
   implementing strategy, 115–120
Fateful Friday, 106–107
FCC, 67, 107, 127
history, 103
Illinois Bell
   Chicago general manager, 91–96
   vice president, 95–97
Indiana Bell
   Bloomington local operations manager, 68–69
   computers, 79
   Evansville, 43–45, 69, 84, 93
   IMDP, 40–46, 84
   Indianapolis district accounting manager, 78–81, 84
   Indianapolis district manager, 69, 84
   Indianapolis general advertising manager, 84–88
   Indianapolis general commercial manager, 84, 88–90
   Lebanon local operations manager, 64–68
   manual telephone service, 44
   technological advancements, 77–81
   Touch-Tone system, 44, 80
Iran (Islamic Revolution), 129–130
level system, 83–84
NCR, 125
Office of the Chairman, 120–122
Olivetti, 124
president of AT&T Consumer Products, 107–108
relocating phone manufacturing, 109–111
resignation, 137–138
Sears, 108–109
strategic struggles, 123–127
technological advances, 111–113
Time Warner (Warner Media), 126–127
Trimline phones, 80, 110–111
vice president for residence services
   note from CEO, 105–106
   promotion, 97, 131–132
   relocating, 99–103
Western Electric, 21, 100, 104, 107–109, 117, 119–120, 126, 128–129

Atkinson, Dutch, 9
ATMs, 125
Auburn University, 281
Augustine, Norm, 213
Australia, 164, 355

B

Baby Bells, 105, 116–117, 119, 126
Baker, Chief of Staff James, 120
Baker, Senator Howard, 297
Ball State University, 381
Ballard, Mayor Greg, 321–322
banking career (Tobias, Roy), 3–6, 16–17
Barden, Dan, 225
baseball, 349–350
Bashore, Kayla, 353

INDEX

basketball, 67, 139, 225, 290
   Indiana High School Athletic Association's Boys Basketball State Tournament, 87–88, 91
   Indiana University, 352–353, 365
   Remington, 10, 13, 19, 25, 27–28
   University of Dayton, 353

Baxter, Assistant Attorney General William, 130
Bayh, Senator Evan, 246
Beering, Dr. Steven, 195
Beesley, Gene, 142
Before Their Time, 221
Bell Laboratories, 100, 104, 107, 117, 120, 124, 126
Bell, Alexander Graham, 103
Bellows, Janet (Janet Biddle), 9, 28, 341, 360
Bellows, Wilson, 9
Bench, Johnny, 62
Bepko, Gerald "Jerry," 318–320
Bezos, Jeff, 112
Biddle, Bill, 9, 28, 341, 360, 363
Biddle, Bryce, 28, 363
Biddle, Chester, 28, 360
Biddle, Edith, 28
Biddle, Janet (neé Bellows), 9, 28, 341
Biden, President Joe, 245–246, 313
Bird, Larry, 225
Birx, Dr. Deborah, 259, 293
Black, Amy, 259, 281
Blackwell, Carla, 379
Bligh, Ed, 149
Bloomington local operations manager (Indiana Bell), 68–69

boards (Tobias, Randall)
   Chemical Bank, 139–140
   Colonial Williamsburg Foundation, 201, 217–218, 231
   ConocoPhillips, 139, 202, 212–215
   Duke University, 139, 198, 201, 215
   Eli Lilly, 139–147
   Indiana University, 318, 325
   Indianapolis Airport Authority, 321–324
   Kennedy Center, 231–234
   Kimberly-Clark, 139, 202
   Knight Ridder, 139, 202
   outside director, 140
   overview, 138
   Phillips Petroleum, 139, 212–215
body men, 281, 292
Bolger, Tom, 105
Bolivia, 307–308
Bolton, Josh, 259
Bono, 303–304, 314
Boo Boo, 338, 344–345, 374
Boren, Senator David, 297
Botswana, 233, 258
Bowen, Governor Otis, 327
Brazil, 163–164, 196
Brim, Amy Rae (Amy Rae Tobias), 332, 346, 350
Brinkley, David, 231
Brokaw, Tom, 208, 210
Brown, Ann Lee, 122–123, 218
Brown, Charles "Charlie," 93–94, 97, 99, 105–106, 112, 115, 120, 122–123, 126–129, 131–132, 217–218
Bryn Mawr College, 249

INDEX

Bryson, Vaughn, 143–150, 153–154, 164

Buckingham, Diane, 49

Buckingham, Fred, 34, 49

Buckingham, Warren, 259

Bugling for Books program, 210

Buhrt, Mike, 336–337

Buhrt, Sandy, 336–337

bureaucracy (Washington), 289–297, 299–300

Bush, Barbara, 198, 200

Bush, President George H. W., 198–200, 203, 284

Bush, President George W., 164, 204, 273, 289, 306, 308

    AIDS crisis, 231–233

    Director of Office of Foreign Assistance, 298–299

    PEPFAR, 246, 254–255, 301, 303–304, 313–315

        creating, 236–242

        Roosevelt Room nomination speech, 241–242

    USAID, 298–299

Business Committee for the Arts, 85–87

Butcher, Helen (neé Tobias), 2, 363

Butler University, 87

Button, Ava, 337, 341, 345–346, 348, 352, 373

Button, Connor, 139, 337, 339, 344, 347–348, 350, 373

Button, Emily, 139, 205, 207, 337–341, 344, 348, 353, 373

Button, Jack, 337, 339, 347–350, 373

Button, Paige. *See* Tobias Button, Paige

Button, Tim, 184–185, 205, 344–345, 350, 373

C

call to change, 365–368, 370–371, 373–374

Cameron College, 63

Camp Potawatomi, 19–21

Canada, 163

cancer

    Gemzar (pancreatic cancer drug), 161

    melanoma (Tobias, Randall), 182

Captiva, 207, 234, 338–340, 347

Card, Chief of Staff Andy, 204, 259

Carmel, 340, 349, 372

Carson, Tracy, 257, 259

Carter, John Michael, 359

Carter, President Jimmy, 128–130

CDC (Centers for Disease Control), 280

Ceclor (antibiotics), 142

celebrities

    PEPFAR, 303–304

    USAID, 302–304

cell phones (AT&T), 111–113

Centers for Disease Control (CDC), 280

chairman and CEO (Tobias, Randall)

    AT&T Communications, 121, 151–152

    Eli Lilly, 150

        achievements, 371

        Bryson, Vaughn, 143–150, 153–154, 164

INDEX

communication style, 155–156
downsizing staff, 158–160
early retirement plans, 158–160
FDA, 162
FIAU clinical trials, 152–155
first days, 152–155
Health Security Act, 165–167
leadership tone, 155–156
Lilly USA creation, 163–164
management team, restructuring, 157–158
medical devices, 162–163
National Academy of Sciences, 155
NIH, 152–155
offered position, 147–148, 150
Office of the Chairman Emeritus, 212
potentially suicidal employee, 189–190
priorities, 156–157
research strategy, 160–162
retirement, 191–198, 200
succession plan, 191–198, 200
Working Mother, 167–168
change, call to, 365,–368, 370–371, 373–374
Chase, Alyssa, 379
Chemical Bank board, 139–140
Cheney, Vice President Dick, 199, 301
Chicago general manager (Illinois Bell), 91–96
China, 151–152, 285
Chitty, Julie, 259
Civiletti, Attorney General Benjamin, 129
Clapacs, Terry, 35
classified data, 305–306
Clendenin, John, 97, 131–134
clinical depression
    mental health system, 330, 333
    potentially suicidal Lilly employee, 189–190
    Prozac, 174–175, 193, 200
    Tobias, Marilyn, 62, 169–179, 181, 189
    Tobias, Todd, 329, 332–333
clinical trials (FIAU), 152–155
Clinton, President Bill, 146, 165, 270
Clowes, George Henry Alexander, 141
colleges. *See* universities/colleges
Colonial Williamsburg Foundation board, 201, 217–218, 231
Columbia University, 196
computers (Indiana Bell), 79
condoms, 245, 254, 269–272, 274–275, 294–295, 313
Congo, 233
Conners, Cathy, 341
ConocoPhillips board, 139, 202, 212–215
Conseco, 229–231
Contos, Larry, 34
Cook, Dory, 348–349, 377–378
Cornelius, Jim, 158, 161, 163
corporate boards. *See* boards
corporate reorganization (AT&T), 120–123, 131–135
Cozad, Jim, 149
Cuba, 355

D

Dalton, Alice (Alice Medley), 18–19, 364
Daniels, Cheri, 164
Daniels, Governor Mitch, 164, 196, 231–232, 234–235, 293, 314–315, 341
Danzman, Sarah Bauerle, 355
Dayton Accords, 279
Deborah Tobias Field (the Deb), 353
deButts, John, 128, 131
Department of Justice antitrust suit (AT&T), 104–105, 128–130
Department of State. *See* PEPFAR
DePauw University, 2, 25, 31, 346–347, 367
depression
    clinical depression
        mental health system, 330, 333
        potentially suicidal Lilly employee, 189–190
        Prozac, 174–175, 193, 200
        Tobias, Marilyn, 62, 169–179, 181, 189
        Tobias, Todd, 329, 332–333
    Great Depression, 3–4, 19, 363, 367–368
Deputy Secretary of State. *See* Director of Office of Foreign Assistance
diabetes, 142, 182
Dilday, William, 259
Director of Office of Foreign Assistance (Deputy Secretary of State)
    appointment, 298–299
    Bush, President George W., 298–299
    celebrities, 302–304
    illegal drugs, 306–308
    meetings, 305–306
    office, 299–300
    resignation, 308–311
    SCIF, 305–306
    strategy, 300–302, 304
    transformational diplomacy, 311
    White House Situation Room, 305–306
divestiture (AT&T)
    creating plan, 104–107
    implementing strategy, 115–120
Dollens, Ron, 163
Dolson, Scott, 353
Double R Stables, 215–217
drinking (alcohol/substance abuse)
    Tobias, Marilyn, 172–173, 176–177
    Tobias, Todd, 330–334
driven shoot (pheasant hunting), 368–369
drugs
    AIDS
        antiretroviral (ARV), 241, 254, 311–312
        generics, 267–269
    Eli Lilly
        Ceclor (antibiotics), 142
        Evista (osteoporosis), 161
        FIAU (hepatitis B) clinical trials, 152–155
        Gemzar (pancreatic cancer), 161
        Humalog (insulin), 182
        Humulin (insulin), 142
        Iletin (insulin), 142
        Keflex (antibiotics), 142

INDEX

penicillin (antibiotics), 142
Prozac (antidepressant), 174–175, 193, 200
research strategy, 160–162
Zyprexa (schizophrenia), 161
illegal drugs (USAID), 306–308
Duke University, 185, 208, 353
Tobias Button, Paige, 176–177, 184
Tobias, Randall, 139, 198, 201, 215
Durham, Tim, 226–227
Dybul, Dr. Mark, 256, 259

E

Edson, Gary, 234, 259
education
Bugling for Books program, 210
Indiana High School Athletic Association's Boys Basketball State Tournament, 87–88, 91
Literacy for Life program, 219
Remington High School Alumni Association, 361
Remington Public Schools, 23–29, 361
Tobias, Deborah (neé Flanagan), 336–353
Tobias, Fern, 3–4
Tobias, Marilyn, 62–63
Tobias, Roy, 1–4
Tobias, Todd, 176, 221, 331
universities/colleges. *See* universities/colleges
Eli Lilly
board, 139–147
chairman and CEO, 150
achievements, 371

Bryson, Vaughn, 143–150, 153–154, 164
communication style, 155–156
downsizing staff, 158–160
early retirement plans, 158–160
FDA, 162
FIAU clinical trials, 152–155
first days, 152–155
Health Security Act, 165–167
leadership tone, 155–156
Lilly USA creation, 163–164
management team, restructuring, 157–158
medical devices, 162–163
National Academy of Sciences, 155
NIH, 152–155
offered position, 147–148, 150
Office of the Chairman Emeritus, 212
potentially suicidal employee, 189–190
priorities, 156–157
research strategy, 160–162
retirement, 191–198, 200
succession plan, 191–198, 200
Working Mother, 167–168
drugs
Ceclor (antibiotics), 142
Evista (osteoporosis drug), 161
FIAU (hepatitis B drug) clinical trials, 152–155
Gemzar (pancreatic cancer drug), 161
Humalog (insulin drug), 182
Humulin (insulin drug), 142

392

Iletin (insulin drug), 142
Keflex (antibiotics), 142
penicillin (antibiotics), 142
Prozac (antidepressant drug), 174–175, 193, 200
research strategy, 160–162
Zyprexa (schizophrenia drug), 161
history, 141–143
elk hunting, 210
engagement, first, 39, 45–46
English pheasant driven shoot, 368–369
Enright, Rev. Dr. William G., 185
Enron, 317
Ethiopia, 233, 274, 285
Evansville (Indiana Bell), 43–45, 69, 84, 93
Evista (osteoporosis drug), 161

F
faith healer (PEPFAR), 282–285
faith-based organizations (AIDS), 274
Fateful Friday (AT&T), 106–107
Fauci, Dr. Tony, 256, 259, 279
FCC (Federal Communications Commission), 67, 107, 127
FDA (Food and Drug Administration)
Eli Lilly, 162
generic AIDS drugs, 267–269
Federal Communications Commission (FCC), 67, 107, 127
Feinstein, Ambassador and Indiana University Dean, Lee, 354
Feinstein, Senator Diane, 325
FIAU (hepatitis B drug) clinical trials, 152–155

field hockey, 353
Finland, 126
firetruck, 209
fishing, 28, 185–186, 192, 199, 207–208
Flanagan, David, 342–344
Flanagan, Deborah. *See* Tobias, Deborah
Flanagan, Diane, 341
Flanagan, Donald, 341
Flanagan, Kaye, 342
Fleischer, Press Secretary Ari, 239
Fleming, George, 61
flying
flights to remote locations, 281–282
pilot's license, 53–55
Food and Drug Administration (FDA)
Eli Lilly, 162
generic AIDS drugs, 267–269
football
Indiana University, 34, 69, 352–353, 365
Remington, 10
foreign aid. *See* Director of Office of Foreign Assistance; PEPFAR; USAID Administrator
Fort Sill, 48–53
Foster, John, 341
Foster, Teenah, 341
France, 164, 196, 355
Franks, General Tommy, 236
Frick, Dave, 35

G
Gaza, 305
Gemzar (pancreatic cancer drug), 161

genealogy, 369–370
generic drugs (AIDS), 267–269
Gerberding, Dr. Julie, 259, 279–280
Gere, Richard, 303
Germany, 163
Gerrold, David, 225
Gerson, Michael, 259, 314
Gibson, Dave and Ginny, 35
Gilbey, Elinor, 369–370, 379
Gillam, Ronnie (attorney), 360
Gillam, Ronnie, Q., 29, 34, 360
Global AIDS Coordinator/AIDS ambassador. *See also* PEPFAR
    ABC (abstinence, be faithful, condoms), 254, 270–271, 274, 275, 295, 313
    achievements, 311–315, 328, 371
    AIDS activists, 265–266, 286–287
    airplane flights to remote locations, 281–282
    body men, 281, 292
    building central team, 256–259
    bureaucracy, 289–297, 299–300
    celebrities, 303–304
    condoms, 245, 254, 269–272, 275, 294–295
    coordinating local teams, 260–264
    creation of role, 232–238
    faith-based organizations, 274
    five-year goals, 254–255, 262
    generic drugs, 267–269
    getting AIDS tested, 285–286
    Global Fund, 265
    host country officials, 266–269
    long hours, 263, 277–278
    meetings, 292–295
    nomination announcement, 238–243
    orphans, 280, 287–288
    prevention, treatment, and care, 254–255, 262
    resignation, 298
    Senate confirmation, 243–251
    sex workers, 286
    South African faith healer, 282–285
    strategy development, 253–262
    strategy document, 249–251, 256, 262
    visiting frontline locations, 278–288
Global Fund, 265
Godfrey, Bill, 42
Golden, Charlie, 158, 195
Goldsmith, Kate, 314
Goldsmith, Mayor Steve, 314
golf, 62, 96
Gonso, Harry, 69
Gonzalez-Mulé, Associate Professor Erik, 327
Gore, Vice President Al, 278
Gorrell, Sarah, 259
Goss, Becky, 196
Granadillo, Pedro, 192, 196
Grandview Lake, 206
Granich, Reuben, 259
Great Depression, 3–4, 19, 363, 367–368
Greece, 201
Grillo, Michael, 259
Gulf of Tonkin incident, 47–48
Gulf War, 199, 203

INDEX

Gunderson, Brian, 309
Guyana, 286

H
Hackett, Ken, 261
Haiti, 286
Hamilton Lugar School of Global and International Studies, 354–355
Hamilton, Representative Lee, 297
Hammond, Alex, 259, 281
Hansell, Roy, 28
Harkness, Jerald, 332–333
Harrell, Jackie (Jackie Morris), 35
Harry, Lou, 225
Harvard University, 187, 249
Harwood, Betty Jean, 59–61
Harwood, Fern. *See* Tobias, Fern
Harwood, Grace (maternal grandmother), 58–61
Harwood, Lois Nadine, 59–61
Harwood, Mark (maternal grandfather), 59–61
Harwood, Nora (neé Weir, maternal stepgrandmother), 60–61
Harwood, Ray, 61
Hayden, Sara, 378
Hayhurst, Dr. Tom, 34
Hazelett, Susie, 218
Health Security Act, 165–167
Heimansohn, Donna, 189
Henry, Chris, 378
hepatitis B (FIAU drug clinical trials), 152–155
Hesburgh, Father Ted, 327
Hewett, Dr. Charles M., 35

hierarchy of AT&T level system, 83–84
Hilbert, Steve, 229
history
   AT&T, 103
   call to change, 365–368, 370–71, 373–374
   Eli Lilly, 141–143
   Remington, 359–361
HIV/AIDS. *See* AIDS
Holbrook, Ambassador Richard, 278–279
homes
   12 Springs Ranch, 207–211
   Bernardsville, 101–102, 330–331
   Captiva, 207, 234, 338–340, 347
   Carmel, 340, 349, 372
   Grandview Lake, 206
   Lake Wawasee, 206–207, 336–337, 342, 351–352, 373
   Remington. *See* Remington
Hoo Hoo, 345, 374
horses (Double R Stables), 215–217
Hoyle, Peggy, 259
Hudnut, Mayor William, 110
Humalog (insulin drug), 182
Hume, Ambassador Cameron, 259, 267
Humke, Ray, 95
Humulin (insulin drug), 142
Hunt, Bill, 35
Hunt, Jay B., 35
hunting
   Bugling for Books program, 210
   elk, 210
   English pheasant driven shoot, 368–369

pheasants, 192, 351, 363, 368–369
quail, 351, 363

I

Iletin (insulin drug), 142
illegal drugs (USAID), 306–308
Illinois Bell
    Chicago general manager, 91–96
    vice president, 95–97
Illinois State University, 4
IMDP (Initial Management Development Program), 40–46, 84
India, 269
Indiana Bell
    Bloomington local operations manager, 66–68
    computers, 79
    Evansville, 43–45, 69, 84, 93
    IMDP, 40–46, 84
    Indianapolis district accounting manager, 78–81, 84
    Indianapolis district manager, 69, 84
    Indianapolis general advertising manager, 84–88
    Indianapolis general commercial manager, 84, 88–90
    Lebanon local operations manager, 64–68
    manual telephone service, 44
    technological advancements, 77–81
    Touch-Tone system, 44, 80
Indiana High School Athletic Association's Boys Basketball State Tournament, 87–88, 91
"Indiana, Our Indiana," 365–366
Indiana University, 86

AMPATH Kenya, 355–357
basketball, 352–353
board, 318, 325
Deborah Tobias Field (the Deb), 353
field hockey, 353
fight song, 365–366
football, 34, 69, 352–353, 365
Hamilton Lugar School of Global and International Studies, 354–355
Indiana University Foundation, 318, 325
Indiana University Press, 224
Indiana University School of Law, 40
IU Air Force ROTC, 49
IU Athletics Women's Excellence Initiative, 353
Kelley School of Business, 318, 320–321, 327, 379
Oral History Project, 327, 379
Randall L. and Deborah F. Tobias Center for Innovation in International Development, 354–355, 372
Tobias Chair in Leadership, 327
Tobias Fellows, 320–323, 327, 372
Tobias Leadership Center, 218, 318–321, 326–327, 371–372, 379
Tobias, Randall, 29–37, 39–40, 318, 325, 365–366, 371
Tobias, Roger, 31, 34, 216
Tobias, Todd, 176, 221, 331
Tobias-Lechleiter Institute for Clinical Trial Excellence, 372
Wells Scholars Program, 318

Indiana University Foundation, 318, 325

Indiana University Press, 224

Indiana University School of Law, 40

Indianapolis Airport Authority board, 321–324

Indianapolis district accounting manager (Indiana Bell), 78–81, 84

Indianapolis district manager (Indiana Bell), 69, 84

Indianapolis general advertising manager (Indiana Bell), 84–88

Indianapolis general commercial manager (Indiana Bell), 84, 88–90

Indianapolis Monthly, 332, 346

Indy Men's Magazine, 221, 225–228, 332–333

Initial Management Development Program (IMDP), 40–46, 84

insulin drugs, 142, 182

Iran (Islamic Revolution), 129–130, 249

Iraq, 203, 236, 290, 305–306

Ireland, 185–186

Islamic Revolution (Iran), 129–130, 249

Israel, 269

IU Athletics Women's Excellence Initiative, 353

J

Jackson, David, 340

Japan, 163, 201

Jiang, President Zemin, 151

John F. Kennedy Center for the Performing Arts, 231–234, 304

Johnson, President Lyndon, 48

Jolie, Angelina, 303

Jones, Elizabeth (Elizabeth Tobias), ix, 364, 369, 373

Juncker, Margrethe, 312

Justice Department antitrust suit (AT&T), 104–105, 128–130

K

Kavner, Bob, 132–133

Keflex (antibiotics), 142

Kelley School of Business, 318, 320, 327, 379

Kennedy Center, 231–234, 304

Kennedy Onassis, Jacqueline, 101

Kennedy School of Government, 249

Kennedy, President John F., 36, 53

Kenya, 233, 249, 257, 355–357

Kesner, Idie, 320

Kimberly-Clark board, 139–202

Kish, John, 323

Kittle, Jim, 35

Klingbeil, Jeannine Syrstad, 60–61

Kmart, 108–109

Knight Ridder board, 139, 202

Kolker, Ambassador Jimmy, 259, 311–313

Kraft, Heidi, 259

Kucera, Christine, 259

L

lacrosse, 350

Lake Wawasee, 206–207, 336–337, 342, 351–352, 373

Lange, Ambassador John, 256–259

Lantos, Representative Tom, 309

Lashmet, Laura, 377–378

Lebanon local operations manager (Indiana Bell), 64–68
Lebegioara, Corina, 379
Lechleiter, John, 196, 371–372, 380
Lechleiter, Sarah, 372
legacy (Tobias, Randall), 373–374
Lehrer, Jim, 231
level system (AT&T hierarchy), 83–84
Levin, Gerry, 126
Lewis, Ward, 360
Lilly. *See* Eli Lilly
Lilly McCutcheon, Rennie, 207
Lilly Nicholas, Ginny, 206–207
Lilly, Colonel Eli, 141–143, 206–207
Lilly, Eli (grandson), 143
Lilly, Josiah Kirby, Jr., 143
Lilly, Ted, 207
Linden, Meg, 377–378
Literacy for Life program, 219
Longy School of Music, 187
Lucent, 126
Lugar, Senator Richard, 110, 243, 246, 259, 297, 327
Lynch, Peter, 192

M

Malden, Karl, 225
Mani, Nithya, 259
Manning Magid, Julie, 320, 327, 379
manual telephone service, 44
Marconi, Dr. Kathy, 258–259
Marine, Frances, 259
marital engagement, first, 39, 45–46
Marshall, Chuck, 97, 120–121
Marshall, Secretary of State George, 299–300
Max, Peter, 225
May, Hollis, 360
May, Jeff, 28, 360
May, Mary and Bill, 24
Mayfield, Ann (Ann Tobias), x
Mayfield, Isaac, x
McBrearty, Lee, 259, 281
McDonald, Barbara, 185–186
McDonald, Gene, 185–186
MCI, 104, 119
McKinney, Frank Jr., 187
McKinney, Jim, 326
McKinney, Katie, 326
McKinney, Marianne (Marianne Tobias, second wife), 187–188, 197, 206, 326, 336
McKinsey & Company, 111–112
McRobbie, Michael, 320, 326, 354
meant to be, 339
Meche, Myron, 259
medical devices (Eli Lilly), 162–163
Medicare, 165
medication. *See* drugs
Medley, Alice (neé Dalton), 18–19, 364
Medley, Bill, 19, 364
Medley, Jeff, 364
Medley, Randy Lee, 19
Medley, Sandy, 364
Meese, Ed, 120
meetings/scheduling
    Director of Office of Foreign Assistance, 305–306

PEPFAR, 292–295
private time/office work, 203–204
melanoma (Tobias, Randall), 182
mental health system, 330, 333
mental illness. *See* clinical depression
Merkel, Mike, 21, 28, 360
Mesa College, 351
Mikus, Kristie, 259
Milhous, Hanna, 2
military
    air force (IU Air Force ROTC), 49
    army, 37, 39, 47
        artillery school, 48–52
        Fort Sill, 48–52
        pilot's license, 53–55
    navy, 47–48
    Pentagon, 47, 92, 305
    ROTC, 21, 36–37, 39, 45, 49, 216
mill, x–xii
Millennium Challenge, 232, 234–235
Miller, J. Irwin, 85–87
Milner, Doc, 17–18
Moi University, 355
Moloney-Kitts, Michelle, 259
Montana (12 Springs Ranch), 207–211
"moose on the table" philosophy, 188–190
Morales, President Evo, 307–308
Morocco, King of, 101
Morris, Jack, 373
Morris, Jackie (neé Harrell), 35
Morris, Jim, 35, 327
Mosbacher, Secretary of Commerce Bob, 203

Mozambique, 233, 255, 287
Museveni, President Yoweri, 270

N

Nadler, Dr. David, 188
Namibia, 271
National Academy of Sciences, 155
National Collegiate Athletics Association (NCAA), 201, 290, 318
National Institutes of Health (NIH), 152–155
Natsios, Andrew, 239, 259
navy, 47–48
NCAA (National Collegiate Athletics Association), 201, 290, 318
NCR, 125
never daunted, 365–366, 370
Never Daunted, 380–381
New Zealand, 355
Nicholas, Peter, 206–207
Nigeria, 233, 267–268
Nigeria, president of, 267
NIH (National Institutes of Health), 152–155
Nixon, President Richard, 2, 382
Nokia, 126
North Sea, 157, 215
Norway, 215
note from CEO (AT&T), 105–106

O

O'Connor, Supreme Court Justice Sandra Day, 231, 249
Office of the Chairman (AT&T), 120–122

INDEX

Office of the Chairman Emeritus (Eli Lilly), 212
Oklahoma College for Women, 63
Okon, Andrew, 341
Okon, Julie, 341
Okon, Matthew, 341
Okon, Michael, 341
Okon, Robert, 341
Olivetti, 124
Olson, Jim, 85–87, 93–94, 97, 120, 122–123, 132–133
O'Neil, Dr. Joe, 234, 250, 256–257, 259
Oral History Project, 327, 379
orphans, 280, 287–288
Orr, Governor Robert, 110
osteoporosis (Evista drug), 161
Our Lady of Lourdes painting, 359
outside director (boards), 140
Overman, Jesse, 40

P

Pacqué-Margolis, Sara, 259
paintings
   Our Lady of Lourdes, 359
   Remington, 359–360
Palestine (Gaza), 305
Pampel, Carl, 361
Pampel, Deloris, 361
pancreatic cancer (Gemzar drug), 161
Parrish Fuentes, Adrienne, 259
Partoll, Al, 128–130, 379–380
Payne, Pat, 217
Peck's grocery, 17–19, 360, 364
Pederson, Barbara, 219

Pelosi, Speaker of the House Nancy, 152
Pence, Vice President Mike, 325
penicillin (antibiotics), 142
Pentagon, 47, 92, 305
PEPFAR (President's Emergency Plan for AIDS Relief). *See also* AIDS
   AIDS ambassador. *See* Global AIDS Coordinator/AIDS ambassador
   Bush, President George W., 246, 254–255, 301, 303–304, 313–315
   creating, 236–242
   Roosevelt Room nomination speech, 241–242
   Engole, John Robert, 311–313
   Global AIDS Coordinator/AIDS ambassador
      ABC (abstinence, be faithful, condoms), 254, 270–271, 274–275, 295, 313
      achievements, 311–315, 328, 371
      AIDS activists, 265–266, 286–287
      airplane flights to remote locations, 281–282
      AMPATH Kenya, 355–357
      body men, 281, 292
      building central team, 256–259
      bureaucracy, 289–297, 299–300
      celebrities, 303–304
      condoms, 245, 254, 269–272, 275, 294–295
      coordinating local teams, 260–264
      creation of role, 232–238
      faith-based organizations, 274

INDEX

five-year goals, 254–255, 262
generic drugs, 267–269
getting AIDS tested, 285–286
Global Fund, 265
host country officials, 266–269
long hours, 263, 277–278
meetings, 292–295
nomination announcement, 238–243
orphans, 280, 287–288
prevention, treatment, and care, 254–255, 262
resignation, 298
Senate confirmation, 243–251
sex workers, 286
South African faith healer, 282–285
strategy development, 253–262
strategy document, 249–251, 256, 262
visiting frontline locations, 278–288

Peru, 306
Pfleger, Claire, 341
Pfleger, Rick, 341–342
Pharmaceutical and Research Manufacturers of America (PhRMA), 165–167
pharmaceuticals. *See* drugs
pheasant driven shoot, 368–369
pheasant hunting, 191, 351, 363, 368–369
philanthropy/public service (Tobias, Randall)
    Bugling for Books program, 210
    Indiana Airport Authority, 321–324
    Indiana University
        AMPATH Kenya, 355–357
        Deborah Tobias Field (the Deb), 353
        Hamilton Lugar School of Global and International Studies, 354–355
        IU Athletics Women's Excellence Initiative, 353
        Kelley School of Business, 318, 327
        Oral History Project, 327, 379
        Randall L. and Deborah F. Tobias Center for Innovation in International Development, 354–355, 372
        Tobias Center for Leadership Excellence, 218, 318–321, 326–327, 371–372, 379
        Tobias Chair in Leadership, 327
        Tobias Fellows, 320–321, 323, 327, 372
        Tobias Leadership Center, 218, 318–321, 326–327, 371–372, 379
        Tobias-Lechleiter Institute for Clinical Trial Excellence, 372
        Wells Scholars Program, 318
    Literacy for Life program, 219
    Randall L. Tobias Foundation, 212, 218–219, 319
Phillips Petroleum board, 139, 212–215
phones
    AT&T Phone Centers, 108
    cell phones, 111–113
    relocating AT&T manufacturing, 109–111

401

INDEX

Touch-Tone system, 44, 80
Trimline phones, 80, 110–111
PhRMA (Pharmaceutical and Research Manufacturers of America), 165–167
pilot's license, 53–55
Pitt, Brad, 303
planes
  flights to remote locations, 281–282
  pilot's license, 53–55
political activists (AIDS), 265–266, 286–287
Powell, Dina, 232, 234, 236–238
Powell, Secretary of State Colin, 199, 234, 239, 241, 249, 251, 257, 259, 278, 289–292, 294, 298, 314
president of AT&T Consumer Products (AT&T), 107–108
President's Emergency Plan for AIDS Relief. *See* PEPFAR
private time/office work, 203–204
prostitution (sex workers), 286
Prozac (antidepressant drug), 174–175, 193, 200
Pruett, Elissa, 259
psychiatrist (Tobias, Marilyn), 169, 174
public service. *See* philanthropy/public service
Purdue University, 21, 31, 78, 164, 195, 314–315, 318
Put the Moose on the Table, xii–xiii, 182, 192, 221–225, 332, 381
"put the moose on the table" philosophy, 188–190

Q-R

quail hunting, 351, 363
Quayle, Vice President Dan, 110, 284
Radcliffe College, 187
Radigan, Maureen, 147, 149, 377–378
Rainey, Susan, 379
ranch (12 Springs Ranch), 207–211
Randall L. and Deborah F. Tobias Center for Innovation in International Development, 354–355, 372
Randall L. Tobias Foundation, 212, 218–219, 319
Rapposelli, Karina, 259
Reagan, President Ronald, 120, 130
Red Cross Water Safety Instructor, 20
Redford, Robert, 208
Remington
  childhood home, visiting, 361–363
  early childhood, xi, 7–14, 16–17
  history, 359–361
  new home, 363–364
  painting, 359–360
  reconnecting, 363–365
  Remington High School Alumni Association, 361
  Remington Public Schools, 23–29, 361
Remington High School Alumni Association, 361
Remington Public Schools, 23–29, 361
reorganization (AT&T), 120–123, 131–135
Reserve Officers' Training Corps (ROTC), 21, 36–37, 39, 45, 49, 216

402

resignation
    AT&T, 137–138
    Director of Office of Foreign Assistance, 308–311
    Global AIDS Coordinator/AIDS ambassador, 298
    USAID Administrator, 308–311
Rice, Secretary of State Condoleezza, 234, 236, 239, 259, 298, 300, 304–305, 309, 314
Richard, Catherine (Catherine Tobias), ix, 369
Ricks, Dave, 371
Rogers, Nadine, 259
Roosevelt Room, 241–242
Ross, Brian, 308–310
ROTC (Reserve Officers' Training Corp), 21, 36–37, 39, 45, 49, 216
Ryan, Caroline, 259

S

Salyer, Cindy, 58
Salyer, Derek, 58
Salyer, Erwin, 57
Salyer, Jerry, 58, 62
Salyer, Marilyn. *See* Tobias, Marilyn
Salyer, Michelle, 58
Salyer, Ruth, 58
Samari Kermani, Nazanin (Nazanin Ash), 248–251, 256, 259, 281, 341, 380
Scarpino, Dr. Philip, 327, 379
Schantz, Carol, 28
Schantz, Dr. Richard, 11
scheduling/meetings
    Director of Office of Foreign Assistance, 305–306
    PEPFAR, 292–295
    private time/office work, 203–204
schizophrenia (Zyprexa drug), 161
Schmults, Deputy Attorney General Edward, 130
Schofield, Ken, 259
schools. *See* education; universities/colleges
SCIF (sensitive compartmented information facility), 305–306
Scott, Mike, 364
Scowcroft, Brent, 199
Sears, 108–109
Second Presbyterian Church, 185, 188, 352, 378
Senate confirmation hearings (Global AIDS Coordinator), 243–251
sensitive compartmented information facility (SCIF), 305–306
Sessions, Senator Jeff, 240
sex workers, 286
Shearer, Robert B., 25–27
Shenefield, John, 128–129
Shinawatra, Prime Minister Thaksin, 204, 224
Sigo, Lanny, 361
Silverberg, Ambassador Kristen, 259
Simic, Curt, 35
Simonds, RJ, 259
Singapore, 109–111
Situation Room (White House), 305–306
skiing, 74
Smart, Andrew, 102

INDEX

Smart, Holly, 102
Smart, John, 102–103, 341
Smart, Lynn, 102–103, 341
Smith, Attorney General William French, 130
softball, 13
South Africa, 233, 255, 261, 267, 280
Southern Methodist University, 28
Spellings, Secretary Margaret, 259
sports
   baseball, 349–350
   basketball, 67, 139, 225, 290
      Indiana High School Athletic Association's Boys Basketball State Tournament, 87–88, 91
      Indiana University, 352–353, 365
      Remington, 10, 13, 19, 25, 27–28
      University of Dayton, 353
      Deborah Tobias Field (the Deb), 353
   field hockey, 353
   football
      Indiana University, 34, 69, 352–353, 365
      Remington, 10
   golf, 62, 96
   IU Athletics Women's Excellence Initiative, 353
   lacrosse, 350
   NCAA, 201, 290, 318
   skiing, 74
   soccer, 96
   softball, 13
   track, 27
Sprint, 119

stables (Double R Stables), 215–217
Stall, Sam, 381–383
Stanford University, 130
State Department. *See* PEPFAR
Steiger, Dr. Bill, 256–257, 259
Stewart, Karen, 259
Stone, Marsha, 323
stores (AT&T Phone Centers), 108–109
Streep, Meryl, 101
substance/alcohol abuse
   Tobias, Marilyn, 172–173, 176–177
   Tobias, Todd, 330–334
suicide
   potentially suicidal Lilly employee, 189–190
   Tobias, Marilyn, 169, 177–179, 186
Supreme Court (O'Connor, Justice Sandra Day), 231, 249
Switzerland, 303

T

Talbot, Kelly, 379
Tanenbaum, Morrie, 120–121
Tanzania, 233, 257
Target, 109
Taurel, Sidney, 166, 193, 195–197, 200–201, 371, 380
technological advancements
   AT&T, 111–113
   Indiana Bell, 77–81
telephones
   AT&T Phone Centers, 108
   cell phones, 111–113

INDEX

relocating AT&T manufacturing, 109–111

Touch-Tone system, 44, 80

Trimline phones, 80, 110–111

Thailand

    AIDS Conference, 224, 286

    Shinawatra, Prime Minister Thaksin, 204, 224

Thomas, Ann, 259

Thompson, Carol, 257, 259

Thompson, Secretary of Health and Human Services Tommy, 239, 257, 259, 268, 278, 284, 286–287, 291

Thrapp, Gary, 338

Time Warner (Warner Media), 126–127

Tobias Bridge, xii

Tobias Button, Paige (daughter), 77, 188, 197, 205, 243, 282, 336, 341, 373, 377

    asthma, 71–75

    Bernardsville, 101–102

    birth, 68–69

    brother's alcohol/substance abuse, 332–334

    children, 344–348

    coping with moving, 170–171

    Duke University, 176–177, 184, 353

    engagement and wedding, 184–186

    meeting Deborah, 337–338

    mother's clinical depression, 169, 175–178, 184

    Never Daunted, 380–381

    Randall L. Tobias Foundation, 212, 218–219, 319

    relationship with father, 94–96, 139

skiing, 74

soccer, 96

Vanderbilt Family Weekends, 350

Tobias Center for Leadership Excellence, 218, 318–321, 326–327, 371–372, 379

Tobias Chair in Leadership, 327

Tobias Enterprises, 41–42

Tobias family history

    mill, x–xii

    Tobias Bridge, xii

    Wales, ix–x

Tobias Family Office, 211–212, 215, 223, 244, 277–278, 337, 349, 372, 377

Tobias Fellows, 320–321, 323, 327, 372

Tobias Leadership Center, 218, 318–321, 326–327, 371–372, 379

Tobias, Abbie Grace, 373

Tobias, Amy Rae (neé Brim), 332, 346, 350

Tobias, Ann (neé Mayfield), x

Tobias, Anna, 373

Tobias, Catherine (neé Richard), ix, 369

Tobias, Clifford, 2

Tobias, David, ix

Tobias, David T., x–xi, 369

Tobias, Deborah (neé Flanagan, third wife), 367–369, 373, 377–378, 380–381

    as part of Tobias family, 345–352

    career, 336

    early relationship with Randall, 335–338

    engagement and wedding, 338–341

    Flanagan, David, 342–343

INDEX

grandchildren, 343–352
Hoo Hoo, 345, 374
meant to be, 339
nicknames, 343–345
Our Lady of Lourdes painting, 359
philanthropy/public service
   AMPATH Kenya, 355–357
   Deborah Tobias Field (the Deb), 353
   Hamilton Lugar School of Global and International Studies, 354–355
   IU Athletics Women's Excellence Initiative, 353
   Randall L. and Deborah F. Tobias Center for Innovation in International Development, 354–355, 372
   Tobias-Lechleiter Institute for Clinical Trial Excellence, 372
Remington home, 363–364
University of Dayton, 336, 353
visiting Randall's childhood home, 361–363
Tobias, Elizabeth (neé Jones), ix, 364, 369, 373
Tobias, Ella, 332, 339, 344, 346–347, 351, 373
Tobias, Enos, 369
Tobias, Eric, 351, 373
Tobias, Fern (neé Harwood, mother), xi, 20, 22, 27, 50, 147, 361, 363–364, 368
   education, 3–4
   family secrets, 58–62
   passing away, 183
   raising children, 7–8, 10–12,

   relationship with Roy, 3–5
   teaching, 4, 12, 27
Tobias, Gordon, 216, 364
Tobias, Harry (paternal grandfather), xi, 1–2, 11, 362, 364
Tobias, Hazel, 2
Tobias, Helen (Helen Butcher), 2, 363
Tobias, John, x, 369
Tobias, Karen, 216
Tobias, Laura, 373
Tobias, Leva Sparks (paternal grandmother), 1–2, 11, 12, 364
Tobias, Margaret (neé William), x
Tobias, Marianne (neé McKinney, second wife), 187–188, 197, 206, 326, 336
Tobias, Marilyn (neé Salyer, first wife), 57, 77, 94–96, 101–103, 138, 148, 202, 207, 217, 333, 345
   alcohol/substance abuse, 172–173, 176–177
   clinical depression, 62, 169–179, 181, 189
   education, 62–63
   family secrets, 58, 62
   grieving her passing, 181–182, 184–190
   Paige pregnancy and birth, 68–69
   Paige's asthma, 71–75
   psychiatrist, 169, 174
   suicide, 169, 177–179, 186
   Todd pregnancy and birth, 69–70
   wedding, 58, 63–64
Tobias, Randall. *See also separate entries for family members*

INDEX

AIDS ambassador. *See* Global AIDS Coordinator/AIDS ambassador
army, 37, 39, 47
   artillery school, 48–52
   Fort Sill, 48–52
   pilot's license, 53–55
AT&T. *See* AT&T
boards
   Chemical Bank, 139–140
   Colonial Williamsburg Foundation, 201, 217–218, 231
   ConocoPhillips, 139, 202, 212–215
   Duke University, 139, 198, 201, 215
   Eli Lilly, 139–147
   Indiana University, 318, 325
   Indianapolis Airport Authority, 321–324
   Kennedy Center, 231–234
   Kimberly-Clark, 139, 202
   Knight Ridder, 139, 202
   outside director, 140
   overview, 138
   Phillips Petroleum, 139, 212–215
Boo Boo, 338, 344–345, 374
call to change, 365–368, 370–371, 373–374
Camp Potawatomi, 19–21
cancer, 182
childhood lessons, 17–22
Conseco, 229–231
diabetes, 182
Director of Office of Foreign Assistance (Deputy Secretary of State)
   appointment, 298–299
   Bush, President George W., 298–299
   celebrities, 302–304
   illegal drugs, 306–308
   meetings, 305–306
   office, 299–300
   resignation, 308–311
   SCIF, 305–306
   strategy, 300–302, 304
   transformational diplomacy, 311
   White House Situation Room, 305–306
Double R Stables, 215–217
Eli Lilly, chairman and CEO, 150
   achievements, 371
   Bryson, Vaughn, 143–150, 153–154, 164
   communication style, 155–156
   downsizing staff, 158–160
   early retirement plans, 158–160
   FDA, 162
   FIAU clinical trials, 152–155
   first days, 152–155
   Health Security Act, 165–167
   leadership tone, 155–156
   Lilly USA creation, 163–164
   management team, restructuring, 157–158
   medical devices, 162–163
   National Academy of Sciences, 155
   NIH, 152–155
   offered position, 147–148, 150

Office of the Chairman Emeritus, 212
potentially suicidal employee, 189–190
priorities, 156–157
research strategy, 160–162
retirement, 191–198, 200
succession plan, 191–198, 200
Working Mother, 167–168
firetruck, 209
first marital engagement, 39, 45–46
fishing, 28, 185–186, 192, 199, 207–208
genealogy, 369–370
Global AIDS Coordinator/AIDS ambassador. *See also* PEPFAR
    ABC (abstinence, be faithful, condoms), 254, 270–271, 274–275, 295, 313
    achievements, 311–315, 328, 371
    AIDS activists, 265–266, 286–287
    airplane flights to remote locations, 281–282
    body men, 281, 292
    building central team, 256–259
    bureaucracy, 289–297, 299–300
    celebrities, 303–304
    condoms, 245, 254, 269–272, 275, 294–295
    coordinating local teams, 260–264
    creation of role, 232–238
    faith-based organizations, 274
    five-year goals, 254–255, 262
    generic drugs, 267–269
    getting AIDS tested, 285–286
    Global Fund, 265
    host country officials, 266–269
    long hours, 263, 277–278
    meetings, 292–295
    nomination announcement, 238–243
    orphans, 280, 287–288
    prevention, treatment, and care, 254–255, 262
    resignation, 298
    Senate confirmation, 243–251
    sex workers, 286
    South African faith healer, 282–285
    strategy development, 253–262
    strategy document, 249–251, 256, 262
    visiting frontline locations, 278–288
homes
    12 Springs Ranch, 207, 208, 209, 210, 211
    Bernardsville, 101–102, 330–331
    Captiva, 207, 234, 338–340, 347
    Carmel, 340, 349, 372
    Grandview Lake, 206
    Lake Wawasee, 206–207, 336–337, 342, 351–352, 373
    Remington. *See* Remington
hunting
    Bugling for Books program, 210
    elk, 210
    English pheasant driven shoot, 368–369
    pheasants, 191, 351, 363, 368–369

INDEX

quail, 351, 363
Indiana University School of Law, 40
Ireland vacation, 185–186
legacy, 373–374
Millennium Challenge, 232, 234–235
mowing lawns, 17
never daunted, 365–366, 370
Peck's grocery, 17–19
PEPFAR. *See* PEPFAR
philanthropy/public service
    AMPATH Kenya, 355–357
    Bugling for Books program, 210
    Deborah Tobias Field (the Deb), 353
    Hamilton Lugar School of Global and International Studies, 354–355
    Indianapolis Airport Authority, 321–324
    IU Athletics Women's Excellence Initiative, 353
    Kelley School of Business, 318, 327
    Literacy for Life program, 219
    Oral History Project, 327, 379
    Randall L. and Deborah F. Tobias Center for Innovation in International Development, 354–355, 372
    Randall L. Tobias Foundation, 212, 218–219, 319
    Tobias Center for Leadership Excellence, 218, 318–321, 326–327, 371–372, 379
    Tobias Chair in Leadership, 327
    Tobias Fellows, 320–321, 323, 327, 372
    Tobias Leadership Center, 218, 318–321, 326–327, 371–372, 379
    Tobias-Lechleiter Institute for Clinical Trial Excellence, 372
    Wells Scholars Program, 318
post-Lilly family time, 205–206
"put the moose on the table" philosophy, 188–190
Red Cross Water Safety Instructor, 20
Remington
    childhood home, visiting, 361–363
    early childhood, xi, 7–14, 16–17
    history, 359–361
    new home, 363–364
    painting, 359–360
    reconnecting, 363–365
    Remington High School Alumni Association, 361
    Remington Public Schools, 23–29, 361
soccer coach, 96
Tobias Enterprises, 41–42
Tobias Family Office, 211–212, 215, 223, 244, 277–278, 337, 349, 372, 377
United Way, 201
USAID Administrator
    appointment, 298–299
    Bush, President George W., 298–299
    celebrities, 302–304
    illegal drugs, 306–308
    meetings, 305–306
    office, 299–300

INDEX

resignation, 308–311
SCIF, 305–306
strategy, 300–302, 304
transformational diplomacy, 311
White House Situation Room, 305–306

Wales
   family history, ix–x
   visiting ancestral roots, 368–370

Tobias, Roger (brother), 27, 59, 341, 347, 351–352, 362, 364
   Camp Potawatomi, 19
   childhood, 4, 8–12
   diabetes, 182
   Double R Stables, 215–217
   Indiana University, 31, 34, 216
   ROTC, 36

Tobias, Roy (father), xi, 8, 10–12, 24, 48, 59, 77, 223, 346, 360, 362–364
   banking career, 3–6, 16–17
   DePauw University, 2, 31–32, 367
   education, 1–4
   Great Depression, 3–4, 367–368
   passing away, 183
   relationship with Fern, 3–6

Tobias, Sam, 332, 339, 344, 350–351, 373

Tobias, Theopolis, xi, 364

Tobias, Thomas, ix, 369

Tobias, Tobias, ix–x, 366–370

Tobias, Todd (son), 70, 186, 188, 197, 202, 282, 335, 337, 339, 347, 350–351, 373, 377, 382
   alcohol/substance abuse, 330–334
   Before Their Time, 221

Bernardsville Jersey boy, 101–102
birth, 69
children, 332
clinical depression, 329, 332–333
coping with moving, 94–95, 170–171
grandparents, 72–73
Indiana University, 176, 221, 331
Indianapolis Monthly, 332, 346
Indy Men's Magazine, 221, 225–228, 332–333
marriage, 332
mental health system, 330, 333
mother's clinical depression, 169, 175, 176–178, 184
"Prodigal Son Diaries, The," 221
Put the Moose on the Table, xii–xiii, 182, 192, 221–225, 332, 381

Randall L. Tobias Foundation, 212, 218–219, 319
West Virginia University, 176, 221, 331
Westview Press, 332
Tobias, Vicki, 379
Tobias-Lechleiter Institute for Clinical Trial Excellence, 372
Touch-Tone system, 44, 80
track, 27
traditional healer, 282–285
transformational diplomacy, 311
Trienens, Howard, 120, 130
Trimline phones, 80, 110–111
Tshabalala-Msimang, Minister of Health Manto, 267
Tuberville, Senator Tommy, 247
Tyson, Mike, 101

410

INDEX

U

Uganda, 255, 280
   Engole, John Robert, 311–313
   Museveni, President Yoweri, 270
United Nations (UN), 279
   Global Fund, 265
   Goodwill Ambassador Angelina Jolie, 303
   United States Permanent Representative to the UN, 238
United States Agency for International Development Administrator. *See* USAID Administrator
United States Permanent Representative to the UN (USUN), 238
United Way, 201
universities/colleges
   Auburn University, 281
   Ball State University, 381
   Bryn Mawr College, 249
   Butler University, 87
   Cameron College, 63
   Columbia University, 196
   DePauw University, 2, 25, 31, 346–347, 367
   Duke University, 185, 208, 353
      Tobias, Randall, 139, 198, 201, 215
      Tobias Button, Paige, 176–177, 184
   Harvard University, 187, 249
   Illinois State University, 4
   Indiana University, 86
      AMPATH Kenya, 355–357
      basketball, 352–353
      board, 318, 325
      Deborah Tobias Field (the Deb), 353
      field hockey, 353
      fight song, 365–366
      football, 34, 69, 352–353, 365
      Hamilton Lugar School of Global and International Studies, 354–355
      Indiana University Foundation, 318, 325
      Indiana University Press, 224
      Indiana University School of Law, 40
      IU Air Force ROTC, 49
      IU Athletics Women's Excellence Initiative, 353
      Kelley School of Business, 318, 320, 327, 379
      Oral History Project, 327, 379
      Randall L. and Deborah F. Tobias Center for Innovation in International Development, 354–355, 372
      Tobias Chair in Leadership, 327
      Tobias Fellows, 320–321, 323, 327, 372
      Tobias Leadership Center, 218, 318–321, 326–327, 371–372, 379
      Tobias, Randall, 29, 31–37, 39–40, 318, 325, 365–366, 371
      Tobias, Roger, 31, 34, 216
      Tobias, Todd, 176, 221, 331
      Tobias-Lechleiter Institute for Clinical Trial Excellence, 372
      Wells Scholars Program, 318
   Kennedy School of Government, 249

INDEX

Longy School of Music, 187
Mesa College, 351
Moi University, 355
Oklahoma College for Women, 63
Purdue University, 21, 31, 78, 164, 195, 314–315, 318
Radcliffe College, 187
Southern Methodist University, 28
Stanford University, 130
University of Alabama, 73
University of California, 257
University of Dayton, 336, 353
University of Minnesota, 187
University of North Carolina, 143
University of Oklahoma, 63
University of Oregon, 349
University of Pennsylvania, 102
University of Science and Arts of Oklahoma, 63
University of Southern California, 69
University of Texas, 281
University of Toronto, 142
Vanderbilt University, 350
West Virginia University, 176, 221, 331
Xavier University, 380
University of Alabama, 73
University of California, 257
University of Dayton, 336, 353
University of Minnesota, 187
University of North Carolina, 143
University of Oklahoma, 63
University of Oregon, 349
University of Pennsylvania, 102
University of Science and Arts of Oklahoma, 63
University of Southern California, 69
University of Texas, 281
University of Toronto, 142
US Department of State. *See* PEPFAR
USAID (United States Agency for International Development) Administrator
    appointment, 298–299
    Bush, President George W., 298–299
    celebrities, 302–304
    illegal drugs, 306–308
    meetings, 305–306
    office, 299–300
    resignation, 308–311
    SCIF, 305–306
    strategy, 300–302, 304
    transformational diplomacy, 311
    White House Situation Room, 305–306
USUN (United States Permanent Representative to the UN), 238
Utter, Donald, 25
Vanderbilt University, 350

V

vice president
    AT&T vice president for residence services
        note from CEO, 105–106
        promotion, 97, 131–132
        relocating, 99–103
    Illinois Bell, 95–97
Vietnam War, 21, 36, 47–48, 50, 52, 365

Vosloh, Channa Beth, 20
Vosloh, Channing and Rowena, 19

W

Wales
  family history, ix–x
  visiting ancestral roots, 368–370
Walmart, 109
Walsh, Tom, 259
Warner Media (Time Warner), 126–127
Warren, Dr. Joe, 123
Washington bureacracy, 289–297, 299–300
Watanabe, Dr. Gus, 160–161, 173, 178, 181–182, 195
Watanabe, Dr. Margaret "Peg," 173
Weir, Nora (Nora Harwood, maternal stepgrandmother), 60–61
Welch, Jack, 212, 228
Wells Scholars Program, 318
Wendt, Gary, 231
Wert, Milo, 67–68
West Virginia University, 176, 221, 331
Western Electric, 21, 100, 104, 107–109, 117, 119–120, 126, 128–129
Wheeler, Dr. J. Clyde, 63
White House Situation Room, 305–306
Whitlock, Carrie, 259
William, Margaret (Margaret Tobias), x
Winfrey, Oprah, 304
Wolfe, Mitch, 259
Wood, Dick, 140, 142–148
Woosnam, Rich, 35

Working Mother, 167–168
World Economic Forum, 303
World War I, 144
World War II, 9, 16, 25, 299, 365

X-Z

Xavier University, 380
Young, Senator Todd, 297, 339
Yugoslavia, 279
Zemin, President Jiang, 151
Zimbabwe, 233
Zyprexa (schizophrenia drug), 161

ABOUT THE PAINTING

1950s DOWNTOWN REMINGTON

This canvas by John Michael Carter hangs in the foyer of my home. It recreates downtown Remington, Indiana, close to the way it looked in the 1950s. The painting, which was based on photographs, existing structures and my memories, presents the view looking north on Ohio Street, the main downtown thoroughfare. It offers nostalgic views of long-gone landmarks such as the State Bank of Remington, where my father worked for 44 years; Peck's grocery, where I worked on Saturdays as a teen; and the farm truck of Chester Biddle, who frequently drove into town to share coffee with the locals, including my dad, at Woody's Snak Shop.

Follow the numbers to see the businesses visible in the painting. Remington shops and businesses that I remember and that aren't visible in the painting are listed on page 415. Buildings and businesses, many of which are long gone, are listed in the locations where they existed to the best of my recollection. If you were to visit Remington now, the view would be quite different.

VISIBLE:

Remington shops and businesses visible in the painting

East (left) side of street:

1. Ronald Gillam, Attorney
2. Bowman's Jewelry Store
3. Hansell's Drug Store
4. Lynch's Five and Dime
5. Shea's Appliance Store
6. Masonic Lodge

West (right) side of street, from north to south:

7. The iconic Remington brick water tower
8. The garage for the Remington Volunteer Fire Department's two fire engines
9. The Remington Public Library
10. Stokes Plumbing Shop

ABOUT THE PAINTING

11. Nelson's Hardware Store (on the corner with striped awning)
12. State Bank of Remington (on the opposite corner)
13. Main Entrance to C.H. Peck and Sons Dry Goods and Grocery (Peck's grocery)
14. Farmers National Bank
15. Charles Biddle Insurance Agency
16. Woody's Snak Shop

NOT VISIBLE:

Remington shops and businesses not visible in the painting

East (left) side of the street, bottom left, from south to north:

Remington Telephone Company, which had a two-position switchboard and no dial phones

Best's Poultry

Helene Guy, Attorney

Lish's Hardware Store (next to Ronald Gilliam, Attorney)

Skelly's Auto Repair (around the corner behind Shea's)

Post Office (next to the Masonic Lodge)

Howard's Furniture Store and Funeral Home

Remington Hotel (six rooms)

West (right) side of street, from north to south from Woody's:

National Guard Armory (formerly Shortway Bus Company garage)

Remington Pool Hall

Dr. Richard Schantz, M.D.

Bahler's Feed Store

REM Theater

Dr. G. T. Landis, Dentist

From west to east from Nelson's on the north side of the railroad tracks:

Abe Lewis's Barber Shop

Ethel Childress Chiropractor

Hammie Hamilton's Barber Shop

Harry's Bar and Restaurant

Remington Lanes Bowling Alley

From east to west in the block south of the railroad tracks:

Holderly's Farm Implements

American Legion Hall

Dr. L. E. Andres, Veterinarian

Shelmon's Dry Cleaners

Louise Lewis Shelmon's Beauty Shop

Frosty's Market

Remington Butcher Shop and Locker Plant

Side entrance directly into Peck's Grocery

ABOUT THE AUTHOR

Randall Tobias has built a professional legacy that ranges from government service to business leadership to philanthropy. He variously served as vice chairman of AT&T, chairman and CEO of AT&T Communications and chairman and CEO of AT&T International during the period from 1986 to 1993. In 1993 he became chairman, president and CEO of Eli Lilly and Company, serving until 1999. In 2003, at the request of President George W. Bush, he became the first United States Global AIDS Coordinator with the rank of ambassador, launching the President's Emergency Plan for AIDS Relief (PEPFAR), now credited with saving more than 25 million lives. In 2006 he was named the first United States Director of Foreign Assistance, as well as Administrator of the U.S. Agency for International Development (USAID). Among his philanthropic interests, he was instrumental in the 2004 founding of the Tobias Leadership Center at his alma mater, Indiana University. Tobias lives in Carmel, Indiana, with his wife, Deborah.

www.ingramcontent.com/pod-product-compliance
Lightning Source LLC
Chambersburg PA
CBHW040440240426
43665CB00051B/2923